Limelight

A Greenwich

Village

Photography

Gallery and

Coffeehouse

in the Fifties

A MEMOIR BY

Helen Gee

University of New

Mexico Press

Albuquerque

Library of Congress Cataloging-
in-Publication Data
Gee, Helen. Limelight : a Greenwich Village photography
gallery and coffeehouse in the fifties / Helen Gee. —1st ed.
p.   cm.
Includes index.
ISBN 0–8263–1783–9 (cloth)
ISBN 0–8263–1817–7 (paper)
1. Gee, Helen.   2. Women photographers —
United States — Biography.   3. Limelight (Gallery :
New York, N.Y.)   4. Photographic art galleries —
New York — New York — History.   I. Title.
TR140.G39A3   1997
770.'92 — dc20
[B]   96–25382
CIP

Designed by Kristina Kachele

FOR THE PHOTOGRAPHERS WHO MADE IT POSSIBLE.

ACKNOWLEDGMENTS

It is Tennyson Schad who is responsible for this book. It is he who suggested I write about Limelight, which preceded his own gallery, Light, by seventeen years. I went ahead and wrote a few chapters, then abandoned the project, busy with other things. But I had made the mistake of mentioning these efforts to friends. Word got around, and for several years, when I attended openings and other places where the clan gathers, I was faced with that awful question, "How's the book coming along?" My response was not always polite. Rather than go on evading the question, I sat down and tried again. But I was a hunt-and-peck typist, and had I not been given a computer by Yula Lipchitz (who became a photographer in her seventies after the death of her husband, Jacques Lipchitz), my efforts would have died once again. I approached this gift horse with much trepidation, but after learning the basics, I was carried away by its magic. Words kept flying all over the screen, but, alas, they did not, and would not, form coherent sentences. I had to face the sad reality: computers, smart as they are, do not do the writing for you—you have to do it yourself. So I buckled down, and from then on tested the patience of my friends. They put up with my complaints and forgave my withdrawal into self and my absence from functions I would not ordinarily have missed.

I want to thank Frank Paulin, with whom I shared many a memory fest, William Rossa Cole, who listened as I struggled with my syntax, and those long-suffering friends—Doris Aach, John Erdman, Ilona Kinzer, Sanne Melgaard, and Gary Schneider—whose ministerings included everything from pats on the head to bowls of soup. To them I owe thanks and deepest gratitude. My thanks, too, to the photographers who so generously contributed their work: first to Arthur Lavine for his coverage of Limelight's beginnings, and to Ellen Auerbach, John Cohen, Ken Heyman, Morris Jaffe, James Karales, Wayne Miller, Frank Paulin, Paul Seligman, Nina Howell Starr, and Sandra Weiner. I want to thank Peter C. Bunnell for his long years of friendship and James L. Enyeart for his encouragement and support. My thanks too to Susan Kismaric, Virginia Dodier, Ellen Kornhauser, Julia Van Haaften, Sharon Girard, Joan Stoliar, and to the many others who helped along the way. A very special thanks to my editor, Dana Asbury, for her patience and support during the many months of work.

THERE'S NO TELLING what an empty stomach can lead to. Had I eaten breakfast that morning, cereal and eggs instead of toast and black coffee, Limelight might never have been born. I would have gone on with my own photography and left the pioneering to others.

Opening a gallery for photography had never occurred to me, and certainly, never a coffeehouse. All I had in mind on that fine Sunday morning in the fall of 1953 was getting in a good day's shooting. It was the week of the St. Gennaro festival on the Lower East Side, a perfect opportunity to start using color. I rushed through my morning rituals—walked the dog, fed the cat, and after seeing my daughter off for her weekly visit to her father, grabbed my camera and took the subway downtown.

The festival was in full swing when I got there. Mulberry Street had been cordoned off and for a half-mile stretch, from Chinatown north through the heart of Little Italy, the streets were alive with color. People came from all over, to eat, to stroll, to play carnival games, but it was the neighborhood Italians, dressed in their Sunday best, that gave the festival its flavor.

I fell in with the crowd honoring the good saint and for the first few blocks did nothing but savor the sights and the smells, trying to get the feel of things. I had studied photography with Lisette Model and was determined to follow her advice: "Don't shoot until you feel it in your gut."

Alongside the food stalls there were games of chance, where for as little as a dime and a bit of luck, you could choose from an array of prizes, everything from Hula-Hoops and Kewpie dolls to plastic Madonnas and bottles of scotch. I was tempted by a teddy bear, having my daughter Li-lan in mind, but I'd never had much luck with a roulette wheel, and preferred playing games of skill. I toyed with the idea of pitching pennies into a gold-fish bowl and coming away with a goldfish. But the fish looked sickly, and if I won, could I handle a camera and a goldfish too?

Besides, it was time to start taking pictures; I was beginning to get that gut feeling. I strolled along, camera poised, and the first to catch my eye was a pot-bellied man in a gaudy Hawaiian shirt. I stepped back to take in his enormous girth and clicked the shutter at the "decisive moment" (á la Cartier-Bresson), just as he bit into a pizza. Next I spotted a Franciscan monk who, with his long brown robe and tonsured pate, looked like he'd stepped from an old engraving; he was happily munching popcorn. (I could smell the butter as I focused.) Then I stopped at a stall where a man was shucking oysters (they looked so pretty in the half-shell on a bed of ice) and took a few shots of him. Farther down the block, teenagers were jitterbug-ging to the beat of a jazz combo. But they moved so fast and color film was slow, so I focused on a baggy-pants zoot-suiter slouching on the sidelines, his pompadour gleaming in the sun. He was swigging a Coke.

Wherever I looked, there was something good to eat. Within the space of a single block, I saw (and resisted) a whole smorgasbord of culinary de-lights: ravioli, lasagna, manicotti, pizzas; corn on the cob, stuffed peppers, and artichoke hearts; spumoni, cannoli, and racks of Neapolitan pastries. But the most tantalizing of all were the Italian sausages, sizzling away on the grills.

Did artists *really* work better on empty stomachs? After several more shots I decided they did not and headed for the nearest barbecue stand. I watched as the man behind the counter arranged the sausages on the grill. I watched as he turned them, gently, so as not to disturb the juices, and watched the skins burst as they browned. I watched as he forked the sausages on to thick slabs of Italian bread and heaped them with peppers and onions. Then I stopped watching and ordered one. First the "sweet" kind—pale-skinned, flecked with fennel and parsley. Next, the "hot" kind—pink-skinned, sea-soned with pepper and paprika. And then, just as I bit into this second sausage, the idea struck.

Why not combine food and photography? Why not open a European-style coffeehouse and combine it with a gallery devoted exclusively to photography? Photographers had never had a gallery of their own, and perhaps it was time they did. There were galleries in New York for almost everything — painting, sculpture, graphics, ceramics — yet none for photography, although the medium was already a hundred years old. Not that it had never been tried. When Alfred Stieglitz opened his gallery "291" in 1905, he had that very thing in mind. But he was eventually seduced by modern art, and photography took second place. Julien Levy had occasionally shown photographs in his gallery in the 1930s, but he never succeeded in selling a print to a client, only a few to friends at ten dollars each.

Hardly anyone bought photographs, but almost everyone drank coffee — so why not subsidize a gallery with coffee beans? Clutching my half-eaten sausage, I wandered off to a side street and pondered the idea.

Coffeehouses — the kind where you could meet friends, read newspapers, write a novel — were catching on in New York. Two had recently opened, the Rienzi on Macdougal Street run by a group of nine artists, and the Coffee Mill in midtown owned by two psychoanalysts. They were based on the idea of the Parisian cafes, where artists and writers made cultural history over coffee and croissants. I thought of Picasso, Modigliani, Jean-Paul Sartre, Simone de Beauvoir — could I create the same kind of place for photographers? But this one would have a double purpose: It would be a place to exhibit, a place to meet.

I put my camera in my gadget bag and took the subway back home. And that night, between bouts of indigestion and gulps of Alka-Seltzer, I made plans for bringing the idea to life.

But had I known what the next seven years would be like as I grappled with the problems of running the biggest and busiest coffeehouse in New York and the first photography gallery in the country, I would never have bitten into that sausage.

Peter Wimmer, daughters Ella and Helen, and son Henry.

I DID NOT CHOOSE photography so much as fall into it. A lifelong aversion to things mechanical (including cameras) made my choosing such a course unlikely. My background didn't help. I was raised by a father who, had he the advantage of position and wealth, would have been viewed in polite society as a "nineteenth-century man." But he was a hard-working house-painter, an immigrant from Austria-Hungary, and with no woman in the house to counter his old-fashioned attitudes — my mother having died in my infancy — he steadfastly clung to the past. He had no patience with modern technology; even a Brownie was beyond his ken. And except for a portrait of the four of us — my older sister and brother, my father and me — taken in a storefront studio when I was ten years old, our family events (birthdays, graduations, an occasional outing) went largely unrecorded. The only appliance we had was a carpet sweeper, and we didn't own a radio until I was fifteen.

Along with sharing my father's aversions, I shared his love of art. He'd been trained in Europe as a church decorator but finding few churches to refurbish when he arrived in New York, he settled for painting apartments instead. He painted pictures on Sundays until his problems proved too much, and at every opportunity (which riled my sister when she had boys to the house), he'd bring out his collection of picture postcards — castles, cathedrals, liturgical art — and foist them on whoever was present. Usually it was me. I liked to draw and wanted to go to art school, but times were hard in the 1930s, and besides, my father had other ideas; education was not for girls. What he wanted for me was a year or two as a waitress or clerk (a step up the ladder, most of the women in the family having worked as servants) and an early marriage to a hard-working man.

He was disappointed. I left home at sixteen, not to work or to marry, but to live in Greenwich Village with Yun Gee, a Chinese modernist painter who I met through an art teacher in a WPA class. (My departure was facilitated by my father's new wife, whose pro-Nazi views were a source of strife, so my leaving suited us both.) Still in high school, I took the subway each morning to Washington Heights (where Wadleigh High was located and where my family, the Wimmers, lived) and graduated in June.

Life with Yun was the kind I had dreamed of ever since I was ten. I was a lonely child—shy, myopic, and underweight—and after discovering Isadora Duncan's autobiography in the adult section of the public library, I decided to pattern my life after hers: I would live for love and art. Yun was charming, gifted, and thirty when we met. He was born in China, had lived in Paris, and exhibited in leading galleries and museums both here and abroad, including New York's Museum of Modern Art.

Yun encouraged me in everything I did. I painted, played Chinese music on the butterfly harp, practiced Chinese boxing (a form of tai chi ch'uan) and continuing my education where school left off, pored through Yun's hundreds of books, reading everything from the Confucian Analects to Freud's Interpretation of Dreams. I also helped care for his forty-odd birds—nightingales, skylarks, canaries, finches, and a giant mynah with a raunchy vocabulary. Yun was a connoisseur cook, and though I'd learned to prepare several Cantonese dishes, I never inflicted these efforts on our guests, many of them Chinese men. The Oriental Exclusion Act was still on the books, and most were here illegally, working at menial jobs to support their families back home, usually without prospects of ever seeing them again. Until I met Yun, I had never so much as spoken to a Chinese, yet I felt more comfortable with these men than with most of Yun's Occidental friends, many of whom (artists as well) looked askance at our living together, probably because of my age. Interracial relationships were relatively rare, and in many parts of the city one could run up against unpleasant or even nasty encounters. Rather than chance an incident (Yun was hot-headed and could lose control), we stayed close to home. And when we did leave the Village and

Yun Gee, mid-1930s.

venture uptown, we often walked separately and sat opposite each other on the subway train.

Other than that, we were happy. But everything changed when Yun was invited to exhibit in Paris, which meant living apart for a while. He had always hoped to return to France, claiming to have experienced less prejudice there, and while waiting to join him, I went to work. I was trained for nothing and jobs were scarce, so I took whatever I could get. I worked as a girl Friday for a Chinese "antique" dealer (but quit when I discovered the Ming Dynasty porcelains were being aged in the basement), waited on tables (two jobs in two days, each a fiasco), and just when I thought I'd never keep a job, I answered an ad for "artists, no experience necessary" and was hired by Whelan Studios.

Whelan's (also known as the American Photograph Corporation) operated a chain of studios in department stores, specializing in low-cost portraiture. Each studio had a different name and appeared to be individually owned. They were staffed by young men who, after taking a crash course at the company headquarters (three floors of an office building at 370 Seventh Avenue) were sent afield, knowing little more than when to click the shutter. Everything was reduced to a formula—the lighting, the poses, even the words to coax smiles from the sitter. ("Say prunes, say cheese.") The film was processed assembly-line style, and after the negatives were retouched—wrinkles and blemishes (and character) removed—all that remained on the foggy faces were the smiles. Few small studios could compete with Whelan's prices, and over half were forced to close.

Whelan's also offered a photo restoration service, which was where I fit in. Hired as a trainee, at ten dollars a week, I was placed in the Airbrush Department, where a group of young women—"the airbrush girls"—worked on enlargements of the originals. Huddled at easels and breathing in dust, we sprayed in backgrounds, cleaned up faces, built in clothes, and turned battered old photographs into new-looking studio portraits. I took to the work because I could draw, and after several months got a five-dollar raise, bringing me up to fifteen. Eventually I developed a specialty: I had opened the eyes of a man in a coffin, propped upright against the side of a house, flanked by members of his family. Because they liked what I'd done, they gave me all the corpses, and since photographing the dead was common-place in the past, I performed these resurrections regularly.

This was not the most inspiring work, and I only hoped I'd survive the dust and long hours (seven days a week in the busy season) and not develop tuberculosis or some other dread disease while waiting for Yun to establish himself in Paris. I had thought of the job as temporary. After a couple of years this was hard to do.

YUN WAS STILL in Paris when World War II broke out. For a while he was trapped, unable to get permission to take along his paintings. But once he did, he took the next boat, and we resumed where we left off, a couple of hundred letters ago.

But nothing was the same. Yun had changed. He was moody, erratic, and prone to depression, yet when we finally married, in 1942, I was still un-aware he was ill. I attributed his behavior to fatigue. He worked six days a week in a defense plant, then stayed up half the night to paint.

I was three months pregnant when Yun broke down. He was hospital-ized, placed under observation in the psychiatric ward of Bellevue Hospital, and diagnosed as schizophrenic, with no chance of cure. I was beside my-self. I couldn't bear to separate him from his paintings and his birds, and rather than incarcerate him in a mental institution, possibly for life, I had him released in my custody on the understanding that he'd return as an out-patient for electric-shock treatment.

Besides, I needed him. I had developed a serious pregnancy disorder and was ordered to remain in bed for the next six months, until the baby was born. But Yun was of little help. He was always on the edge, fluctuating be-tween frenzy and apathy, and since most of the time he was unable to work, I found I had to support myself. Having planned to freelance after the baby was born, I owned all the necessary equipment—an airbrush, a compres-sor, and drawing tools. Whelan's agreed to keep me on salary (at eighteen dollars a week) and delivered a new batch of photographs each day. But working in bed was difficult, and what would ordinarily have taken seven or eight hours took ten or twelve.

Much of the time I was hungry. A pot of rice by the bed kept me going,

but it often ran out and Yun was seldom around to replenish it. But I could always depend on a pig's knuckle. He boiled a dozen a week in a large restaurant pot, adding occasional variety with ears and snouts. While this may have been a time-honored dish in China—rich in nutrients and of benefit to the unborn—my stomach turned at the sight of the quivering mass, whether I was hungry or not.

The chance of sustaining the pregnancy was slim. But I managed to hang on and give birth to a big baby girl, one ounce shy of nine pounds. (Yun attributed her size to the pigs' knuckles; I weighed less than a hundred.) She looked completely Chinese, with thick, black hair, almond-shaped eyes, and the bluish color at the base of the spine that Asian babies are born with (and which fades in a couple of months). We called her Li-lan, meaning orchid that grows on the Li River, a name Yun found thumbing through the Chinese-American dictionary.

For a while Yun improved. But the disturbance returned, and when his behavior began to border on violence, I took the crib, some clothes, and a few books, and left. I had a dollar and a quarter and the offer of a job.

THE OFFER FELL through, but rather than return to the dust and long hours at Whelan's, I took a job in a factory painting chinaware. I painted l'amour and rosebuds on heart-shaped porcelain boxes, at twelve dollars a gross. As a piece-worker, I was able to leave in mid-afternoon and pick up Li-lan at her nursery school, the Church of All Nations on the Lower East Side. To make up the time, I brought home a suitcase full of hearts each day, and painted them at night when Li-lan was asleep. I returned them in the morning, but navigating the subway rush hour, a toddler in one hand, a suitcase full of porcelain in the other, was a balancing act.

The work dried up after St. Valentine's Day, so I took a job painting roses on hampers and garbage cans, at ten and a quarter cents a can. I could paint a full-blown rose in less than a minute, and working at full speed, gross forty dollars a week. But the money didn't go far, and when I thought of the future, I became very depressed. All I saw ahead of me was roses, thousands and thousands of roses.

But photographs, not roses, were destined to be my lot. Out of the blue came a call from John English, the art director of *Today's Woman*, a new home-

Helen Gee and Li-lan, 1943.

maker's magazine. I'd met John's wife, Frances, when Li-lan was a baby (we were the only mothers in Washington Square Park who believed in breast-feeding and were looked upon by the others as peasants). She apparently told John about my airbrush experience. Could I handle a food shot?

The Englishes lived nearby — we were on Fourteenth Street, they on West Twelfth — so I ran over to their apartment, worked on the photograph when Li-lan was asleep, and returned it on the way to nursery school in the morning. A few days later, he brought home a fashion shot. I had no trouble adapting the techniques I'd used on corpses to fashion models, and soon I was retouching all of the magazine's black-and-white prints.

But John grew uneasy with the arrangement. "Helen, you've got to quit your garbage can job and show your face at the magazine," he said. "I bring the work home at night and return it in the morning. The editor thinks that I'm the one doing the retouching."

Today's Woman didn't have enough work to keep me going, but I took a chance and quit the garbage cans, banking on finding additional clients. Taking on Madison Avenue was difficult. My hands shook when I showed samples of my work, and every interview left me limp. Art directors were unwilling to take chances with a beginner, and the only one who offered any hope (and didn't keep me waiting forever in the reception room) was Alexey Brodovitch, the illustrious art director of *Harper's Bazaar*. He promised to call me should his regular retoucher fall ill.

Nothing developed on Madison Avenue, so I rooted around in the neighborhood and picked up some work from Angela Calomiris, a photographer with a studio on Jane Street. She was illustrating a children's book about a flying fish, and I had to paint in the fish, leaping out of buckets and swooping through the air. Calomiris was pleased and promised more work, but when I learned that she'd been a spy for the FBI, reporting on members of the Photo League, I crossed her off as a client. Though I'd never heard of the Photo League and knew nothing at all about social documentary photography, I had only contempt for anyone who would participate in Senator Joseph P. McCarthy's witch hunt.

John English urged me take up transparency retouching, a new, lucrative field, promising to give me additional work should I master the skills. But the techniques involved were a mystery, and the only three retouchers who did this work—William Way, Estelle Friedman, and Tulio Martin—were not about to share trade secrets. Transparency retouching required some knowledge of chemistry, so I spent several days at the Eastman Kodak plant in Rochester. Though the technicians were able to supply me with some information, I experimented a year before taking on a job.

By 1951, I was doing quite well. I had given up black-and-white print retouching, specialized in color, and my clients included not only *McCall's* (where John English was now art director), but four-star advertising agencies and leading magazines. I had a pleasant apartment in midtown, a secretary named Queen Nonnamaker, and could afford to send Li-lan to a private school. I'd given up thrift shops, wore designer clothes, and even had a bit of a social life.

Yet, despite all this, I was restive. Was success on Madison Avenue enough?

MY ROMANCE with photography began, as romances often do, by accident. I had gone to the Museum of Modern Art to see a foreign film, and while waiting at the entrance to the auditorium, an area adjacent to the ladies' room, where the photography shows were generally held, I became fascinated with the exhibit on view. It opened my eyes to the possibilities of the camera, and on every subsequent visit I went downstairs, hoping to find another photography show. I was hooked.

I toyed with the idea of taking pictures myself and, at the advice of the photographer Paul Radkai, purchased a Rolleiflex and registered for Alexey Brodovitch's course at the New School for Social Research, held at the Radkai Studio. Brodovitch was not only the country's most influential art director, but he was esteemed as a teacher as well. Yet I realized after a few sessions that the course was not for me. Most of the students were working photographers, and I was still studying the instruction manual, trying to fathom the workings of the camera. Brodovitch was harsh, imperious, impatient with the students, suspecting, perhaps (as I did), that most were there simply to draw his attention to their work, in the hope of an assignment from *Harper's Bazaar*. Too intimidated to bring in pictures—or even to take them—I quit in the middle of the course.

But the time had not been lost. I came away knowing about Lisette Model. Brodovitch had mentioned her name a number of times, usually when discussing his efforts to include one or two images by a great photographer, such as Cartier-Bresson, Brassai, Walker Evans, Bill Brandt, and Lisette

Model, in every issue of the magazine. I looked for her work at the Museum of Modern Art, and though none of her photographs was currently on view, I did learn something about her. She was born in Vienna to well-to-do parents, studied music with the composer Arnold Schoenberg, and continued her studies in Paris in the 1920s. In the mid-1930s, finding herself in financial straits, she purchased a camera, hoping to find work as a darkroom technician. She had no formal training, but on a trip to Nice in 1937, she took the photographs of wealthy idlers on the French Riviera that brought her instant recognition when she moved to New York. Brodovitch was one of her early supporters, and her work appeared regularly in *Harper's Bazaar*. On checking back issues, I found that I liked her brash, hard-hitting style, and particularly those pictures of stout, aging, ill-clad women, incongruous in a fashion magazine. After 1946, her work seldom appeared. Had she stopped photographing? Was she difficult? Or was it related to a remark that Brodovitch had made in class: "Lisette Model is a great photographer, but alas, she cannot make a good print."

While it was reassuring to know that even great photographers have weaknesses, it hadn't rekindled my interest in taking pictures, and I relegated my Rolleiflex to an upper shelf, alongside a guitar, a chess set, and other relics of past enthusiasms. And there it might have remained were it not for a chance encounter with a stranger at a party, a man whose name I didn't learn, and who I never expected to see again.

The party was one of those glitzy Madison Avenue affairs, buzzing with art directors, account executives, and commercial photographers, all busy promoting themselves. While wandering around, looking for someone to talk to, I noticed an interesting-looking man on the sidelines. He had longish black hair, a marvelous face, and soft, dark eyes, but what made him stand out in this sea of crew cuts and gray flannel suits were his clothes: black corduroy pants, a black Eisenhower jacket, and tossed around his neck, a kelly green scarf.

He could only be an artist, and not having talked to an artist for a very long time, I maneuvered my way to his side. Soon we were deep in conversation. He had a curious accent—it sounded Russian with a tinge of French—and other than the fact that he was indeed a painter, I learned little else. He preferred to talk about me. When did I first become interested in art? I told him I'd been interested as far back as I could remember and that I'd once even thought of becoming a painter myself.

"Why not start now?" he said. "It's never too late."

"I can't," I said. "I work for a living, and I'm raising a child. Art is a luxury I can't afford."

"Making art is no luxury. It's as important as bread."

"But I have no time."

"You must *make* time."

He went on and on, trying to convince me to "make art" on the side, when we were interrupted by a client, the account executive of Van Camp's Beans. He scribbled his name and number on a paper napkin and as I stuffed it in my purse, he said, "Why don't you come visit the studio? We're there most of the time."

Having taken note of the "we," I decided not to call. My life was on an even keel—at last—and I was not about to court trouble. But I couldn't forget him. For days I was in turmoil, trying to sort out my feelings—was it the man, or was it the memories he evoked? Whatever it was, he'd brought back the past, and I found myself thinking of Yun, reliving those days in the studio before he became ill. I saw him at his easel, a memory so vivid I could almost smell oil paint. I heard him play music, heard the birds chime in, heard the singsong sound of Cantonese as he talked with his Chinese friends. How I missed all that.

But what I missed most of all was art in my life. The painter was right. I should do *something*, but what? Should I paint? Painting was lonely, hard work, and after being tied all day to a retouching stand, did I want to be tied to an easel? Should I photograph? I'd gone that route and it hadn't worked out. Should I try again? With photography, I'd at least get fresh air and exercise. But was that a good enough reason?

Unable to decide, I thought I'd call the painter and ask for advice. But when I looked in my purse, the napkin was gone. And I couldn't remember his name.

I WAS STILL undecided, vacillating between painting and photographing, when I came across an item in Jacob Deschin's column in the *New York Times*

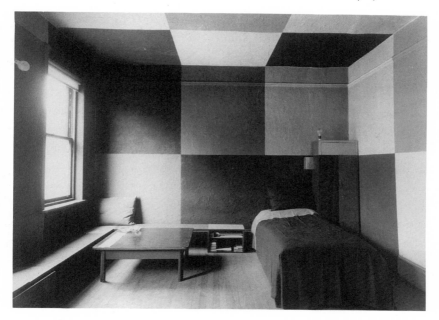

Lisette Model's studio, 1951, by David Vestal.

announcing a course by Lisette Model. I picked up the phone and made an appointment to see her that same afternoon.

I took a cab to Greenwich Village, but as I mounted the stairs at 55 Grove Street, a small, nondescript building off Sheridan Square, I had qualms. Would Model accept me as a student? She had asked me to bring work, and I had none. But it was too late now; there she was, standing at the door, a small woman of about fifty or so, with a pert, heart-shaped face and short, wavy, white hair. Dressed in a simple black sweater and skirt, she nevertheless looked elegant.

"Come in, my dear." She had a deep, rich voice and a manner both regal and gracious. She led me through a foyer, which was painted black, into a room so filled with color I gasped. It was like nothing I'd ever seen. The entire room, walls, ceiling, everything but the floor, was divided into squares, each measuring about three or four feet, and each painted a different color—red, yellow, black, white. The afternoon sun, pouring through uncurtained windows, intensified the reds and the yellows. It was like stepping inside a painting by Mondrian.

"It's beautiful!" I exclaimed, finally finding my voice.

"I'm glad you like it," she said. "Some people find it too strong."

What little furniture there was had been painted black—a few chairs, a coffee table, and a low, narrow bench built against one wall. A narrow cot was covered in black, and, except for the color, the room was monastic. Nowhere was there a work of art—not a painting, a photograph, not even a plant or a book.

She motioned me to a chair, and as we talked I became aware of her eyes. They were the eyes of a clairvoyant—hooded, mystical; they looked at you and at the same time through you, a most unsettling sensation. Even more unsettling was a sudden strange thought: if Lisette Model had been born centuries earlier, she would have been burned at the stake as a witch.

"Why do you want to study photography?" she asked.

"Because I love it," I blurted, unprepared for the question.

"Good. That's the only reason to study. Now let's take a look at your work."

I confessed that I had none; all I had in my bag was a camera.

"Good! Then you have nothing to unlearn." She took my Rolleiflex and, peering into the viewfinder, pretended to take my picture. "My dear, using a camera is like playing the piano," she said, tapping the casing as if playing a few notes. "It comes alive in your hands." As she handed it back, I noticed her ring, a conventional wedding band with tiny diamond chips, oddly out of sync in this setting.

"I have no equipment. Should I buy a light meter?"

"No. If you depend on a meter, you'll never develop a sensitivity to light conditions. Photography is all in the eye, my dear. Come, I'll show you my darkroom and you'll see how little you need."

She led me to the bathroom. Squeezed into a niche at the foot of the tub was an enlarger, bottles of chemicals, and some developing trays. I thought of the spacious, well-equipped darkrooms in the uptown studios, all gleaming with stainless steel, and wondered: is this how a great photographer is fated to work?

"Then you will accept me as a student?" I said, edging out of the bathroom.

"Of course, my dear. But don't depend on me for technical advice. I have no patience with that sort of thing."

I took out my checkbook, and was filling it out—fifty dollars for a three-month course—when I heard a key turn in the door.

"Evsa, where have you been?" she called.

"Walking in Washington Square, mon cherie." The voice sounded vaguely familiar. I looked up, and there was the man I'd met at the party—the man in the kelly green scarf.

SIX OTHERS enrolled for Lisette's class, and she started us off on a Sunday afternoon with a trip to the Lower East Side. We assembled on the corner of Delancey and Grand, and after delivering her dictum, "Don't shoot until you feel it in your gut," she disappeared into a coffee shop.

The Lower East Side was a street photographer's paradise, vying in popularity with Coney Island and Times Square. The tenements had not yet been replaced with giant housing projects, and life was still lived on the streets. Television had not made inroads, and the drama was all outside. Women hung out of windows, keeping an eye on their kids; boys played stickball and cops-and-robbers; girls skipped rope and played hopscotch; old people sunned themselves on camp chairs; and neighbors gossiped on stoops. Everybody knew everybody else, much like in the small towns of Europe. Czechs, Poles, Russians, Hungarians, all were part of a rich ethnic mix. On Saturday, the Jewish Sabbath, most stores were closed. But on Sunday, the big shopping day, people came from all over, to haggle with the vendors, pick up bargains in the mom-and-pop stores, and gorge themselves on blintzes, knishes, and the best kosher frankfurters in town.

Though still uncertain of the workings of the camera, I plunged in, excited by everything I saw. Pushcarts offered all sorts of things—cabbages, corsets, antique jewelry, old clocks—and while I would ordinarily have rooted around for bargains, I was more interested in the vendors than their wares. They had wonderful, craggy faces, and since they couldn't leave their pushcarts, I had time to figure out exposures and such. But I was taken aback when one reached out his hand for a modeling fee—fifty cents was the going rate—and another announced no purchase, no picture.

Giving up on the vendors, I concentrated on shoppers, and for the rest of the afternoon went charging around, bursting with newfound confidence. My only frustration was having to duck into doorways and reload the camera every twelve shots, and after shooting eight rolls in less than two hours, I decided I was too prolific a photographer to stay with a camera as cumbersome as the Rolleiflex, and thought of buying a Leica.

But when I picked up my contact sheets at the developer's that week, I found that I'd produced mostly blurs. "You're very uninhibited," Lisette remarked kindly, when I showed the sorry results in class. "All you need is practice."

Halfway through the course, Lisette's husband Evsa (still sporting his kelly green scarf) decided to give a class of his own. Lisette urged her students to join. "Painting will help your photography," she said. "It will put you in touch with your feelings."

Feelings were not my problem. Time was. Free to photograph only a few hours a week, how could I find time to paint? But finally I agreed, and on Tuesday nights splashed away with the others. Evsa's method of teaching was similar to Lisette's; the emphasis was on feeling rather than technique. He would suggest a subject—a nude, an eye, possibly Times Square—and give us twenty minutes to work. He insisted we use only cheap newsprint paper and poster paints, and while this made us feel like kindergarten students, the results were fresh and spontaneous. I brought Li-lan to class a couple of times, and her work showed talent, portending a future as a painter.

The class was fascinating and, unfortunately for me, so was Evsa. I found it hard not to stare when he leaned back in a chair, eyes half-closed, and took a long, sensuous drag on a cigarette. Lisette painted along with us, but nothing escaped her. I felt increasingly uncomfortable, and guilty, too, smitten as I was by Evsa. That the attraction was mutual soon became evident, and after he started following me into his bedroom when I went to pick up my coat, I knew it was time to quit class.

Lisette suggested I quit hers as well. I did, but with regrets. First Brodovitch, now Lisette Model—would I ever complete a photography course?

Lisette Model and Helen Gee on the Lower East Side, 1953.

"YOU'VE GOT TO study with Sid Grossman!" Lou Bernstein slammed his fist on the counter, startling the customers waiting to be served. "He'll change your life."

"I don't want my life changed," I protested, having gone to Peerless only to buy film, not to be lectured by a salesman and told what to do with my life. But one had to forgive him. Lou was a serious photographer, a disciple of Grossman's, and he was simply spreading the word.

This was not the first time I'd heard of Sid Grossman, of course, though it was usually in connection with the Photo League; he had been one of its guiding lights. Described by a former member as "part school, part club,

Sid Grossman, 1951, by David Vestal.

part exhibition space," the Photo League had, for a full ten years, served as a rallying ground for serious photography. Despite its advocacy of social documentary work, it had attracted, both as members and participants in its lectures and exhibits, photographers as disparate as Ansel Adams, Barbara Morgan, Aaron Siskind, Edward Weston, Richard Avedon, Lisette Model, W. Eugene Smith, Berenice Abbott, Walter Rosenblum, Paul Strand, and Helen Levitt. Grossman had headed its teaching program, yet he was often at odds with those who espoused a social-activist approach. Grossman was committed to personally expressive work, yet because of his radical political views, it was he who bore the brunt when the Photo League was declared "subversive" and placed on the attorney general's list of Communist-front organizations. At first photographers rallied—Eugene Smith became its president in 1947—but black-balling had its effect, and the membership declined. The league was disbanded in 1951. Afraid of being accused of "guilt by association," a common McCarthy ploy, Sid was deserted, even by close friends. Though no longer badgered by the FBI, he was still considered a pariah.

He eked out a living teaching in his loft, and when I heard that he was about to start a new class, I took Lou Bernstein's advice and joined. "You better think twice," a former student of Sid's warned, "Grossman's a tyrant. He'll either inspire you or crush you."

I paid the usual fifty dollars for a three-month course and arrived at Grossman's loft on East 24th Street at eight o'clock on a Friday night. There were six students in all, though one, I suspected, was a friend, sitting in to flesh out the class. (She kept dozing behind dark glasses.) Sid sat at the head of the table, and, cigarette in one hand, coffee cup in the other (frequently refilled by his adoring wife Miriam), he launched into a monologue. Carried away by his eloquence, I lost track of the time, and when he finally stopped, it was ten o'clock. But this was only a coffee break; Sid was just warming up. I kept checking my watch, having told my baby-sitter I'd be home by eleven. At midnight Sid was still going strong.

I went through quite a few baby-sitters in the next three months. The class seldom ended before two in the morning, and Sid never ran out of words. He looked like a stevedore—dungarees, work shirt, chunky shoes, an image in keeping with his proletarian views—but out of his mouth came poetry. In one breath he'd say, "You must know that the day welcomes you, that the sun shines generously, that the rain means you no harm . . ." and in the next, he'd lash out, attacking some favorite target. He railed against the photo magazines, picture magazines, camera clubs, photo agencies, advertising agencies, Edward Steichen and the Museum of Modern Art. Although I shared many of his views (particularly about the hack work in the picture magazines), I found his tyrannical behavior hard to take.

We clashed from the start. But after weeks of verbal fencing, I gave up and said nothing. Rather than quit the class (not again!), I swallowed hard and tried to ignore the pains in my stomach, which grew worse as the evening progressed. I tried slipping out one night during the coffee break, but Sid spotted me at the door, and after overhearing him remark about "bourgeois women in expensive clothes" (I was wearing a coat I'd designed and had made), I never tried to escape again.

Sid seldom looked at the students' work (he looked at mine once, and I was elated when he praised it), but what he gave us was more valuable than individual criticism. His passion and commitment were lessons in themselves. For Sid, photography wasn't a thing apart, not something you did with only half a heart; it called for total involvement. He urged us to live for photography, and if not for photography, then for whatever else we believed in. "On the day of your death," he thundered one night, "will you say to yourself, I've thrown my life away?"

Sid inspired either love or hate. In me, he inspired both. I loved his integrity, his zeal, his sense of mission; I hated his intolerance and need to disparage others. My feelings kept changing from week to week, and by the end of the course, I'd lost fifteen pounds and was much too thin. Rather than go on riding an emotional roller-coaster—and risk getting an ulcer—I decided not to repeat the course in the fall.

Besides, I had other plans. I had hit on the idea of my coffeehouse cum photography gallery and had to start looking for space. Lou Bernstein was right: my life would change.

THE ABANDONED nightclub, its facade a patchwork of faded posters and peeling paint, spoiled the appearance of the entire block. Overhead, like a swinging tombstone, a sign marked the remains of what had once been The Place.

I'd been looking for space in Greenwich Village, a section of the city where I felt most at home. I'd been searching for months, and though I'd passed The Place a number of times, I dismissed it as a prospect after reading the posters plastered out front. One advertised a concert held in 1949, another a play long since closed; others were too faded to read. Something had to be wrong with a place empty that long.

I'd walked every block, answered all the ads, but everything was too small, too high-priced, too out of the way. After many disappointments, I went back to the West Village and took another look at The Place. One thing in its favor was its size. It was a one-story building running diagonally through the block, with an entrance on Seventh Avenue South, a back door on Barrow Street. Another advantage was location. It was in the heart of the West Village, one block from Christopher Street and a half-block from Sheridan Square. It was surrounded by Off Broadway theaters: the Sheridan Square Theater on the corner, the Actor's Playhouse across the street, the Cherry Lane and the Theater de Lys just blocks away, and the Circle in the Square, the granddaddy of them all, around the corner on 4th Street. It was also within blocks of several popular bars—the Riviera on Sheridan Square,

Louis' on West 4th, Chumley's on Bedford, and the White Horse Tavern (where Dylan Thomas was said to have had his last drink) on Hudson Street.

Why, then, had it been empty so long? The way to find out was to ask around the neighborhood. I dropped in at Aphrodite, a flower shop across the street, and while purchasing a bunch of zinnias, worked around to the subject of the club.

"The Place? Don't touch it," the florist warned. "It's been empty for seven years."

"Why? What's wrong with it?"

"It's jinxed."

He wouldn't elaborate, so I stopped in for a hamburger at a luncheonette two doors away. But there I learned even less. The owner was more interested in talking about his own spot, which had been owned by Harry Belafonte before he became a star. From there I went to a book store, a drugstore, a delicatessen, a shoemaker's, and picking up tidbits here and there, finally put together a picture of The Place. A striptease joint in the 1940s, it was shut down after a shooting, in what was rumored to be a gangland murder. Intrigued, I tracked down Romano, the agent of the building, and asked him to take me inside.

"Don't waste your time. It's a wreck," he said. Now I know a nice little spot on Bleecker Street. Just right for a tea room."

"A *coffeehouse*."

"Okay, a coffeehouse."

He finally agreed to show me The Place after I promised to travel to Bleecker. But he never stopped grumbling as I stood shivering in the cold on a January morning while he tinkered with an unyielding lock. "Damned thing's busted. Can't remember the last time I showed this joint."

The door grated open, and I walked into a vestibule, down a few steps, and stood peering through the half-light at what remained of the club. I could make out a bar and a long row of booths. Everything was covered with layers of dust, and I kept sneezing as I picked my way across the badly warped floor.

"Watch out!" Romano yelled. "Don't stand under them skylights!" The glass in one was hanging in shards, perilously close to crashing down, and the other had caved in and was open to the sky. Glass lay shattered at my feet.

Behind the bar there were two large mirrors, one with cracks radiating from a small round hole. (From a bullet?) Glasses and beer bottles still stood on the bar, strung together with cobwebs. The cash register hung open, bar checks were strewn all over the place, and a couple of coats, moldering in the cloak room, suggested hasty departures.

At the back of the room was a bandstand, which was probably where the strippers had worked, and behind the bandstand, another room, the vandalized remains of a kitchen. Broken crockery, pipes ripped from walls, and everything but the stove turned upside-down.

"See what I mean?" Romano said. "Come on, let's go. I'll show you that spot on Bleecker Street."

"But this is wonderful! It's just what I want." I'd transformed the place with my eyes. I'd torn out the bar and the row of booths, ripped away the plasterboard and exposed the brick, dismantled the bandstand and built a gallery in its place, and hanging in the spot where the strippers had performed were Edward Westons, Eugene Smiths, Robert Franks.

Romano looked puzzled. "You got any experience in the food line?"

"Well, sort of. . . ." I was not about to admit that my experience was limited to sneaking into the kitchens of the Rienzi and the Coffee Mill and taking a quick look before being ushered out.

Limelight premises before renovation, February 1954, by Arthur Lavine.

"Okay. I'll talk to the landlord. But don't get your hopes up. Big Ben ain't eager to rent this joint. You're wasting your time."

I knew he was right, but it was worth a try. Yet, if by some miracle he did agree, how could I afford a place of this size? I figured it could seat about two hundred people and still leave room for a nice-sized gallery.

I had resigned myself to yet another disappointment when Romano called and said yes, Big Ben had agreed. But the big surprise was the rent—only two hundred and seventy-five dollars a month!

Romano couldn't believe it.

Neither could I.

Neither could my attorney, Meyer Sheinfeld. "There must be a catch in it somewhere," he said. "Rents are sky-high in the Village. A place that size is worth at least a thousand."

Sheinfeld had hoped I'd give up my plans, not only because I was young and female and inexperienced in business, but because the mortality rate in the restaurant field was extremely high; most failed within the first year.

I had to remind Sheinfeld that mine was to be no *ordinary* restaurant.

And Big Ben, I now discovered, was no *ordinary* landlord. I'd heard rumors of nightclubs and nefarious dealings, so I wasn't surprised when he showed up at Sheinfeld's office to sign the lease with three "associates," dark-haired men in snap-brims and dark suits, right out of an Edward G. Robinson movie. Sheinfeld winced, and seemed for a moment to lose his cool legal stance as the three plunked down on his big leather couch and Big Ben sank into a wing chair.

While Sheinfeld looked over the lease, I looked over the men. Big Ben was attractive in an oily sort of way. He was tall and heavy-set, with the kind of Italian good looks that you saw every day along Bleecker Street. One of his "associates" must have spent years in the ring, and however much I tried not to stare, I couldn't take my eyes off the only cauliflower ears I'd ever seen. (Actually though, they looked more like Brussels sprouts.)

Sheinfeld wrangled his way from clause to clause, with an occasional grunt from Big Ben. Everything seemed to be going well. We won a ten-year lease, starting February 1, 1954. But just when I thought all was settled, we ran into a snag. Big Ben insisted that I get his approval to transfer the lease should I ever decide to sell. Sheinfeld objected, beckoning me into a side room.

"What difference does it make?" I argued.

"Can't you see this is a trap? He can ruin a sale if he wants to."

"But I don't intend to sell the place. Ever."

"You may feel that way now. But no one knows what the future holds."

"I'll worry about the future when it arrives," I said. "Let's go ahead and sign."

Sheinfeld shrugged. "You're a stubborn girl, Helen. But remember, I warned you."

We signed the lease—Big Ben with a flourish, me with a trembling hand. If for a moment I lost my nerve, it was quickly restored when all four men started pumping my arm and wishing me luck. Already I felt a success. As they trooped out, Big Ben turned and wished me a final "Good luck!"

"You'll need it," Sheinfeld said. "The last thing Ben wants is for you to succeed."

"Why not? What's he got to gain if I don't?"

"A newly renovated place, which he can either use for himself to open another club or rent out for quite a lot of money. That's probably why he decided on you as a tenant, because he's sure that you'll fail."

Fail? The possibility had never occurred to me. But then I remembered the florist's warning. "The Place? Don't touch it. It's jinxed." I pushed the words from my mind.

SIX THOUSAND dollars wouldn't go far, but it was all I was able to raise. Part had come from the sale of stock, and part from the settlement of Gee v. Yee (a lawsuit my attorney said sounded like a tong war). I'd been injured while picking up work in the studio of Tom Yee, a commercial photographer (one of the few Chinese in the field). His help had gone home, and he was constructing a set for *Bride's Magazine* when he climbed on top of a ceiling-high pile of props, dislodging a crate. Everything came down on me. My foot was crushed, I limped for a year, and during that time, slipped and broke my coccyx too. My attorney urged me to settle, claiming that a jury would not look kindly on a woman with an "Oriental" child. That hurt almost as much as the accident itself, but at least I had the satisfaction of putting the money to good use. I'd have a gallery to show for those months hobbling around on crutches and sitting on a doughnut-shaped rubber cushion.

The money crunch eased when Peggy Tallmer, an interior designer just starting out, offered to design the place for a pittance. Peggy was a friend, and I admired her taste. She had little in the way of conventional good looks—a long, thin face, a toothy smile—yet she gave the illusion of beauty. Dressed in blue jeans, her hair pulled back in a single braid, she could have appeared on the cover of *Harper's Bazaar*.

We visualized the place in much the same way—simple, elegant, yet warm and inviting, and with none of those corny, "bohemian" touches one associated with Greenwich Village—no candles in chianti bottles, no red-checkered table cloths, no cobwebs in corners. The dining room would be softly lit, even a bit romantic in feeling, and the gallery, in contrast, cool, stark, and brightly lit.

Since this all had to be done on a shoestring, we needed just the right contractor—one we could afford, one we could trust. We'd heard all the usual horror stories, how contractors ran over their estimates, did shoddy work, and didn't finish on time. After interviewing several, I decided to play it safe and hire Moe Rubin, an elderly man with long experience, recommended by Sam, my accountant. He was a friend of his father's and, as Sam put it, "a man of the old school; his word is his bond."

But I still preferred a legal bond, so we drew up a contract. Rubin agreed that for four thousand dollars, he would gut the premises, strip the walls and expose the brick, lay a new floor, install new plumbing and wiring, replace the two broken skylights, restore the front window (which had been bricked up when the place was a strip-tease joint), make repairs in the kitchen and rest rooms, construct the gallery, and paint.

This was a very good deal. But Rubin was inclined to be touchy. He wasn't accustomed to working with women (especially young women), so Sam advised using tact. "Remember, he's a man of the old school."

But the trouble with a man of the old school, we discovered, was that his ideas were "old school" too. Rubin was horrified when he saw Peggy's plans. "What, no chrome? I built dozens of cafeterias in my day, and they all had nice, shiny chrome."

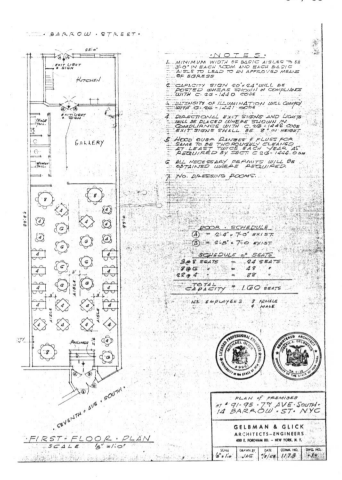

Peggy said nothing, but she decided to keep an eye on Rubin and his crew to make sure they didn't slip in his chrome. She lived nearby, so every day, ostensibly on her way to the library, the laundromat, or Washington Square, she strolled in and took a quick look around.

Meanwhile, we set about equipping the place. Neither Peggy nor I had the foggiest idea of how much to order of anything, but whenever I was able to break away from the studio, we went downtown to the Bowery and poked around in the restaurant supply stores, figuring things out as we went along. These trips could be depressing. Alongside the stores were the Bowery "hotels," flea-bags with names like Excelsior, Paradise, or Uncle Sam's, and sprawled on the streets, lying in urine and reeking of vomit, were the unfortunates of New York's Skid Row. Nowhere else in the city did people live on the streets; even the poorest had homes.

What helped raise our spirits were some very good buys. The stores all seemed to be run by cantankerous old men, who, together with their cantankerous wives, had been selling pots and pans in these very same stores for twenty or thirty years. Peggy was good at haggling, a necessary rite in the secondhand stores, so we often came away with great bargains: two hundred beautiful (if a bit wobbly) bentwood chairs at three dollars each, old cafe tables with wrought iron bases and white milk-glass tops at ten dollars, and a group of sturdy wood tables (originally from the Central Park boat house) at fifteen. Some of our best buys came from basements. In one, we found a barrel of old silverware, each piece from an exclusive restaurant or hotel, dating back to a time when only fine silver would do. Persnickety as brides, we picked through hundreds of knives, forks, and spoons, selecting those with the prettiest patterns, at ten cents a piece.

The shopkeepers considered us crazy—meshugge, they muttered, in Yiddish—and whenever we asked for anything out of the ordinary, like white chinaware (which was seldom used at the time) or white oval side-dishes (which we planned to use as ashtrays, instead of the usual black plastic ones), they would shrug, roll their eyes, and mutter "meshugge."

There was one time, however, when the tables were turned, and it was we who decided that the dealer was meshugge. I had thought of using a Chemex pot for "American" coffee. I liked the ingenious double-coned design and approved of the principle behind the pot: the coffee was filtered through chemists' paper, and with the oils removed, it always tasted fresh. I had one at home and liked it.

We visited the Chemex showroom uptown, and when the salesman heard that I was opening a coffeehouse and was interested in the giant, fifty-four-cup model, he announced that Dr. Schlumbohm, the inventor of the Chemex, just happened to be in the office. Schlumbohm was a bit of a celebrity, having been profiled in the New Yorker, and having made a fortune with his pot. A tall, massively built man with a halo of iron-gray hair, he charged out of the office and, talking nonstop, led us into a room in the back. Inspired by the success of his Chemex pot, he'd designed a new set of products, each incorporating chemist's paper and cone. They were displayed on pedestals, like works of art.

"You ladies smoke? Ever try to stop? Want to cut your nicotine consumption in half?" Without waiting to find out, he thrust a strange-looking object at us. "This is the revolutionary Schlumbohm cigarette holder." Clamping the thing in his jaw, he gave a muffled description of how it worked. You inserted the cigarette into one cone-shaped end, and as you inhaled through the other end, the paper inside filtered the smoke. It just so happened that I *was* trying to stop smoking and was interested in anything that would cut my nicotine consumption in half, but I couldn't see myself walking around with something in my mouth that looked like plumbing, regardless of the rewards.

"You ladies live alone?" He hadn't observed Peggy's wedding ring. "Here's just the thing, my Cinderella garbage can." It was the tiniest garbage can I'd ever seen—cone-shaped, of course, and lined with filter paper. It was just the thing, provided you ate like a bird.

We moved on to the next feature. "So you're going to open a coffeehouse? Well, summer's coming, and here's just the thing, the Schlumbohm personal electric fan." It had a cone-shaped base and "blades" of filter paper. "Place one of my fans on each one of your tables, and you won't need to invest in air-conditioning."

"But what about all the wires on the floor?" Peggy asked, finally managing to get in a word.

For a moment, Dr. Schlumbohm was silent, a far-away look in his eyes. Was he pondering the question? Did he see what we saw—a room full of tables and crisscrossed wires, and customers trying to pick their way through?

We didn't wait to find out. We declined politely and backed out of the room, leaving Schlumbohm with yet another cone-shaped object in his hand.

A MONTH went by and the renovation was in full swing when we were suddenly besieged by inspectors—health inspectors, building inspectors, fire inspectors, inspectors from city agencies that I didn't realize existed. I was unprepared, not yet having learned how to grease palms (or "shoot silver bullets," as the Chinese say). It was as if every city agency was focused on 91 Seventh Avenue South, determined that it should not open.

When we weren't besieged by inspectors, we were besieged by people looking for jobs—actors, dancers, poets, and painters (three Abstract Expressionists in a single week), all professing talents that had little to do with restaurant work. I liked the idea of hiring young women who "did things," but it was hard to choose from the array of Vassar graduates, Bennington drop-outs, and Theater Wing aspirants who showed up each day, eager to support their careers by working part-time as waitresses. The one photographer was Lilo Raymond (then still in the fledgling stage), and we hired her on the spot. Though we were still holding off on the kitchen help, we also hired her husband Herb, a painter. Herb had worked at the Coffee Mill uptown. Since we had just purchased an espresso machine—one thousand dollars, a sizable chunk of the budget—he went to work concocting the various coffees, helping us decide which to include on the menu.

To me, a coffee bean was simply a coffee bean. But now I learned from the ubiquitous salesman who descended en masse that there were all kinds of coffee beans: Jamaican, Italian, Colombian, French roast, to say nothing of all the blends. This was also true of food. Salami was not just salami: there was kosher, Genoa, Italian dry. Pickles were not just pickles: there were sweet, sour, Russian, dill. Hamburger was not just hamburger, mustard not just mustard, relish not just relish. . . . It seemed that everything had endless variations, each, of course, affecting the price.

"Thank heavens for Rubin," I murmured, when the inspectors, the salesmen, and the prospective employees proved too much. "At least I don't have to worry about him. The renovation was progressing on schedule, the plumbing and electrical work already half-done.

So I was surprised when he showed up at the apartment one day, saying something about "problems."

"Problems? What kind of problems?"

"This job is taking more time than I thought. I'm going to have to charge you extra."

"Extra? What about our agreement?"

"You never know what you're going to run into on a job." He handed me a list of hieroglyphics, none of which I could decipher. "It's going to cost you another two thousand."

"*Two thousand?* But the contract specifies *four*."

"Well, that's life. Things don't always turn out like you want."

"But I'm running out of money. There's hardly enough left for a refrigerator."

"Don't worry. dear, I'll make it easy for you. You can give me promissory notes."

Frantic, I telephoned Sam. He warned about changing horses in midstream, and though I was hardly in the mood for platitudes, it did make sense.

"But how could he have made such a big mistake?" I asked. "Six thousand dollars instead of *four?*"

"Helen, I'm sure it's something he couldn't help. Remember, we're not dealing with a stranger. Rubin's an old family friend."

I signed the notes with a sinking heart, consoling myself with the thought that any other contractor, running into these same problems, might not have accepted notes.

I went back to work, juggling the hours I spent at the studio and those downtown. There was still endless work to be done. The kitchen had to be organized, the menu planned, the rest of the staff hired—and most pressing of all, an exhibition arranged. The photographer I had in mind was Robert Frank. I loved his work and could think of no better way of launching a gallery than with a Robert Frank show. I'd phoned several times and left messages with his wife, Mary. But she sounded cold. I was afraid she was putting me off.

I decided to write and was framing a letter when Rubin appeared. He'd made considerable progress, but there were . . .

"Problems?" I asked, apprehensively.

"Yep, there's much more work than I expected. It's going to cost you another two thousand."

"So now it's *eight* thousand, double your estimate! Do you take me for a fool?"

"No, I think you're a very nice girl," he said, patting my arm. "I'll make it easy for you. You can give me notes."

"I won't give you anything," I said, jerking my arm away. "There's something fishy about this."

I marched to the phone and called Sam. But he was at his psychoanalyst's and wouldn't be home until late.

"Now don't do anything foolish," Rubin warned. "You wouldn't want a picket out front the night you open, would you?"

"*A picket line?* For what reason?" I'd never crossed a picket line and was appalled at the very thought.

"The union will send pickets if I ask them to. And you know what that will do to your business. You'll be finished before you even start."

"So if I'm finished, you can't collect on the notes."

"Oh yes, I can. Remember, you gave your personal guarantee. You've got to pay if you're in business or not."

I told Rubin to get out; I would never give in to his outrageous demands.

SAM SEEMED even more shaken than I was. We met at Jack Delaney's, a restaurant and bar on Sheridan Square. I wasted no words. "The man's a crook. All that stuff about his word is his bond. A man of the old school, indeed. . . ."

"Shhhh. . . ." Sam kept lighting cigarettes and glancing around. I'd always thought of Sam as a teetotaler (a rare bird in this hard-drinking age), but he ordered a scotch and gulped it down.

"And now he's threatening to picket the place. And you say he's an old family friend?"

"Yeah, until a few weeks ago." He crushed another cigarette, eyes darting around the room. "I guess I'll have to level with you. But you've got to promise that you'll keep it to yourself. Nobody must know. *Nobody.*"

Sam's father, it seemed, had a political past, and though Rubin had previously shared the same radical ideas, now he was threatening to expose him.

"That's terrible," I said. "But what has that got to do with me?"

"If you don't pay what he asks, he'll go ahead. He claims he made an honest mistake."

"That's blackmail!"

Sam doubted that Rubin would go so far as to report him, but spreading the word in the neighborhood would do damage enough. "You know what happens to people when they're accused of being 'reds.'" Of course I knew; everybody knew. I'd been following the hearings of the House Un-American Activities Committee, and what I found most appalling was how friends betrayed friends, either out of misguided patriotism, or simply to save their own skins. You caught glimpses of the hearings in newsreels, and as you watched Senator Joseph McCarthy play Grand Inquisitor, and saw people cave in, you couldn't help but wonder what happened to those American values—loyalty, honor, fair play.

I decided to fight. Not only to save my place, but to show up Rubin for the slime he was. But then I realized, after a sleepless night, that it was a fight I was certain to lose. Even if I won, I would lose: Sam's father would lose, his family would lose, and since I didn't have the money for a long, drawn-out battle, I would have to cancel my plans for a gallery. And so, in the end, photography would lose.

I signed the notes, told Rubin to finish in two weeks, and get out.

JUST AS I'D given up on reaching Robert Frank, he called. Surprised, I stumbled all over my words.

"Why don't you come to my studio?" he said. "We can talk about it then. How about nine o'clock Sunday morning?"

Nine o'clock on a Sunday morning? It was an unearthly hour to meet. I was never at my best in the morning, and these days I was at my worst—tired, cranky, unable to think clearly. I was sleeping less than four hours a night, dropping into bed in my jeans. Queen was worried. She hoped I could get through the next few weeks without ruining a transparency or losing an account. Li-lan was complaining about seeing me so little. It was weeks since we'd observed our Sunday morning ritual—Li-lan, dog Penny, and Mia the cat all piled on my bed while I read the papers.

Come Sunday morning, I gulped down a cup of coffee, stripped off my jeans, put on a skirt, dashed outside and hailed a cab. I'd heard that Robert Frank was difficult; I didn't want to offend him by arriving late.

"You sure you got the right address, Miss?" The cab pulled up in front of a deserted-looking loft building, the entrance barricaded with a metal gate. I checked my address book, and finding that this was indeed 130 West 23rd Street, I looked for a way to get inside. Finding no doorbells or name plates, I assumed this was one of those industrial buildings where artists lived illegally, needing space and low rent. The usual way of announcing one's arrival was to stand on the sidewalk and yell. I looked up at the windows and yelled till I was hoarse, but there was no sign of life—or Robert Frank. Had he forgotten the appointment? Had I arrived on the wrong day?

I looked around but couldn't find a phone. The stores along the block, most of them dealing in second-hand office furniture—beat-up old desks and swivel chairs—were closed, and the bars didn't open till noon. On weekdays, this was a busy thoroughfare, teeming with crosstown traffic, but now the streets were deserted.

Then I remembered the old Chelsea Hotel and called from a booth in the lobby.

"Who? Oh yeah. I'll be down in a minute," Frank mumbled.

About ten minutes later, he finally appeared, rumpled and puffy-eyed, like he'd been pulled out of bed. He unlocked the gate, and on the way upstairs, I remembered a friend's comment after visiting the Franks: "You can't tell if they're moving in or moving out."

I saw what he meant. The loft looked tentative, not quite settled in. The furniture—what there was of it—looked as though it had been carted in and dropped rather than arranged. Clothes were strewn all over the place—shoes, socks, underwear, and in front of a bureau with its drawers hanging open, lay a pair of lacy, lime-colored panties. "Careful," Robert Frank cautioned, side-stepping a toy truck and a pile of blocks. His small son, Pablo, a wistful-looking child with large dark eyes, went whooping his way around the room. He'd been using the floor as an easel; pictures and paints were scattered everywhere.

Yet despite the disarray, the place had charm. At the far end of the loft, framed against a bank of windows and a cascade of hanging plants, sat Robert's wife, Mary. I knew her from his photographs—Mary nursing Pablo, Mary lying in bed, Mary bathed in a magical light. She sat without moving, her face turned away. But I was already familiar with the pale oval face, the aquiline nose and light-colored eyes, and the tangle of long, frizzy hair. Hugely pregnant, she looked due any day.

"Coffee?" Her high, thin voice sounded far away. Coffee was just what I needed. On the table, along with three cups, was a bowl of fruit, a half-loaf of bread, a wedge of cheese, and a clump of tiny flowers in a jelly jar.

As the Franks sat silent and Pablo raced around the room, I launched into my gallery spiel. I was tired of repeating it and couldn't wait for the day when I no longer had to make speeches. But this time it really mattered. I had to convince Robert Frank that I was serious, that I was deeply committed to photography, and, if I was not too shy and could find the words, I would tell him how I loved his work and what it would mean to me personally to open with a Robert Frank show.

I went on and on, but with dwindling hope, talking to a man who was half-asleep and a woman who seemed lost in her own private world. For all I knew, I was talking to myself.

Then, just as I was about to come to the point, Robert Frank asked, "Do you know Bill Brandt's work?"

Yes, I did. In fact, Brandt was one of the photographers I planned to show.

"How about Edouard Boubat?"

I knew Boubat's work, and he was on my list too.

"Gotthard Schuh?"

I knew nothing about Schuh except that he was Swiss, like Robert Frank himself.

"They're friends of mine. I think they'd be happy to exhibit in your gallery. I'll write to them if you'd like."

"But what about *you*? That's really why I came."

"Thanks for asking, but I can't . . . I'm not ready . . . there are too many things. . . ." His voice drifted off.

Crushed, I couldn't find words. Not that words would help. I could tell, even in the short time I'd been here, that Robert Frank was a man who was not easily swayed. There was a no-nonsense directness about him. No game-playing, no guile, a man who meant what he said.

Perhaps sensing my disappointment, he added, "But I think you have a very good idea. Let me know if you want me to write to my friends."

Pablo had fallen and bruised his knee, and wailing, climbed on to his father's lap. It was time to leave.

NOW I *really* had a problem. What if others should turn me down too? And how could I find time to visit photographers when I scarcely had time to eat? I berated myself for having become so submerged in all the other problems that photography — the very reason for the whole venture — was sidetracked.

Then I thought of Joseph Breitenbach. He had recently returned from Korea, and having heard that I was opening a gallery, had appeared at my door with a whole body of work, mounted and ready to show. He'd been on assignment for the United States Reconstruction Agency, but these were photographs he'd taken on off-hours, as a kind of "personal notebook." What came through was his love of the Korean people, particularly in the pictures of children. Yet I had mixed feelings about the group as a whole. When I thought of work he'd done in Berlin in the 1920s—his portrait of Berthold Brecht came immediately to mind—I felt these couldn't compare.

But Korea was a timely subject, and I had strong feelings about the war. America had suffered 165,000 casualties (including 45,000 dead), and all to no purpose, I thought. Most of the pictures we'd seen were of American G.I.s; the most memorable was a photo essay by David Douglas Duncan published in the Christmas week 1950 issue of Life. We saw very few picture of the Koreans themselves, and these by Breitenbach, showing the efforts of the people at rebuilding their country, made an important statement. Or so I told myself as I settled for an exhibition that was not up to the standards I hoped to establish in the gallery, an exhibition better suited for the halls of the U.N.

At work on the exterior of Limelight, by Arthur Lavine.

Helen Gee and
Peggy Tallmer, by
Arthur Lavine.

Friends helping out,
by Arthur Lavine.

Li-lan painting a table,
by Arthur Lavine.

A WEEK went by and I was still brooding about Robert Frank when the doorbell rang one morning, and there he stood. I fell all over myself letting him in.

"I was just passing by," he said, shifting awkwardly from foot to foot, "and thought I'd drop in for a minute. I want to tell you how sorry I am. I have too many problems. I can't think about a show."

Now that I had no mission in mind, I was able to observe him more closely. He had a shy smile, soft dark eyes, fly-away hair, and several day's growth on his chin. His suit was baggy, his shoes scuffed, and his black turtleneck stretched at the neck. But there was something about him that was very appealing. He looked like he'd stepped out of a foreign film, the melancholy young lover in a doomed liaison.

He declined my offer of coffee, and as he turned to go, he handed me a large manila envelope he'd been holding behind his back. "I want you to have this," he said, and left.

The minute the door closed I tore open the envelope. There, to my surprise and great delight, was one of my favorite Robert Frank photographs: a young man, waiting for his lover in a park in Paris, holds a tulip behind his back.

RUBIN LEFT after the allotted two weeks, but there was still a lot to be done. Having exhausted what little money there was, I called on my friends for help. Peggy organized a series of work parties, and with a crew made up of actors, writers, painters, and Li-lan (I avoided asking photographers, not wanting to feel obligated), we tightened the legs of chairs, polished silverware, painted tables, built kitchen shelves, and did whatever electrical work we could, short of risking electrocution. Peggy spent most of her time on a ten-foot ladder (even my pilot friend, "Sky" Shapiro, was nervous past the fifth rung), and following the instructions of technicians at the Museum of Modern Art, installed the gallery lighting.

I was everybody's girl Friday, and when I wasn't holding nails or running around with buckets of paint, I took on the more onerous job of paperwork. But not yet having come up with a name for the place, it was hard to write a press release, send out announcements, or even arrange for a listing in the telephone book. Jerry Tallmer, Peggy's husband, was a member

Work crew at lunch, by Arthur Lavine.

Jerry Tallmer and Helen Gee, by Arthur Lavine.

of the crew, and I hoped that he, or one of the others, would think of a name. Whenever we sat down to lunch (Chinese dim sum as a reward for their work), I asked for suggestions. But they were all too busy munching the dim sum, and whenever someone did think of one—Le Bido, The Flying Saucer, Helen's Folly—it was just for laughs.

For a while I thought of opening without a name and awarding the customer who came up with one a year of coffee on the house. I was half-listening to the radio while retouching one day, when a newscaster reported (erroneously) that Charlie Chaplin had offered to adopt the two sons of convicted "spies" Julius and Ethel Rosenberg. In the months since they were executed, I sometimes wondered how the children could survive the trauma and grow up to lead normal lives. I wasn't thinking of Chaplin—or of his film Limelight—when I went to bed, but in the middle of the night it came to me. "Limelight! That's it!" and went happily back to sleep.

"JUST TWO MORE weeks, and life will be back to normal." I was trying to assure Li-lan and Queen (as well as myself) that I would settle back into my old routine the moment Limelight opened its doors. The strain was beginning to show. I'd lost twelve pounds I could ill afford (try opening a coffeehouse, I told my overweight friends), and where I'd once had hips, I had only hipbones. Coffee kept me going, and I hoped I could go on depending on a caffeine high to get me through until May 13, the day of the opening party.

Peggy and I stepped back and viewed our work. Limelight was beautiful. It was simple and understated: white brick walls, a gleaming black floor, and the one touch of color, a vivid red on the gallery's outer wall. A cluster of white Japanese lanterns, suspended from the ceiling like a piece of hanging sculpture, cast a soft light over the tables and chairs. (Friends had sat for hours while Peggy adjusted the wattage, studying the effect on a woman's face.) The gallery, in contrast, was brightly lit, and the front of the building, a sharp lemon yellow, was illuminated with a row of white globes. We kept the window simple: a short cafe curtain, a bowl of fruit, and a placard announcing the exhibition on view.

"Well, we made it," Peggy said. "Never thought we would, but we did."

"Keep your fingers crossed," I said, glumly. In the three months since I signed the lease, I'd had adequate proof of Murphy's Law: Everything that could go wrong had. What worried me now was the gallery. I'd been waiting for Breitenbach to come hang his show, getting nervous at the sight of the empty walls.

I had been planning to help with the various details, such as fastening hinges on the backs of the photographs (a method I'd found of securing them to the wall without any evidence of a hanging device). But when he finally appeared, he waved me aside, scoffing at the idea of needing help. So I decided to go home and spend time with Li-lan.

When I left he was unpacking his photographs and bustling about. Breitenbach was a man of great energy. He was short, squat, had a handshake that could crush, and was full of warmth and enthusiasm. He loved the outdoors, and having heard that he frequented nudist camps, I had a picture of him in my mind that I couldn't quite shake. I saw him stealing through the woods, naked as an egg, with nothing but his camera, horn-rimmed glasses, and a big cigar.

After a couple of games of Chinese checkers which, as usual, Li-lan won, I called to see how he was coming along.

"He's finished," Peggy said. "He had tickets for the theater and had to rush off."

"How does the show look?"

"You'd better come see for yourself."

I walked into the gallery and burst into tears. Having held myself together all these weeks, once I started crying I couldn't stop. The photographs were all so haphazardly hung, they could have been blown on the wall by a giant Schlumbohm fan.

What should I do? Should I re-hang the exhibition and risk Breitenbach's wrath? What if he stormed out with his work and left me with empty walls?

Reluctantly, I called Sid Grossman. I hadn't seen him for several months, and hearing a baby crying, I remembered that Miriam was pregnant at the time. I had gone to tell him about my plans for a gallery, and also to thank him for his having inspired the idea. Without his class (difficult though it was), the concept might never have sparked. Sid was enthusiastic and had

Helen Gee in kitchen, by Arthur Lavine.

offered to help. But I knew what that meant; he would hover in the background and monitor my every move. I had to feel free—even to make my own mistakes. The Breitenbach show was my first mistake.

"Maybe it's not as bad as you think," he said. "Joe's a fine photographer and a very good man. I'm glad you're showing his work." (Breitenbach was one of the few who continued to visit after he was denounced as a red and hounded by the FBI.) "I'll be glad to go look at it. This is Miriam's first day home from the hospital."

He arrived at midnight. Seeing him at the door, shoulders hunched, head thrust forward like a boxer in the ring, I felt a flood of affection. Sid always looked like he was taking on the world.

"Hmm, nice place," he said, swaggering in. Sid seldom paid compliments, and I was not so worn out that I couldn't feel a thrill.

He walked into the gallery, and without a word, took down the photographs and spread them on the floor. He arranged them and rearranged

Helen Gee and
Joseph Breitenbach
exhibition (after
Sid Grossman's
installation), by
Arthur Lavine.

them, playing one image against another, and as the layout developed, I began to understand the importance of sequencing. The photographs were trimmed flush, mounted on board (which was how they were usually shown at the Museum of Modern Art). Lacking the visual separation of frames and mats, the juxtaposition of the images was crucial. Sid hung the photographs in formal rows, double-stacked because there were so many, and I was surprised to see how much stronger the work looked now that it was properly displayed.

"Miriam! The baby! I've got to get home." Sid grabbed his jacket and headed for the door. He stopped midway, and for the next ten minutes gave me additional pointers on hanging shows. He stressed simplicity. "The emphasis should be on the photographs, not on dramatic design. The layout should whisper, let the images talk."

I would remember these words, not only because of the sound advice, but because they were among the last that I'd hear from Sid. He died a year later of a heart attack, at the age of forty-one.

PEGGY GROANED. "I can't take another crisis," she said, having just experienced what we hoped was our last. She had been up on a ladder adjusting the lights when a fire inspector walked in and ordered them down, claiming the wire was not up to code. We said we would comply but prayed that we'd get through the opening party before he returned to check. The invitations had been mailed, and there was no time for rewiring.

There was one day to go and still lots to do. I had to write wall text for the gallery stating its aims and letter a sign with Breitenbach's name.

"Go home," Peggy said. "You'll be able to concentrate a lot better there." She knew I was worried. Li-lan was refusing babysitters, feeling at eleven too old for them. Penny was a wonderful watch dog, alert to every sound, and I had a friend in the building look in now and then. Still, whenever I was downtown, my mind was half at home.

"Make sure you get enough sleep," Peggy said. "You've got to be in shape for the party." It would take more than a night's sleep to get me in shape, but tonight, at last, I'd get a full eight hours.

But on arriving home, I couldn't get in. Li-lan had put the chain on the door. I'd had the chain installed at the advice of the police when a neighbor went berserk and threatened us. He'd since been institutionalized, so we no longer used it. I kept ringing the bell, and when Li-lan didn't respond, not even to Penny's loud barking, I went downstairs to a phone booth and called.

The answering service broke in. "You have a message, Miss Gee. Someone from the Manhattan State Hospital called, saying a patient has escaped and to be on the alert. He might be headed your way."

I called the police, and sat trembling in the hall, waiting an eternity until they arrived.

"How do you know he's in there, Miss?" one of the cops asked.

'My daughter never leaves the chain on . . . something terrible's happened . . . please help me . . . don't wait . . . go in. . . ."

"Why would she let him in? Who is he? Your boyfriend?"

"Please, please, break the door down."

"We can't go breaking down doors, Miss. We'll be responsible if we damage the frame."

"You're worrying about frames and a madman's in there with my daughter?" I threw myself against the door but it wouldn't give.

"Okay, but don't blame us for any damage," said a cop, and lunging forward, he hurled himself against the door. There was a thud, the crackle of splintering wood, and the door flung open. Hands on holster, they crept inside.

I waited, frozen with fear.

Within minutes, they were back, full of smiles. "Nobody's in there, and your daughter's okay."

Li-lan was sitting up in bed, rubbing her eyes. "Mom, I had a bad dream. Some cops came in the room. . . ."

"It wasn't a dream. You put on the chain on the door. . . ." I didn't ask why. She was safe; that was all that mattered.

She went back to sleep but I couldn't calm down. I propped a chair against the door and tried to work. My hands kept shaking as I lettered the sign, and though I found it hard to concentrate on the text, I managed to write a few lines:

Limelight is dedicated to photography. Limelight exists primarily to show the work of those photographers, both known and unknown, who have made an outstanding contribution through their serious creative endeavor. We intend to present continuing shows, each running five weeks, including the work of both European and American photographers. The public will have an opportunity to purchase the works on display.

That morning, after receiving word from the police that the man had been picked up, I took the sign and the text and went downtown, arriving just as the cases of champagne were wheeled in. I paid the bill and with my last remaining dollar bought toilet paper for the restrooms.

THE PARTY WAS a success, or so I was told. Champagne and adrenalin carried me through, but all I could remember when I woke up the next day was standing in the middle of an enthusiastic crowd—photographers, writers, editors, friends—happily soaking up kudos. But out of the blur a lovely image emerged, the tiny persimmon face of our youngest guest, the Franks' three-week old daughter Andrea, cradled in her mother's arms. That Robert had come and brought along his family was the greatest compliment of all. But the real test was yet to come. The public opening was at six o'clock, and I wondered how the staff would handle its debut. We planned to remain open until one in the morning, so I prepared for a long hard night.

Everything was set. Herb was at the espresso machine, an exhibition of his drawings tacked on the wall; Arnold was at the stove (he'd applied as a strolling guitarist but settled for short-order cook); Frank (a set designer pinch-hitting as kitchen helper) was at the sandwich board; and the dishwasher (recruited that afternoon from a Bowery hotel) was sober and at the sink. Cheri, Leticia, and Lilo, the three waitresses we'd selected from a long list of applicants, were standing out front, glamorous in their Limelight "uniforms"—black stockings, ballerina-type shoes, and blue denim wraparound skirts. Myron, our part-time cashier (a psychology major at New York University), was at the cash box, anxiously watching the door.

After what seemed like hours, a customer arrived. She hesitated at the sight of the sea of empty tables, then settled at a table for two. A waitress approached, handed her a menu, and stood patiently by as she studied our long list of offerings: There were ten different coffees, nine kinds of tea, and all kinds of hot and cold beverages; there were sandwiches, salads, cheeses, and soups; there were pastries, sundaes, sodas, and ice cream; and there was the specialty of the house, Limelight pizza, made with French bread instead of the usual rubbery dough.

The customer decided on an espresso and a fruit cup, and as she waited for the order to be filled, I became painfully aware of the silence in the room. Was it a mistake ruling out background music? I'd grown tired of the constant bombardment of sound; wherever you went there was music—Muzak in elevators, "dinner" music in restaurants, and there was hardly a bar where you could have a quiet drink without the blare of a jukebox. The only sound I wanted at Limelight was the sound of the human voice.

But what I was hearing now was a hissing sound, coming from somewhere in the back. I rushed to the kitchen, and there, clustered around the espresso machine, which was hissing and wheezing and making all sorts of strange sounds, were all three waitresses and the kitchen men. I hovered at the door, afraid the machine was about to explode, while Herb, armed with a battery of makeshift tools—a knife, an ice pick, whatever he could get his hands on—tried to repair a faulty valve. Everyone had a suggestion—tighten this, loosen that, screw this, unscrew that—and just when it looked like that nothing would ever work, there was a burst of steam, a final wheeze, and the machine began to make coffee. The help then turned to the fruit salad, which Arnold had forgotten to prepare. He'd also forgotten where he stashed the fruit. Everyone pitched in. They searched the refrigerator, bread box, pastry cooler, and freezer. They looked on shelves and under the sink. They rummaged through paper bags, found potatoes and onions, and finally, in one bag, the fruit. They sliced and diced, and after preparing enough fruit salad for fifty, the waitress scooped a portion into a sherbet dish, topped it with whipped cream, and swept out with her tray.

But the dining room was empty. Our customer was gone.

"You must admit," said Myron, "the staff has a fine sense of group spirit. Togetherness of this sort is rare."

He had a point, but I was less concerned with "togetherness" than with the thirty-one empty tables and two hundred empty chairs. It was already

Helen Gee on the way to the opening of Limelight, May 13, 1954, by Arthur Lavine.

six-thirty, and the only money in the cash box was the twenty-five dollars I'd borrowed so that Myron could make change. But a few minutes later, a couple walked in, and no sooner were they seated when others appeared. What started as a trickle turned into an avalanche, and in less than an hour the place was filled, and people stood out front, waiting to get in. Myron hit on the idea of using the gallery as a waiting room, but herding them to the back was difficult. They stood around in clumps, blocking the aisles, waiting for tables to empty. But those who were seated stayed on and on, stoically waiting for service.

The espresso machine was still holding up; what worried me now was whether the waitresses would. As they struggled through the room with their loaded trays, I kept expecting a cappuccino to slide into a customer's

Opening party (Helen Gee and Peggy Tallmer in center), by Arthur Lavine.

lap. I grabbed a tray, meaning to help, but afraid of adding to the chaos, I tried clearing the tables instead. But there weren't many to clear. Half of those seated hadn't been served, and the rest kept nursing cold cups of coffee, having given up on ordering anything else. Still, there were few complaints. People seemed to enjoy the pandemonium, the excitement of being in on something new.

The kitchen was in no better shape. But the men carried on valiantly, despite the garbled orders and the waitresses' outbursts and tears. If they sent out a cheese sandwich when the customer ordered ham, if they sent out hot chocolate when the order called for tea, if they sent out orzata instead of lemonade, it was because they were running short of everything and wanted to send out *something*.

By midnight everyone was in a state, and rather than remain open until one, we closed. Leticia was in tears, Lilo looked dazed, and Cheri was gulping aspirin. The kitchen men were exhausted and could only tackle the clean-up after a couple of quarts of beer. There seemed to be as many dishes

Limelight, May 1954, by Arthur Lavine.

Helen Gee, by Arthur Lavine.

Limelight Gallery, by Arthur Lavine.

Limelight, by Arthur Lavine.

lying broken on the floor as stacked up in the sink, and as many pastries squashed underfoot as had made their way to the customers out front.

Only Myron was calm; he hadn't been overworked at the cash box. The receipts were paltry despite the crowd; not only had fewer than half been served, but some, I suspected, had left without paying, unable to fight their way to the desk.

Myron stood at the kitchen door, a smile congealed on his face. "Great team work," he said. "You're a wonderful crew. You have a fine sense of togetherness, a great . . ."

"Balls," Arnold growled.

And thus ended Limelight's first night.

ADDITIONAL HELP was hired—three more waitresses, a part-time kitchen man, and because the dishwasher had disappeared, we hired one from the Mills Hotel, a single-room occupancy on Bleecker Street, which was a step above the Bowery hotels and would serve as a source from now on. We tripled the number of pastries, doubled the coffee and tea and, as the weeks went by, made other adjustments as well. We replaced the Chemex with a less interesting but more durable restaurant-type urn, the dishwashers having broken both the original pot and two replacements as well. Our hand-picked silverware was another mistake; the silver turned green unless hand-dried, and I had to settle for stainless steel. Anyway, half of the tea-spoons were already gone, swiped by customers as souvenirs. Our lovely white cups were also disappearing, but I refused to replace them with standard restaurant ware. And at the rate my little white ashtrays were going, I imagined there was one on every coffee table in the Village, not to mention uptown.

What I *hoped* would disappear was our newly acquired collection of cats. Seven customers had had a single thought, and in less than a month, we were given seven kittens: two tortoise shells, a silver-gray Angora, and four of indeterminate origin. None were toilet-trained, and I had other things to do besides teach seven kittens where to piddle. Arnold filled a pan with torn-up strips of the *Villager*, a neighborhood newspaper that nobody read (and which now found a use), but the kittens preferred the dining room floor. The customers loved them, and I watched in dismay as they poured them saucers of pure, heavy cream and the kittens lapped up the profits.

I made up my mind: they had to go. I tacked up a sign offering them to anyone who could supply a good home (not that I was about to investigate), and they were all adopted in less than a week. The waitresses were just as relieved as I was—no more stepping on tails and slipping in puddles. And it freed us to work on other problems—the bottleneck in the kitchen, the flow of food to the front.

Gradually, the operation started running more smoothly, and I considered it progress when only one waitress broke down during the course of a night.

LIMELIGHT was fast becoming the "in" place, attracting people from all walks of life. But most were drawn from the photography world—editors, writers, and photographers of all kinds. It made for an interesting mix: At one table you'd find Philippe Halsman drinking coffee with friends; at another Arnold Newman with his pleasant wife, Gus; Cornell Capa at an eight-seater with a contingent from *Life*; and Weegee at no table, just roaming around. And to my surprise, considering the circumstances of my departure from class, there was Lisette Model, together with Evsa and a group of their students, at a large round table in the middle of the room. (I skirted that table and avoided Evsa's eyes.) You never knew who might appear next. Eugene Smith? Cartier-Bresson? Robert Frank?

Everybody knew everybody else, and while this made for a feeling of warmth and camaraderie, it drove the waitresses to distraction. No sooner were people seated when they saw others they knew and wandered off to their table. There was a constant reshuffling of seats, a rerouting of cappuccinos, and adding to the confusion, a never-ending trek to the gallery. The young photographers were the worst offenders, table-hopping, milling about, talking nonstop.

I was too busy to pick up a camera these days, but I still identified with that network of young photographers, both professional and nonprofessional, for whom photography was a passion. We were imbued with a sense of mission, a belief in photography as an instrument of change (both social and psychological), a feeling that through our personal vision, we could make a better world. I was happy that so many were coming around, some in fact making Limelight their "home." Arthur Lavine, Lew Parrella, Leon Levinstein, May Mirin, Louis Stettner, David Vestal, Hella Hammid, Simpson Kalisher, Morris Jaffe, Jerry Danzig, David Heath, Suzy Harris, Ray Jacobs, Lee Friedlander, Sid Kaplan, John Cohen, Morris Engel, Walt Silver, Harold Feinstein, Paul Seligman, Ruth Orkin, Martin Dain, Leo Stashin, Norman Rothschild, Ed Wallowitch, Victor Obsatz—these were but a few.

Sitting in their midst, on the nights he was in town, was their friend and impassioned supporter, Jacob "Jack" Deschin, the camera editor of the New York Times. A short, gnome-like man with a prominent nose and thinning gray hair, Deschin could be seen at every photographic event, whether in the grubby basement quarters of the Village Camera Club on Bank Street, or at a meeting of the American Society of Magazine Photographers in some posh midtown hotel. Getting around, Deschin said, was part of his job. But now that I was getting to know him well—we'd met at the Village Camera Club about a year ago—I realized that his job on the Times was more than a job: it was his life. He'd been married for many years and spoke lovingly of his wife, yet he seemed never in a hurry to get home. He was forever losing his hat, forgetting his overcoat, taking a drink too many, and missing his train.

Deschin was the only camera editor on a newspaper whose opinion mattered. His column in the New York Times was avidly read, not only for information on products and photographic events, but also for his reviews of shows. Though he spoke of himself as a "photo reporter" and didn't consider himself a critic, his primary concern was the image. The others dealt mostly with technical matters, the so-called nuts and bolts, and none wrote on photography exclusively. John Adam Knight, the camera editor of the New York Post, wrote a column on cooking called The Man in the Kitchen, under his real name, Pierre de Rohan, and Mabel Scacheri, the camera editor of the New York Post, also wrote a column on cats. Few seemed to share Deschin's sense of commitment, nor were they given the leeway he enjoyed on the Times.

Deschin shared my reservations about Breitenbach's work, and his review of the exhibition was mixed. While commending him for providing us with a picture of the Korean people, he felt that Breitenbach had weak-

Sam Falk,
Philippe Halsman,
by Arthur Lavine.

Jacob Deschin in
Limelight Gallery,
by Morris Jaffe.

ened his statement by failing to include pictures showing the devastation of the war. But he found the pictures of children "some of the most heartrending in documentary history."

Though I would have liked to have launched the gallery with a rave review (which might have occurred with a Robert Frank show), I was glad that Deschin had been forthright. Knowing how he wanted the gallery to succeed, I was afraid that he might not be tough enough, that he would lean over backwards and soft-pedal his criticism. We had discussed this before Limelight opened, and had agreed that, even if he were to pan an exhibition, it would in no way affect our friendship. I would rather that an exhibition be attacked than ignored, if only to stimulate controversy.

Breitenbach was given short shrift in *Aperture*, the only journal devoted to the aesthetics of the medium, which had been launched on a shoestring in 1952, and was still struggling to survive. Its editor, Minor White, referred to the exhibition as an "unfortunate choice because photographs made for publication in magazines rarely look well on walls." I agreed with Minor White—it was an unfortunate choice—but not for the reason he mentioned. I was interested in a wide range of styles and approaches, regardless of genre, and had no intention of limiting my choices to work that looked good on walls.

DESCHIN LIKED nothing better than to discover new talent, and the next exhibition, by Rudolph Burckhardt, made up for his previous disappointment. Burckhardt was little known in the photography world. He earned a living photographing works of art and made avant-garde films on the side. A wisp of a man, full of sly wit, he was the only person I knew, other than the artist Saul Steinberg, whose words hung in the air like a balloon in a cartoon, words you wished you could remember and quote.

Burckhardt's one hundred photographs covered two decades of work, beginning with his arrival from Switzerland in the 1930s. There were street scenes taken in New York and Rome and a group of still-life compositions which appeared to have been inspired by the surrealist constructions of his friend Joseph Cornell. The single portrait in the exhibit was of the poet and dance critic Edwin Denby, sitting on a rooftop in Chelsea (not far from Robert Frank's loft).

Rudolph Burckhardt exhibition, July 1954, by Jacob Deschin.

Deschin often used a review to make a point and, in writing about Burckhardt, cited him as an exception to what he saw as a common problem:

A distinctive style is rare in photography. The lack of it is particularly noticeable among the younger photographers today, many of whom appear to be more concerned with kinds of material—which, incidentally, are treated with little variation in approach—

than in developing an individual manner. The result is a monotonous repetition of state-
ment that, with a refreshing exception now and then, keeps telling us the same thing
over and over again in almost the same way.

The rest of the review was a rave. Deschin lauded Burckhardt for his "uniqueness of seeing," for his "utter simplicity and delicacy of feeling," and for a style that was "remarkably consistent and therefore readily identifiably as the photographer's manner."

Rudy had never before seen his name in print, and he was so startled when he came across it while sitting in a bus reading the newspaper, he missed his stop and rode miles out of the way.

I EXPERIENCED the same pleasurable shock when I came across an article headed "Galleries Needed," in the August 1, 1954 issue of the *New York Times*. Deschin complained of the "continuing incongruity of the scarcity of photographic galleries in this biggest city in the country, the center of American photograph activity," and used Limelight as a model for others. In summing up the situation, he wrote:

> *The Museum of Modern Art, where Edward Steichen used to offer periodically the leading shows in town, has not had one in so long that it almost seems the museum has abandoned photography altogether. True, the job of assembling* The Family of Man *exhibition, which will finally be hung in January, has taken all of Mr. Steichen's time and energy, but the fact remains that the No. 1 gallery in town has been inactive.*

The Brooklyn Museum appeared to have given up after a series of infrequent shows, and the focus of the exhibitions at the Museum of Natural History and the Museum of the City of New York was too slanted, he claimed, for general interest. The city's two progressive camera clubs, the Village Camera Club and the Camera Club of New York, had put on a few interesting shows, but they were open to the public only a few hours each week. And the Kodak Information Center, which had wall space for photographs on the east balcony of Grand Central Terminal, lacked a program and direction. A few libraries had attempted shows, but they were of dubious quality, hung over bookcases and in totally inadequate light. The one exception was the

Hudson Park branch on Seventh Avenue South, which devoted two months of the year to quality shows.*

This left only Limelight, and in conclusion, he wrote: "In tallying up, one finds that as of today the city has only one gallery with a truly responsible attitude toward the medium related to a continuing program for showing photographs. . . . The Limelight Gallery has set the pattern and the standard. The city could use more such galleries."

The article more than made up for all these months of travail. Limelight had arrived. It was less than a year since I had the idea, and less than three months since it became a reality. I looked at the people sitting in the room. I looked at the crowd out front waiting to get in. I looked at the press clippings piled in the desk drawer. I looked in the cash box at the burgeoning receipts, and thought, "Ah, smooth sailing, at last."

How wrong I was.

---

*It was Deschin himself who was responsible for the exhibitions at the Hudson Park Library. He advised Alice Viehler, the librarian in charge, and helped in the actual organization of the shows, just one of the many things he did with no other reward other than the satisfaction of bringing creative photography to the fore.

IT WAS THE middle of August when I first noticed the change. I had barricaded myself in the gallery, painting the panels for the Louis Stettner show, when the cook's aprons I'd strung across the entrance parted and a head poked through. I looked up, expecting to see a photographer—they were always peering in when a show was going up—but this was no one I recognized. It was a bleary-eyed fellow with tousled hair. "Is this the way to the john?" he mumbled.

At first I thought he'd had one too many, another stray from the corner bar who I'd have to take by the hand, lead out the back, and deposit on a stoop on Barrow Street. But when I saw the dungarees, the sandals, and the dirty feet, I knew he was a bohoe, a stray from Washington Square. I pointed the way to the men's room and gave it no further thought.

But later that night I saw him again, sitting at a table with others. They all looked "beat." One, a pimply-faced kid with down on his lip, sat slumped in his chair, and the girl sitting next to him, an apparition in white pancake make-up and soot-black eye shadow, could hardly hold her head up.

It was strange seeing bohoes at Limelight; it just wasn't their kind of place. You didn't see them in any of the West Village hangouts, not at Louis', Chumley's, the Riviera, Julius', and never, certainly, at the White Horse. Even if they were of drinking age, it would be hard to imagine them hobnobbing with the likes of Norman Mailer, Daniel "Pat" Moynihan, or, for that matter, any of the intellectuals (and pseudo-intellectuals) who held forth in these bars. Since there were no coffeehouses in the West Village other than Limelight, the bohoes stuck to their usual haunts, the scruffier joints around Macdougal Street and rarely ventured as far west as Sheridan Square.

So why in the world were they here? They could not have come for the coffee; there were a dozen of them squeezed around a table, and I didn't see a single cup. Certainly not for the gallery; whenever they got up and drifted to the back, it was simply en route to the rest rooms. And they couldn't have come for the social life; they hardly spoke to each other, much less anyone else. All they did was sit and stare into space.

Bohoes, which was what they were called before "beatnik" was coined, were not exactly new to the Village. They had been popping up for a year or two, but it was only this summer that they descended in droves. They sprawled around the fountain in Washington Square, straggled along Macdougal and the neighboring side streets, squatting on curbs and in doorways. They were already something of a tourist attraction, and on weekend nights, when the streets were so crowded you couldn't push your way through, Macdougal was virtually a parade.

Nobody knew what to make of them, or even, for that matter, what to call them. Some wag at the San Remo or other writer's bar, had dreamed up the word "bohoe," a cross, perhaps, between bohemian and hobo. Actually though, they were neither. They weren't hoboes since they had roofs over their heads; some shacked up on the Lower East Side, and others crept in from their homes in Queens. And they hardly qualified as bohemians, at least not the kind that old-time Villagers, hearkening back to a day when artists lived in garrets and wore berets, thought of as bohemian. They had none of the charm or color, say, of Romany Marie, a self-styled gypsy and former restauranteur, who still managed to turn heads as she swept through the streets in her long swishing skirts, wrists jangling with jewelry. Or Joe Gould, a bald, gray-bearded, toothless old man, who went from bar to bar, peddling poems, cadging drinks, and collecting material for his on-going epic, *An Oral History of the World*.

In any case, whatever they were—bohoes, bohemians, or just a bunch of rebellious kids—I gave them no further thought. My concern was photography, not sociology. I went back to the gallery and continued with my work.

THE STETTNER exhibition opened on August 17, attracting the usual crowds. But to my consternation, the bohoes were back, and this time with others in tow. They took up several tables, a few ordered coffee, and the rest spent the night sipping water. The waitresses were miffed, but I asked them to be patient; the bohoes would soon be gone. Come Labor Day, they would be back in school, their summer of rebellion over.

But Labor Day came and went and the bohoes stayed on. And there were more of them every night. Word seemed to have spread through the digs of the Lower East Side; they had found a new place to roost. They arrived early, stayed until closing, and it was getting harder and harder to find seats. Customers were beginning to complain.

The only one who seemed pleased was a professor of sociology from an out-of-state college. Delighted with the opportunity to study them at first hand, he joined the bohoes every night, taking voluminous notes on a pad. After weeks of this, I asked if he'd gained any insights. Not quite, he replied; he hadn't yet determined just how they fit in to the various changes in American society, what with rock-and-roll, the growing rate of juvenile delinquency, and that new phenomenon, the "generation gap." But he had arrived at the reason for their apathy: "These are the children of the atomic age. This is the first generation of young people faced with the threat of global destruction. They live in the shadow of the hydrogen bomb and thus feel powerless and afraid. That's why we call it the Waiting Generation."

So what are they waiting for? For the bomb to drop? For Godot? I suspected they were waiting for checks from home; someone had to support this indulgence.

One thing was clear: they were not waiting for service. Sonya, the head waitress, was threatening to quit. "The only thing these slobs order is water. They tie up your tables all night long and don't even leave you a dime. I'm sick and tired of being stiffed." I was afraid the others were just biding their time. Cheri was coming to the end of a lengthy novel and Leticia was purling the last few rows of a sweater.

I could understand their frustration just looking around the room. There were very few cups on their tables, and only once did I see food. I came in one night and saw ten of them squeezed around a table, wolfing down pickles, potato chips, cheese, salami, cole slaw, and bagels—all of it pulled out of paper bags. Limelight supplied only the pepper and salt and hot water for tea. One of the "chicks," a chubby-faced girl about thirteen years old, kept running into the ladies' room, filling a pot from the hot water tap.

The kitchen help had little to do, but none lamented the slowdown. Herb was busy sketching, Arnold was practicing a new piece on his guitar, and Benny, the dishwasher (or was it Danny?—we'd already gone through five) was dozing, a beer bottle at his side.

I knew we were headed for trouble, but the real shock came when Sam presented a financial report. In September, a month when business should have improved, the receipts were down by half. And along with the statement was a stack of bills, including a note from Rubin, reminding me that a payment was due.

More depressing even than the drop in receipts was the change in the clientele. There was hardly a photographer left in the place. When I first became aware that certain ones were no longer around—Dan Weiner, Erich Hartman, Philippe Halsman, Elliott Erwitt, Arnold Newman, and the many others who'd been so supportive from the start—I assumed they were off on assignment. When the Models didn't appear—and they had been coming in every night—I figured they'd scraped together the money and were off vacationing in Provincetown. But as the weeks went by and fewer and fewer photographers appeared, I knew that Limelight was in trouble.

Something had to be done. Taking count one night, I found all but two of the thirty-one tables occupied by bohoes. A contingent from the Village Camera Club was roaming around looking for seats, and when the after-theater crowd arrived at eleven, it had to be turned away.

I berated myself for not having been more vigilant and not spending more time downtown. I'd been inundated with retouching, and I'd also been working on several new shows—Minor White in the fall, followed by Grant La Farge, a turn-of-the-century amateur photographer (a brother of the painter John La Farge) whose work I considered a find. It had been brought to my attention by Lew Parrella, a young photographer and former editor at U.S. Camera, and since the exhibition was to include a group of rare Lumière color plates, he'd offered to design the installation and build light boxes for their display. But the exhibition that was taking up most of my time was Great Photographs, a Christmas group show, my first real effort at selling prints. Through ads and a special mailing, I hoped to promote the idea of photographs as Christmas gifts.

But now I had to shift gears. Unless I acted quickly, there would not only be no Christmas show, there would probably be no Limelight. I went to see Manuel Neves, the owner of the Blue Mill Tavern, a popular restaurant on Commerce Street (in the same building where Berenice Abbott lived), his having helped with advice in the past.

This time he just shook his head. "Freeloaders are always looking for a place to roost. And once they're entrenched, they're hard to dislodge."

"It happened so quickly . . . not even two months . . . what should I do?"

"What most restaurants do to get rid of deadbeats is slow down the service, and if that doesn't work, kill them with kindness. They keep the waiters hanging around, pouring water, brushing off crumbs, and offering them menus over and over until they finally get fed up and leave. But I doubt that it will work with your bohoes."

I thanked Manuel and went back home, feeling even more helpless now.

TO MAKE matters worse, Minor White was coming from Rochester to hang his show. Though I'd sworn after the Breitenbach fiasco never again to leave the installation to a photographer, it would have been presumptuous, in this case, to refuse. Minor White was a seasoned curator, and I, after all, was a novice.

But as the day approached, I kept hoping that something would interfere, that he'd come down with a cold, or even the flu—anything to keep him in Rochester. Yet from everything I'd heard about Minor White, I knew he'd arrive on a stretcher rather than leave the installation to anyone else.

How would he react to a room full of bohoes? Would he regret having agreed to exhibit? Would he continue his support of Limelight in *Aperture?* He had been talking about running an article, and while a line in *Aperture* was hardly like a line in the *New York Times*, the magazine was important to those who mattered—Beaumont Newhall for one. As curator at George Eastman House, as well as our leading photo historian, he could be helpful. And since I hoped to work out an arrangement for exchanging shows, it was important that Minor White return to Rochester with a favorable report.

Since the less he saw of the bohoes the better, I gave up plans for a

Minor White, 1956, copyright © by Marvin Maslow.

Courtesy the Minor White Archive, Art Museum, Princeton University.

preview. But I sent out a sizable mailing—two thousand announcements instead of the usual twelve hundred—in the hope of luring the photographers back. Yet, even as I sat addressing the cards, I knew this would not be a popular show, not like a show, say, by W. Eugene Smith. Photojournalism was more of a draw. An urban audience, more attuned to the action-packed drama of Life and Look, was less likely to respond to quiet images of rocks and limpid pools, exquisite though they might be. White meant these images as metaphors—a stone was not just a stone, a leaf not just a leaf, but expressions of feeling and mood. Arranged in sequences, he saw them as visual poems. He was also a bit of a mystic. He'd embraced Catholicism, more recently Zen, and it was this search for a deeper meaning that was at the heart of his work.

The day Minor was due, I went downtown and cleaned. We could no longer afford even a part-time porter, and though the dishwasher was supposed to clean up after closing, by then he was usually too deep in his cups. I mopped the dining room, swabbed the toilets, and wiped graffiti from the restroom walls, all the while cursing the bohoes. This was not what I had envisioned when I bit into that sausage on Mulberry Street!

But luck hadn't failed me entirely. Minor arrived on Monday, the one day of the week we were closed. And the minute he walked in he apologized: Between *Aperture* and George Eastman House, he was swamped with work— would I mind if he cut short his visit? I tried not to show my relief.

I had come to know Minor White through letters, and now that we'd met, I found that I liked him. He was a charming man, if a bit remote, and though he was seemingly calm, what I sensed beneath the surface was the passion and intensity he brought to his work. I also sensed a certain defensiveness; as a homosexual he was always on guard. Behind his boyish grin, I saw loneliness and pain.

Having designed the exhibition in advance of the trip, installing it went very quickly. The wall text, written by Nancy Newhall, the wife and associate of Beaumont Newhall, seemed a fitting tribute:

Who is Minor White? He is a tall, shambling guy who has been the quiet observer of many places and an increasingly important participant in others. He has been vers libre poet, G.I., barman, teacher. He lives a life Van Gogh would recognize. And yet, as Ansel Adams said when Minor came to take up his teaching at the California School of Fine Arts, "He fits in as a glove fits on."

Minor White learned from great photographers—Stieglitz, Weston, Adams, and he brought to what he learned the education of a poet in the twentieth century. Currently he is assistant curator at George Eastman House of Photography in Rochester, New York and the editor of Aperture, which at this moment is probably the one magazine in the world devoted to creative photography.

Why should anyone look at his photographs? Minor White is an explorer. His terra incognita is the streets we walk down, the faces we see changing, the rocks, waves, trees, clouds that say to us when we cannot put in words. His unknown world is us.

After the show opened and Minor left town, I turned back to my problems. There was another one now: Limelight had been discovered by a motorcycle gang. Bikers had been a problem in the Village all summer, roaring through the streets at all hours of night. Nobody knew what to do about them. There had been talk in the neighborhood of vigilante action, yet no one, not even the Italian toughs around Bleecker Street, who were always ready to defend their turf, didn't want to tussle with a motorcycle gang. The bikers were hard and mean, and they moved very fast. I shuddered when I heard them pull up out front and held my breath as they roamed around the room, ogling the bohoes' "chicks." After slugging down coffee and using the men's room, they'd leave, often without paying the check.

I was beginning to wonder about the men's room. It had suddenly become a popular spot, not only with the bikers but the bohoes too. They trekked to the back, sometimes in pairs, often in groups, and I found this rather odd. Suspicious, I took a table in the back of the room, ordered a lemonade and pretended to read, glancing now and then at the men's room door. I didn't exactly know what I was watching for, but then I discovered I had company. Snake Eyes was watching too.

Snake Eyes had been coming around for the past few weeks, and I could see why the waitresses called him that. He had small eyes, dark pitted skin, and the cold calm of a cobra in wait. He'd arrive around ten, go straight to the men's room, linger over coffee for an hour or so, then return to the men's room and leave.

After observing this pattern for several nights, I knew he was up to something, and whatever it was, it was happening in the men's room. I knew I should investigate, but I was reluctant to barge in and surprise some male at the urinal. I thought of sending in a kitchen man, but not wanting to convey my suspicions to the help, I kept on watching and waiting. I watched for a week, but nothing much happened, though I did take a turn when I looked up from my book and saw Snake Eyes sharpening a switch-blade on the bottom of an overturned cup.

Then one night, after a group of bohoes trouped to the rear, I mustered my courage and ran to the men's room.

"Christ! I told you to keep an eye out!" someone hissed, and they all started scrambling, trying to squeeze into the one empty booth. But I'd seen enough. I'd glimpsed an arm with a tourniquet and caught a whiff of something pungent and sweet.

I backed out, returned to my table, and went on pretending to read. But my hands shook and the print blurred. I was too frightened to look over at Snake Eyes, but I pulled myself together, left through the kitchen, and telephoned the Tallmers from the corner bar. They told me to come over; this couldn't be discussed on the phone.

"For God's sake, keep this under your hat," Jerry warned. "If the cops get wind of drugs, they'll shut the place down."

"How could I be so blind? Junkies right under my nose."

"Stop blaming yourself. Who thinks of drugs? Nobody we know uses that stuff. Norman Mailer, maybe, but only marijuana and a little hash. You know what Norman's like. He's always looking for kicks."

Jerry was right. In this day of the double martini, hardly anyone bothered with drugs. Drugs were associated with jazz musicians and tragic figures like Billie Holiday, not with white middle-class kids. Even in Harlem, with all its problems, drug use wasn't widespread. But knowing all this didn't help me now.

"If I can't go to the police, what should I do?"

"I've got it!" Peggy said. "Shut down the men's room. That guy you call Snake Eyes is probably a dealer, and he's using the men's room as a drop. Cut off the supply, and the hopheads will leave."

Early next morning I went downtown. I searched the men's room, feeling for loose tiles or some other spot where Snake Eyes might be stashing his supply. But all I found, lying behind the toilet, were a few small empty cellophane bags. I barricaded the entrance with a stack of chairs and tacked up a sign, reading, "Closed for repairs."

That night, I took up my post in the back of the room, sipped a lemonade (fortified with brandy), opened my book, and waited.

Snake Eyes arrived at the usual time. He walked to the back, stopped short when he saw the sign, then swung around and left. I rushed to the phone and called Peggy. "It worked! He's gone! You'll have coffee on the house for the next ten years."

"Wait, don't start celebrating so soon." she said. "It can't be as easy as that."

Snake Eyes was back the next night. When he saw the sign and the chairs still in place, he turned and walked out, but I was afraid he saw through my scheme. He came in again the following night, and the next and the next for over a week. Each time he appeared I averted my eyes, unnerved by his menacing stares. But then he stopped coming, and after several days, I felt he was gone for good. Yet I kept the men's room closed, just in case.

"Great!" Peggy said, when I called with the news. "But that's not the end of your problems. You still have to get rid of the bohoes. They're not all junkies, you know."

GOOD NEWS: A photograph had been sold! Not to a collector (was there such a thing?) but to a young man who had read Deschin's review of the Minor White show, and spent an hour in the gallery deciding which to buy. He'd chosen *Nude Foot* (the legs and buttocks of a male nude) and wanted to buy it right off the wall. When I told him he'd have to wait until the end of the show, he pleaded, "It's a present for a friend. It's his birthday."

Knowing how seriously Minor took sequencing, I telephoned reluctantly, certain he'd refuse.

"*What?* Somebody wants to buy a photograph? *And he wants you to take it off the wall?*" I was about to apologize for suggesting such a thing, when he said, "Of course, take it down. Why wait?"

The photograph was ten dollars, and after deducting the gallery commission of 25 percent, I sent Minor a check for seven dollars and fifty cents. He was delighted, and thrilled when he got a three-page letter from the recipient of the gift, telling him his reaction to the image.

The sale cheered me up, and I felt better than I had in weeks. That night, as I stood on the stairs looking down at the room full of bohoes, I didn't get quite as depressed as usual. It was always that first sight that came as a shock, seeing how the place had deteriorated. The floor, once black and gleaming, was gray and caked with dirt. Napkins were strewn all over, and bits of food lay squashed underfoot. Roaches scurried about, and it was not unusual to see a big, hardy specimen meandering up the leg of a table, headed for somebody's plate. They had even invaded the gallery, and one night, while I stood contemplating Minor White's photographs, I saw something on one of them move.

Getting rid of the bohoes seemed an impossible job, but I felt I could handle it now. I had no plan, nor had Peggy come up with one, but I was sure that something would occur to us soon. So when I came in one night, stepped over the bohoes sprawled on the stairs, and walked past all the others slumped in their chairs, I didn't let it get me down. I went to check on the Minor White show, but on reaching the gallery, I stopped. A man was standing at the entrance, and there were several others inside. And they didn't seem to be looking at pictures.

When I tried to walk in, the man blocked the way. I demanded he move. He refused. I tried to side-step him, but whichever way I moved, he moved too. We kept dancing back and forth, and then to my horror, right over his shoulder, I saw a familiar face. Snake Eyes!

I ran through the kitchen and out the back door, headed I didn't know where. I didn't care how I looked or what anybody thought as I wandered through the streets, tears streaming. Drug dealers in my gallery! It was all too much.

Finding myself on Commerce Street, I walked toward the Blue Mill Tavern. Manuel had closed for the night but was checking receipts, and came to the door when he saw me outside. "You look terrible. What's happened?"

I told him; he looked grave. "You don't want to fool around with those guys," he said. "They've been trying to get a foothold in the West Village, and I guess they settled on your place because you're young and kind of green. What you need is a full-time manager. A place can't run itself."

"I can't afford one. What should I do?"

"The first thing you can do is stop crying." He handed me a napkin, and waited till I stopped. "I'll try to track down Pat Fagan. He used to be the bouncer at Louis'. Maybe he can help."

I got a call from Pat Fagan the very next day, and we arranged to meet at Jack Delaney's. "You won't have no trouble finding me," he said. "I'm a dead-ringer for Marlon Brando."

Having seen On the Waterfront, I watched for a stevedore with a Greek-god profile. And though I failed to see the resemblance, I knew it was Fagan the minute he walked through the door. He swaggered to my table, plunked himself down, and without my asking, told me all about himself. He was interested in acting and worked as a bouncer to support his career. He'd been raised in Hell's Kitchen, had done time in prison, and intended to specialize in tough-guy roles. He had one eye on Hollywood, the other on Broadway. (But here, at Jack Delaney's, he kept both eyes on the mirror, watching himself as he talked.)

"Feel," he said, raising his sleeves and flexing his biceps. "You won't have nothin' to worry about, not with Pat Fagan on the job. I'll send those drug pushers flying, and those bohoes too. I hate those bums. They got no class."

"Isn't it illegal to keep them out?" Manuel had warned me about lawsuits and cries of "discrimination."

"This is how you get around it. You hang a curtain in the window so no-body can look in. I stand outside and if I don't like a guy's looks, I tell him the joint's filled. Get it?"

"So you'll screen everybody at the door?"

"Right. I know those hopheads. They'll do anything for a fix. And that guy you call Snake Eyes is a dealer. He's gonna be mad when he can't get back in."

"I hope there won't be any rough stuff."

"Nah, I use psychology. I learned it in group therapy. I used to use my fists, now I use my head."

"How long will it take?"

"A couple of months. I'll get the place clean by Christmas."

But could Limelight hold out until Christmas? The last time I saw Sam, he spoke about filing for bankruptcy. "Another month like the last one, and you'll have no choice."

I was sewing a curtain for the window, preparing for Fagan to take over, when Deschin called and asked me to join him for a drink. We met at the Oyster Bar in Grand Central Station, and I saw right away he was troubled.

"I've got bad news," he said, glumly. "There's been talk at the paper about what's happening to your place. Even Sam Falk says it's gotten pretty rough, and if a newspaper photographer says that, you can imagine what the others think. I know you're having problems, Helen, but isn't there any way you can clear out those bums?"

I told him about Fagan but said nothing about Snake Eyes. Deschin was trustworthy but drink tended to loosen his tongue.

"Well, I hope your plan works. Because if it doesn't, I can't go on reviewing the shows."

"If it doesn't, there won't be any shows to review," I said.

"Damnit." He gulped another Scotch. "It burns me up. You have a great
idea, you bring it to life, and then it's ruined by a pack of grimy kids. There
wasn't a soul in the gallery when I went to see Minor's show."

"That was a very nice review you gave him."

"I did my best. But you know how I feel about Minor's work. Excuse the
pun, but I consider it minor."

The review had been respectful, even complimentary, but I knew when
Deschin was hedging. He had concealed his lack of enthusiasm by building the article around print quality, contrasting Minor White's meticulous
craftsmanship with the current tendency to "sidetrack craftsmanship . . .
and to concentrate on content alone." The review, together with reproductions in both the Times and the Herald Tribune, had brought in a crowd. But, as
usual, people left, put off by the sight of the bohoes.

Everything would change, I assured him, with Pat Fagan on the job.

THE NIGHT Fagan started work, I paced the floor, anxious to see just who
he'd let in. So far, no one; the place was empty. The waitresses were sitting at
their usual table, reading, knitting, doing crosswords. I kept wandering into
the gallery, trying to become engrossed in New England in the 1890s by Grant La
Farge. Most of the pictures were of nature—strange, brooding landscapes
and woodland scenes, the mood even more somber in the color plates. It
was the kind of work that called for contemplation ("not easily understood,"
Deschin wrote), but contemplation was beyond me now. I kept running to
the front, parting the curtain and peeping out, watching as Fagan, resplen-
dent in a bold, checkered jacket, turned away bohoes one after another.

Would anyone pass muster? We had been open two hours and the place was
still empty. But then, at around nine, a couple walked in. Seeing the room
empty, they turned to go. I urged them to stay, using the gallery as a lure,
and no sooner had they sat down when others appeared, and I inveigled
them into staying too. The trickle continued, but when I counted heads at
eleven o'clock, I found there were less than fifty. At this time, a peak period
on a Saturday night, there would ordinarily be close to two hundred, and

another two hundred would already have passed through. Rather than confront Fagan directly, I went out the back, walked around the block, stood in a doorway, and watched. Fagan was surrounded so it was hard to see, but when I heard him arguing with a young man, I edged closer.

"What do you mean, I can't get in?"

"Not in them clothes, you don't," Fagan growled.

I saw no reason for keeping him out. He was in a handsome tweed jacket. a sport shirt, and dungarees. I took Fagan aside when the crowd thinned out. "Why did you keep that fellow out? He looked perfectly fine to me."

"Didn't you see he was wearing *dungarees?*"

"What's wrong with that?"

"The bohoes all wear 'em, so I got a rule. Nobody gets in wearing dungarees. If you let in one, you gotta let them all in."

"But I like dungarees. I wear them at home all the time."

"Listen, I know what I'm doing."

It was too much for me; I went back inside. But I kept thinking of the fellow in the nice tweed jacket. He seemed typical of those young men (and a few women, too) who, after returning home from their nine-to-five jobs, changed into dungarees before hitting the pubs. And though I found something ironic in clerks and accountants dressing like stevedores and farmers, it was a refreshing change from the gray flannel suit.

I stayed inside for the rest of the night. Yet I had to admit, Fagan was effective. There was no sign of Snake Eyes, nor was there a single bohoe in the place. But neither were there any customers.

"Don't worry," Fagan said, as I looked at the empty tables and the empty cash box. "This is just the beginning. I ain't started yet."

I WAS SITTING at a table watching the door when Robert Frank popped up beside me. "What the hell's going on around here? That guy out front wouldn't let me in."

"Oh, my God . . ."

"I guess he doesn't like my looks. But that's okay. I came in the through the back."

Robert had been helping with the Christmas show. He'd agreed to exhibit several of his prints and had once again recommended his three European friends — Bill Brandt, Edouard Boubat, and Gotthard Schuh. He'd written to each, and though I had not thought of including Schuh, Robert had gone to the trouble of getting several of his prints from the Museum of Modern Art, including the one of a Balinese boy playing marbles which was to be shown in the Family of Man.

What I hoped Robert would do, and I'd broached it several times, was use his influence with his friend Walker Evans. I had invited him to participate, but he hadn't answered my letter.

"Walker's in a terrible mood," he said. "I think it's better to wait."

"What's wrong? It sounds to me like he's always depressed."

"Just the usual, women and booze."

Robert himself seemed rather depressed, though his problems were not quite the same. He drank very little and didn't womanize. I sensed he was experiencing marital strain, but his problems were primarily financial. Whenever I asked about his work, I got the same gloomy report: things were terrible, he had no money, and there were few assignments in sight. Having given up fashion (he'd been a Brodovitch find), he was restricting himself to editorial reportage. Robert was known as "the poet of the camera," but art was not what magazines like Life and Look wanted. And he didn't play the game — no liquid lunches, cocktail parties, gifts of scotch. One of the few who gave him work was John English, and for the very reason that others did not, because he was an artist. But McCall's was hardly the vehicle for Robert's kind of work, and the assignments were only occasional.

"Have you seen John lately?" I asked. Robert had been surprised to learn that John and I were friends, and that it was John who had started me off on my retouching career. He didn't respond. I gave up trying and settled back in my seat. He sipped his espresso, said nothing at all, and when he finally got up, I felt that I'd come to know him better. I was reminded of the story of the two composers who, after sitting in a cafe for hours without speaking, one turned to the other and said, "Now we understand each other perfectly."

"Should I go out the front or the back?" he said, wryly. Robert's humor never deserted him.

The minute he left (via the back), I stormed outside. "Do you realize you barred one of the world's great photographers? And he was *not* wearing dungarees."

Fagan scratched his head, thinking back. "You mean that fat, greasy guy with the big cigar? He was carrying a camera but he looked like a bum."

That sounded something like Weegee.

"No? Was it a little guy with sloppy clothes and hair sticking up?"

That sounded exactly like Robert.

"That guy's a *photographer?* You're kidding. I thought he was a dishwasher looking for a job."

I threw up my hands, went inside, and spent the rest of the night brooding. What if de Kooning or Franz Kline showed up? They never wore anything but dungarees. (Actually, though, I had little to fear. Their bailiwick was the Cedar Tavern, and the only time they were likely to appear was when they were drying out.)

In any case, worrying didn't help. For the time being I was stuck with Pat Fagan — dungaree obsession and all.

ONCE AGAIN I went to see Manuel Neves, not so much to complain about Fagan as to grouse about business in general. I had assumed that once the bohoes were gone, the place would go back to normal. Manuel was not reassuring. "December's the slowest month of the year. People are too busy shopping and they spend all their money on gifts."

There had been a flurry of activity at the beginning of the month, but I attributed this to the Christmas exhibition *Great Photographs.* I'd sent out a special mailing and run an ad in the *Villager* (the only paper I could afford), but despite all my efforts at promoting photographs as Christmas gifts, so far only three had sold. The show did, however, attract photographers, and I hoped they'd return for good.

Great Photographs included the work of nineteen photographers: Berenice Abbott, Ansel Adams, Edouard Boubat, Bill Brandt, Brassai, Manuel Alvarez Bravo, Harry Callahan, Imogen Cunningham, Robert Doisneau, Robert Frank, Izis, Lisette Model, Gotthard Schuh, W. Eugene Smith, Paul Strand, Jacob Tuggener, Sabine Weiss, Edward Weston, and Minor White.

Walker Evans hadn't come through. Dorothea Lange was ill, and Steichen refused in a gracious letter, saying he was deeply submerged in *The Family of Man*, and all his energies were directed toward its completion. He thanked me for the "honor" and hoped that at some future date he would not have to decline.

Pricing was a problem. I left that task to the photographers (as well as the choice of the images themselves), but most would have preferred to leave it to me. There was no precedent; no one knew what to charge. Julien Levy had asked only ten dollars, and Stieglitz's business practices had been too whimsical to go by. He'd ask what he thought the client could afford, or however he felt at the moment—and there were no records of how many, if any, he sold. The Museum of Modern Art held a sale of color photographs in 1940, but the prints were priced at under ten dollars, a figure not worth considering.

Bill Brandt couldn't decide, and in a letter enclosed with his prints, he wrote: "I don't know what to ask since I've never sold a photograph to a collector. Do you think I could expect the same as Edward Weston?" Having left it to me, I decided on twenty-five dollars, the same price as the Robert Franks. Imogen Cunningham asked ten (twelve for her portrait of Stieglitz), Minor White held to ten (he'd sold three from his show); Ansel Adams's prices varied, from twenty-five to sixty; Berenice Abbott, thirty-five; Eugene Smith and Edward Weston, fifty; and Paul Strand, a staggering one hundred and twenty-five.

Deschin's lackluster review had not helped sales, but having come close to losing *Times* coverage altogether, I was grateful for even a line. He was disappointed in the selection of images, though he did single out exceptions: "Adams' dramatic Mt. Williamson, Sierra Nevada, Calif., Abbot's tall and narrow photograph of New York's financial district, Cunningham's Stieglitz and ferns, Frank's prints, Model's elegantly dressed woman in a flowered hat, Schuh's Bali boy playing marbles, White's broken stovepipe picture." He found some of the pictures (the Brandts in particular), "too dark for home display," and others "too journalistic for a show of this character."

Deschin may have had a point, but in selecting the photographers for the exhibit, I had decided on those whose work I admired, regardless how it looked in home settings. (Lisette Model's women would hardly enhance decor.)

One thing was clear: Photographs were not exactly a hot Christmas item. I brought the gift wrappings back home.

MANUEL NEVES was right—the closer to Christmas, the worse things got. Sam didn't think we could hold out much longer. The rent was due, suppliers would no longer extend credit, and everything—pastries, coffee beans, cold cuts, even paper towels for the rest rooms—all had to be paid for in cash. And I knew what that meant. When money was short, and it generally was, I had to pay out of pocket.

I'd been doing this for months, and now I was broke. Not since I'd worked in a factory had I been so short of money I couldn't even buy Christmas gifts. Now, of course, I had charge accounts (an achievement for a woman, according to Sam), so I could buy now, hope to pay later, and somehow get through the holidays.

I'd waited until the last minute, and one afternoon, just as I was about to rush off to a department store, the doorbell rang, and there stood Robert Frank. It was the first time he'd come by since giving me the photograph. "I was just passing by, so I thought I'd drop in," he said, which was exactly what he'd said before.

I told him I was sorry, that I had to rush off. Christmas was only a week away.

"Why don't I come along?"

"*Shopping?*"

"Why not? I'll help carry your packages."

I was delighted, of course. Not that I needed help; I was just glad to have company. I always felt lonely at this time of year, imagining (as single parents often do) that the world was full of big happy families and that you and your offspring were the only ones alone. There was so much that I loved about Christmas—wrapping the gifts, trimming the tree, and seeing Li-lan leap out of bed on Christmas morning and rush to open her presents. But there was something rather sad about being a family of only two.

We walked to Fifth Avenue, went weaving our way though a horde of shoppers, and after replenishing my supply of Christmas tree ornaments at Woolworth's (the cat batted them off), we ended up in the children's department at Lord & Taylor's. Robert stood patiently by, like a dutiful spouse, and as I picked through slippers and petticoats and little girls' dresses, he juggled an ever-growing pile of packages. When my charge plate reached its limit, we left.

It was a shopping spree I would not soon forget.

"**UNLESS THERE'S** a miracle by the end of the year, you'll have to file for bankruptcy," Sam warned. I no longer believed in miracles, and wished that he had waited until after the holidays before springing this news.

Yet I kept up my spirits on Christmas Day, heartened by Li-lan and her thoughtful, loving gifts. She had written me a poem, made a stool for me in her carpentry class, and saved enough out of her allowance to buy me a blue leatherette jewelry case, which, to our surprise, was identical to the one I gave her.

The day after Christmas I came down with a cold and could no longer ward off depression. I lay in bed, buried in blankets, trying to shut out the world. When the telephone rang, I let it ring, afraid it was a tradesman hounding me about a bill.

"Shucks, it's for you, Mom." Li-lan had picked up the phone, expecting a call from a friend.

"Say I'm sleeping. Say I'm not home. Say anything you want. I'm not coming to the phone."

"It's a woman. She's in the gallery and says something about buying a photograph."

"Are you *sure?*" I took the phone warily, knowing to what lengths bill collectors go to trap their prey.

"This is Dorothy Meigs Eidlitz. I'm a photographer, and . . ." I was about to beg off when she added, "and I'm also a collector. I'm here at the gallery. Can you join me?"

"Mom, you're too sick," Li-lan protested, as I threw on some clothes and made for the door. I jumped in a cab, and not until it pulled up at Limelight did I realize I was wearing my bedroom slippers. Mrs. Eidlitz was too busy to notice. She was studying the photographs and making notes on a pad.

A collector, at last! Mrs. Eidlitz was a pleasant-looking woman, simply dressed, nicely coiffed, a typical Westchester matron. Yet she had to be somewhat unusual. Photographs were a poor investment; it was not as it was in the art world, where if you bought a few paintings and called your-self a collector, you had dealers (and artists) eating out of your hand. Collecting photographs was an act of love. I tried to look cool, as if dealing with collectors was an everyday occurrence. Rather than betray my excitement, I stood to one side as Mrs. Eidlitz deliberated, moving from panel to panel. I could hardly wait to see what she'd choose—if anything.

She stopped in front of a Harry Callahan. "I'll take this one," she said, and after checking her notes, singled out seven others—a Bill Brandt, Eugene Smith, Edouard Boubat, Lisette Model, Doisneau, Brassai, and Izis. I held my breath as she lingered in front of the Paul Strand. "I would take this one, too, but the price is outrageous. One hundred and twenty-five dollars for a *photograph?*"

The price did seem out of line when on tallying up her figures, she found the price for all eight was only two hundred and twenty-five dollars.

I was elated. The sale of these eight, together with the Minor White that Li-lan planned to buy (splurging with what was left of her savings), and the Lisette Model that I hoped to buy (provided I could scrape together the money), and the three photographs already sold (an Abbott, an Izis, and a Robert Frank), made a total of thirteen. And the exhibition was not yet over.

MY FEELINGS of euphoria didn't last long. I began brooding on my problems the minute I arrived home. It seemed a sad twist of fate that Limelight was faced with closing just when I'd made this incredible sale. My cold turned into the flu.

I was too sick to retouch, yet Queen came to work every day. I appreciated her loyalty, but I'd already learned from previous bouts with the flu not to expect sympathy. Queen was a Christian Scientist, and whenever she poured me a cup of tea, I could see the rebuke in her eyes; you wouldn't be sick, they seemed to be saying, if only you thought the right thoughts. I was always relieved when Li-lan returned from school and took over, and Queen and her right thoughts left for the day.

My temperature dropped by the end of the week, but I was still feeling weak the night a waitress called and asked me to hurry downtown. "I can't talk now," she said, and hung up. I pulled on some clothes and took a cab downtown. Had Snake Eyes returned? Was Fagan out of hand? Had Rubin made good on his threats?

Seeing a crowd out front, I went around to the back, feeling too weak to push my way through. When I opened the kitchen door, I was amazed at what I saw—the help was working. All three waitresses were dashing in and out, snapping at Arnold, snapping at Herb, and snapping at each other as they vied for the orders the men tried frantically to fill. Herb was foaming milk, whipping cream, and working all three spigots of the espresso machine. Arnold was trying to do five things at once, but mostly he was burning the hamburgers, as I saw from the charred heap on the stove. Even the dishwasher was working, sloshing away at the sink.

Cheri shoved a tray at me. I put on an apron and went out front, but almost backed off when I caught sight of the crowd. People were roaming around looking for seats, others stood blocking the aisles. Adrenalin took over and I went charging around, whisking dishes off tables and carting them to the kitchen.

Fagan was acting as maitre'd. He greeted the customers, herded them into the gallery, and as tables emptied ushered them to seats. I was glad to see the gallery filled, even if only as a waiting room; it could lead to sales. It was December 30, the final day of the Christmas show. Nineteen of the photographs had already been sold; a couple more and half would be sold.

While weaving my way to the kitchen, I noticed Fagan waving a newspaper, trying to attract my attention. Whatever the reason, it had to wait. I deposited a load of dishes in the sink, and I was returning to the dining room when I heard a crash. A man lay sprawled on the floor.

"I don't take no guff from nobody," Fagan growled, clenching and unclenching his fists.

Before I could figure out what happened—everyone had a different version, none quite agreeing with Fagan's—the police arrived.

"Officer," said the man, pocketing his shattered glasses. "Arrest him. He assaulted me."

"I told him he had to leave 'cause he was wearing dungarees."

"You hit a guy for wearing *dungarees?*"

"We got rules here," Fagan said. "Just like the Rainbow Room. You don't go in there looking like a hayseed."

The cop turned to the man. "You want to press charges?"

"Yes, Officer, I do. And I want the name of the owner of this place."

I set down my tray, which I'd been gripping so hard my fingers were numb.

"*You're* the owner?" He looked skeptical, but handed me a card. Under his name was "Attorney-at-Law."

"C'mon, you guys," the cop said. "Let's go talk it over at the station house."

After they left, the customers returned to their seats. I worried about a law suit, and since we'd run out of pastries and almost everything else, I decided to close. The waitresses were near tears, the dishwasher was reeling, and I was once again feeling the effects of the flu.

As I was tallying the receipts, Fagan reappeared. He was smiling. "Ain't this something?" he said, shoving a newspaper under my chin.

Despite the sudden, inexplicable boom in business, I was not in a smiling mood. "If you *had* to hit somebody, why an attorney?"

"Aw, that's nothin'. Read this." He opened the *Daily Mirror* to Walter Winchell's column. "Even the cops was impressed."

Skimming through Winchell's column, I learned, among other things, that Frank Sinatra was to receive $80,000 for a twelve-week tour of Australia; Tennessee Williams had been spotted in a restaurant displaying his new diamond tooth fillings to Sherwood Anderson; Christine Jorgensen of sex-change fame was about to make her stage debut in the role of a pregnant woman; and Marilyn Monroe was having troubles with Joe.

"So what?" I said. "I couldn't care less."

"Keep reading," he said. "You'll see."

Halfway down, I came across the item he meant: "The Limelight in Greenwich Village (a coffeehouse) has gone ritzy. . . . On weekends they bar gals wearing dungarees. . . ."

"So that's what did it!"

"Yep," Fagan said, beaming. "Didn't I tell you to leave everything to me?"

THANKS TO Walter Winchell, a columnist I despised (for his red-baiting rather than the trivia he reported), Limelight might survive after all. But we could still go under, Sheinfeld warned, unless the place were professionally run. "Get rid of your bouncer and hire a full-time manager. And make sure he's not one of those bohemian types." He recommended Bob Borchers, and the minute I met Bob, I knew he was the right person. He didn't paint, sculpt, act, dance, nor was he writing the great American novel. He was clean-cut, a conservative dresser; no "hip" blue jeans for him. He was twenty-six, yet he'd already had two years of managerial experience. Running restaurants was his main interest in life.

I didn't know how the help would respond to someone so young—and so "square." Or, for that matter, whether they would listen to anyone, having been virtually on their own all these months. I introduced Bob at a meeting in the kitchen, and after an initial pep talk, during which he asked everyone to pull together and help save the place, he stressed the need for stricter controls.

First he ordered a clean-up, in which all were "invited" to participate. I expected defections at this point, yet everyone showed up, even the parttimers. They scrubbed floors, washed walls, scraped the accumulated crud from the kitchen, and by the end of the afternoon, Limelight was as clean as the day it opened.

Next he tackled the roach problem. He arranged for the services of an entomologist (which was what the new breed of exterminators was called). The men wore white coats, charged medical prices, and their services included a lecture. I learned more about roaches than I wanted to know— there were several different types (ours, the Norwegian Brown); they had been around for millions of years and would probably survive an atomic war. I found this depressing, but not nearly as depressing as the thought of all the transparencies I'd have to retouch to pay for the entomologist's services. But it was comforting to know that roaches would no longer be seen diving into customers' plates or found perching on photographs in the gallery.

From pest control Bob turned to food control. Herb's desserts were works of art, but by the time he finished sculpting a banana split—three scoops of ice cream, two bananas, syrup, and a mountain of whipped cream—it was no longer a dessert but a meal. Each time one was served, we lost money. Bob advised a less creative approach; each portion was to be clearly prescribed, from the ounces in a hamburger to the pickles on a plate.

"We can make it," Bob said, "if we watch every penny."

I hated watching pennies, having spent most of my life doing just that. So I felt fortunate having a manager who was not only a penny-pincher, but a compulsive worker as well. Bob worked twelve hours a day. He'd arrive a few hours before opening, take inventory, check deliveries, weigh produce, complain to suppliers about quality and price, and then, after every onion and cream puff was accounted for, he'd post himself at the cash box and wait for the help to appear. Next he'd supervise the preliminary set-ups — the filling of cream pitchers, sugar bowls, mustard jars — and all the other details that go into running a food operation. At six o'clock, he'd turn up the lights, open the doors, and, as customers arrived, lead them to tables and hand them menus.

Bob never stopped moving and was everywhere at once. He would wrest an overloaded tray from a waitress and carry it to a table, rescue a hamburger burning under the broiler, run out to the delicatessen for an extra loaf of bread, yet he'd always be back at the cash box, ready to collect the next check. Then, after we closed, he'd count the cash, tally the night's receipts, and plan the next day's purchases. And this he did, day after day, six days a week, for a salary of one hundred dollars.

For the first time in months, I began to relax. The kitchen was running smoothly, the waitresses were less harried and were raking in tips, and for the first time since we opened, the coffee was served hot.

PHOTOGRAPHY HAD arrived! On January 26, 1955, *The Family of Man*, lauded as "the greatest exhibition of all time," opened at the Museum of Modern Art to acclaim seldom awarded any exhibition. And certainly never one of photography.

If not the greatest (this would be debated for years to come), then surely the most ambitious. At an age when most men had long since retired, Steichen embarked on his major opus, embracing all of humanity in one full sweep. His objective, as he described it, was threefold: "To show the relationship of man to man; to demonstrate what a wonderfully effective language photography is in explaining man to man; and to express my own firm belief that we are all alike on the earth, regardless of race or creed or color."

To illustrate his theme, he'd scoured the world for photographs. He traveled to eleven countries, visited twenty-nine European cities, and with the help of a very small staff, screened between two and three million images. From this mass of material he selected 503, the work of 273 men and women in 68 countries, both amateurs and professionals, known and unknown, half of them American.

Photographers were euphoric. They piled into Limelight the night of the preview, and it was one great party night after night, everyone milling about, table-hopping, roaming in and out of the gallery. Hardly anyone talked about anything else, and all you heard were superlatives: "spectacular . . . magnificent . . . great." Even Lisette Model, who invariably took the

opposite tack, joined in the raves. One photographer, swept away, called it "the greatest thing since the hand-held camera."

Every newspaper covered the event, from the staid New York Times to the gossip-mongering New York Daily Mirror. The Mirror ran quotes from speeches made at the preview by Nelson Rockefeller, special advisor to President Eisenhower, and Carl Sandburg, Steichen's brother-in-law and author of the preamble to the exhibit. News services spread word of the exhibition nationwide, and Eleanor Roosevelt wrote in her syndicated column "My Day," "I could not have enjoyed anything more. . . ." But the line that had photographers tossing hats in air appeared in an article by Don Langer in the Herald Tribune: "It can truly be said that with this show, photography has come of age as a medium of expression and as an art form."

Yet despite all the excitement, I felt out of things. While others were cele- brating The Family of Man, I was at home, working my way through a pile of transparencies, glamorizing models in synthetic fabrics. Batten, Barton, Durstin, and Osborne (BBDO), my most lucrative account, had launched a Dupont campaign that very week, and the few times I managed to get downtown, I kept ducking the question on everyone's lips, "What do you think of The Family of Man?"

I was curious to hear what Robert Frank would say. He had dropped in several times since our Christmas shopping spree, but I hadn't seen him since the exhibition opened. He'd attended the preview, and from what I heard, he and Mary had cut quite a swathe, Mary in flamboyant "attic" clothes—swirling skirts, Spanish shawl, cabbage rose in her long frizzy hair—and Robert, though dressed as usual, had compromised and shaved. He had more pictures in the show than anyone else, except Steichen's assis- tant Wayne Miller (Robert had seven, Miller eight), but this was no surprise. Steichen doted on Robert. He admired his work, liked him personally (he called him by a pet name, "Roberto"), and apparently valued his judgment too. He'd consulted with him while organizing the exhibition Post-War Euro- pean Photography, shown at the museum in 1953. Robert happened to be in Zurich at the time, so he took Steichen to the various studios, steering him, of course, to the work of his friends.

Robert was perverse, and it would not have surprised me if he blasted the show, simply because he was favored. The next time he appeared—on his

Edward Steichen, by Wayne Miller.

way to see an editor about a possible assignment—I asked him that same tired question, "What do you think of *The Family of Man?*" He answered in his usual succinct fashion, "It's good, very good. Not one hundred percent, but good." This, from Robert, was rare praise indeed.

He suggested we go see the exhibition together, but I knew that if I waited until he was free, what with the complications of his personal and professional life (problems with the children, with money, with work), I'd wait a very long time. What I planned instead was to dash up to the museum during a lull in my work, and see it with Robert another time.

But then I got a call that changed all that. "It's for you," Queen whispered. "It's a Captain Something-or-other. Could it be the police?"

The *police?* Trouble at Limelight? Had my crazed neighbor escaped? I managed a faint hello.

But the "Captain" was none other than Steichen himself. Having headed photographic units in both world wars, he apparently clung to his rank. "I've been hearing about you. I want to meet you."

Steichen wanted to meet me? It was I who should have called to meet him. Friends had been urging me for months to see Steichen, but I'd always found reasons for putting it off—I was too busy with Limelight, he was too busy with *The Family of Man*—never owning up to the real reason: I was too unsure of myself.

"Are you free tomorrow? Let's have lunch," he said. "If you can get here early, we can look at the exhibition before the crowds arrive."

Put on the spot, I agreed. But the minute I hung up, Queen handed me a picture of roast beef. "What about *McCall's?* John English needs this transparency tomorrow afternoon."

"Don't worry," I said. "I'll finish it even if I have to stay up all night." Which was exactly what I found myself doing. Trimming fat from a roast until four in the morning didn't leave me in very good shape. I was groggy and jittery and coffee didn't help. So I decided to walk the fifteen blocks, hoping it would help clear my head.

On the way I tried bolstering myself up. Every photographer I knew had gone to see Steichen, and they all had good things to say. He was warm, supportive, generous with his time, and despite the imposing epithet—"dean of

Robert Frank, ca. 1957–58, by John Cohen. Courtesy

Deborah Bell Photographs, New York, copyright © by John Cohen.

American photography"—he was neither pompous nor self-congratulatory. Visiting Steichen was like visiting a friend.

But then when I thought of his long career, his fifty years of experience compared to my few, I lost whatever confidence I'd mustered. Steichen had been active in the arts decades before I was born. He'd been both a painter and photographer at the turn of the century, an associate of Stieglitz in gallery "291," an early champion of modern art, a top commercial photographer in the 1930s, and for the past nine years, as director of the photography department at the Museum of Modern Art, the country's leading exponent of creative photography.

Steichen grew more formidable with each passing block and by the time I reached the museum, I was shakier than when I'd started out. I was ushered through the empty museum to the second floor, and there, at the entrance to the exhibit, stood Steichen.

He strode toward me, arms outstretched. "So you're Helen Gee! I hadn't expected anyone so young."

Nor had I. Steichen was tall, lean, showed few signs of age, and had I not known of his long history in the arts, I would never have guessed he was seventy-four. It was his warmth and exuberance that created the illusion; I felt I was meeting a very young man.

"Come," he said, taking my arm and leading me inside. "Let's not spend time talking. Let's go look at the photographs."

SEEING *The Family of Man* with Steichen was like being shown around St. Peter's by the Pope. It took a while before I could focus on the photographs, and the opening panels were lost on me. But the message was not. The subject was love, and what I gathered from the many pictures of couples in many different lands, hugging, kissing, courting, and bonding, was that love was the same all over—in Kilamanjaro, Oshkosh, or Brooklyn. There among the couples was a familiar pair, Robert and Mary Frank at a street festival in New York, taken by their friend Louis Faurer. Accompanying the panels was a familiar quote, some of my favorite lines from the Molly Bloom soliloquy in James Joyce's *Ulysses:* ". . . and then I asked him with my eyes to ask again yes and then he asked would I yes. . . ."

From love we moved on to pregnancy and birth. Here again we encountered the Franks—two photographs of Mary, presumably pregnant, taken by Robert in their New York loft. Babies abounded: babies being born, one with the umbilical cord still attached (a picture considered quite daring), babies being nursed (the mother's nipples discreetly obscured), babies cuddled and cared for. Next came children, doing what children do everywhere in the world—laughing, crying, romping, running, leaping, playing, fighting. Here fathers were more visible: a father in America reads the papers with his son, a father in Bechuanaland teaches his son to spear game. Each panel was accompanied by an appropriate quote, drawn from literature, folklore, and the world's bibles. Repeated at intervals, setting the tone, was the smiling face of a Peruvian piper.

Not having to comment was a great relief. Yet I felt constrained with Steichen at my side and would have preferred to move around freely. This was not the kind of show that followed a simple path, with photographs hung in predictable rows. Many were on stanchions, blown up large, so you stepped forward and backward, and even around them, almost as though they'd been choreographed rather than designed. The installation was the work of the architect Paul Rudolph, and though I found it somewhat over-blown, the overall effect was dramatic. Perhaps, too dramatic. But then, how else could one get an uninitiated public to plow through five hundred photographs, however appealing the theme? This was not an exhibition in the usual sense, but more like a giant, three-dimensional magazine spread.

The museum had opened, people were crowding in, and somewhere along the way Steichen disappeared, waylaid by fans. No longer feeling con-strained, I was free to look, to wander about, and to think about what I was seeing. I had come to the exhibition with some reservations. I was skepti-cal of a world seen through Western eyes, and leery of all this "oneness." It was like tossing all of humanity into a giant blender, and coming up with pap, a bland, homogenized pap. While I could appreciate the sentiment be-hind the show—both its antiwar bias and humanistic concerns—it seemed to me that Steichen was really saying, "Look, see how much *they* are like *us!*"

Yet I tried to be objective and to maintain a cool, critical stance. But the longer I looked, the more difficult this became. The images took over. Some were extraordinary, most were good, others served as a kind of glue, fusing them all into a coherent whole. It no longer mattered that the show was overdesigned, or that I had reservations about the theme. There I was, like everyone else, agog as I traveled man's journey through life.

By the time Steichen returned, I'd covered most of the show—education, labor, worship, music, dance—and had reached fun and games, images so exuberant they seemed to leap from the walls. While dwelling on the panels devoted to food—a picnicker in France salting an egg, a peasant in Yugoslavia hugging loaves of bread—I began to think about lunch. But I wasn't hungry so much as suffering from visual fatigue, having looked at hundreds of pictures, too many to experience in one day.

Until now, the mood had been upbeat, reflecting a more or less optimistic view. But then the mood changed: life's dark side emerged. Presaged by a line from the Chinese poet Chen Chi—"I am alone with the beating of my heart"—we faced loneliness, sickness, old age, and death. Couples turned away, not toward each other, and people, though together, seemed apart. War had barely been touched upon, but the sight of a soldier belly-down on the ground was an ugly reminder of World War II and the fifty million who died. One of the photographs that moved me most (taken by an anonymous photographer) was of a group of Jews being marched by German soldiers through the streets of Warsaw, ultimately to their death. Marching in front, looking fearfully at her captors, was a little girl in a plaid coat. And it was this tiny figure that gripped the heart, more devastating in its impact than the giant blow-up of the explosion of a hydrogen bomb, displayed in color in a darkened room.

The exhibition could have ended right there. But Steichen chose to end on an affirmative note. After a photograph showing the United Nations in session, there were portraits of children from all over the world. The last one you saw as you filed out the door was *A Walk Through Paradise Garden*, Eugene's Smith's photograph of two small children walking hand in hand toward a clearing in the woods.

The only sound was the shuffling of feet; it was like leaving a temple or church. "You don't have to say anything," Steichen said, "I can tell by your face how you feel."

There was nothing, really, that I could say. To mouth the usual superlatives would only diminish the experience. I would have preferred to go home and not face lunch, but it was too late to beg off. Steichen led me to his office, where we were joined by Wayne Miller and another of his assistants, Kathleen Haven.

I was glad that Kathleen was coming along. I'd met her recently through Robert Frank—she was one of those people he called "one hundred percent"—and I knew she was clever at small talk. I discovered this during a visit to her loft, which she shared with a husband and a small menagerie. Nothing fazed Kathleen, but I found conversation difficult with a Doberman nuzzling my elbow, three chimpanzees rattling the bars of their cages, and a small nocturnal monkey perched on my shoulder, reaching its tiny brown hand into my drink, fishing for an ice cube.

Lunch with Steichen was somewhat less daunting. Kathleen prattled on with her usual wit, Steichen said little but ate a lot, and Wayne, with the air of a man who had been through this before, patiently plowed through his pasta. I was relieved when we finally reached the last course, hardly having spoken at all.

Steichen was gracious and as we parted said, "I'm glad we met. Let's get together again soon." But I doubted he'd call again.

AFTER THE euphoria of the first few weeks, photographers looked at The Family of Man with more critical eyes. Most retained their enthusiasm, pleased with the presentation and overwhelmed by the public's response. Some differed but few spoke up, reluctant to attack as popular (and powerful) a figure as Steichen, or to disparage an exhibition that had raised the status of photography virtually overnight. People crowded into the museum every day—six thousand visitors on Washington's Birthday alone—and if this kept up during its three-month run, the exhibit would break all records. The first of the "blockbusters," it rivaled the Van Gogh exhibition in 1934, when after the publication of a best-selling biography, people lined up to see the work of "the crazy artist who cut off his ear."

There was more carping, actually, than criticism. Some wag dubbed the exhibition Tits and Tots, and Steichen, its creator, "Da Lawd." Writers were more openly critical. Minor White was working on an issue of Aperture devoted to the "controversy" surrounding The Family of Man (I had yet to see signs of real controversy), and among those he invited to contribute a piece was Dorothy Norman (who had selected the quotes accompanying the photographs) and the photographer Barbara Morgan (whose enthusiasm for the show bordered on fervor), and George Wright, a freelance writer on photography who was bound to add a dissenting voice.

George had recently married Cora Alsberg, also a freelancer, and on occasion they collaborated on writing projects. George's primary concern was the aesthetics of the medium, but finding few outlets for in-depth criticism, he wrote technical books instead. Cora's expertise was the nuts and bolts (she later wrote a column for *Popular Photography* under the name of Cora Kennedy), but she shared George's interest in creative photography.

George had been mulling over the article for *Aperture*, and to clarify his thoughts, he and Cora came in one night. I listened as they tossed ideas around. I regretted they weren't taped, but they went home afterwards, sat at their typewriters, and reconstructed the conversation. It appeared as *One Family's Opinion*, under both their names, in *The Family of Man* issue of *Aperture*.

Among the points they discussed was the role of the museum itself: Wasn't it the museum's responsibility to educate the public about photography, as it did with painting, rather than deal with social themes, regardless of how noble the intent? Was expanding the audience for photography sufficient justification for presenting a show that was better suited for the lobby of the U.N.? They also questioned the legitimacy of using single images from a photographer's body of work to illustrate a popular theme. In one particularly eloquent passage George wrote:

> *Any really great photographer, like a great painter, creates his own visual universe. . . . You can distinguish a Gene Smith from a Cartier-Bresson without a signature. You can instantly recognize an Adams, a Weston, a Laughlin print, or that of any mature worker whose previous work you've seen. They are all pointing lenses at the same universe but each selects that area or aspect which is most real to him. When we see a group of pictures made by one of these men, we enter his subjective world to look at reality through his eyes. But mixed with others in a show, he surrenders this individuality—just as a writer might if he gave permission for single paragraphs to be quoted by an editor in any sequence and in any context.*

Cora was ambivalent. While objecting to various aspects of the show—it had little to do with creative photography, she maintained—she acknowledged its emotional impact. "I can't remember when I'd been so moved by an exhibition of any kind. I get goose flesh every time I see it, and it is only after that I begin to have doubts."

Both agreed that, despite its failings, the exhibition was impressive, and George concluded, saying, "It could stand for a hundred things that I didn't believe in and I'd still be happy it was put together. . . . I'm only sorry I can't wait for ten years to write this piece — my hindsight has always been a remarkable 20/20." George, unfortunately, did not live that long.

MY REACTION was similar to Cora's. I was swept away each time I saw the show, and it was only afterwards that I began to have doubts. I had misgivings about the prints. They were made by Compo, a large commercial lab, and had a standardized, mass-produced look. Gone were the nuances, those subtleties that distinguish a photographer's work. Another reservation was scale. Although the size of the prints was impressive, and some indeed overwhelming, I felt scale was a decision best left to the photographer. Yet I could imagine how thrilled Wynn Bullock was when he saw his small, gem-like moonlight scene, *Let There Be Light*, enlarged mural-size. (That image was chosen the most popular in a poll of 644,844 visitors when the exhibition was shown at the Corcoran Galleries in Washington, D.C.) I remembered Arthur Lavine's excitement when he saw his picture of workmen's hands enlarged to a monumental nine feet. (It was later reproduced as a first-edition issue by the post office, and even when tiny, it held its own.)

Setting aside these purist notions, I could appreciate the exhibition for what it was, an "editorial achievement rather than an exhibition in the usual sense," as Deschin described it in his rather bland review in the *Times*. This may have explained why most working photographers, accustomed as they were to working with editors, were satisfied with the show. They found nothing unusual in Steichen's appropriation of an editor's role, deciding on scale, layout, and the context in which their photographs were used. Steichen had made no secret of his methods or plans, and no one seemed to have objected — not even the irascible Eugene Smith or Ansel Adams (whose dislike of Steichen was well known). Without the cooperation of the photographic community, there would have been no *Family of Man*.

"HAS PHOTOGRAPHY replaced painting as the great visual art of our time?" Had this question been raised by a photography buff, it would have been brushed off as nonsense. But it was Aline B. Saarinen, a respected art critic, who advanced the idea in a provocative article in the Sunday *Times* titled *The Camera versus the Artist.*

Painters were outraged. Bad enough that they'd been upstaged by *The Family of Man.* Bad enough that the article had appeared on the art page, in space they considered rightfully theirs. Bad enough that *real* artists had to take a back seat until this photography craze blew over. But *for a critic to challenge the primacy of painting? Sacrilege!*

One could imagine the furor at the Cedar Tavern when Saarinen raised yet another question: had painting become so intellectualized that it had lost both its emotion and its power to communicate?

"Suppose," she went on, "we had to choose between all the rest of the paintings of our time and the rest of the photographs?" She would choose the photographs. "For surely, as against the mass of painting, photographs in their totality have a validity, a directness, and a powerful statement the paintings lack."

Having outraged the painters, she then succeeded in alienating photographers, concluding with the statement, "Painting is in our time, as it has always been, in the hands of giants, a great and strong means of expression. But photography is the marvelous, anonymous folk-art of our time."

Folk art? Stieglitz, Weston, Eugene Smith, Cartier-Bresson — were they in the same league as Grandma Moses? Saarinen was dismissed as a fool, both by photographers and painters alike. Painters decided she should "stick to her knitting," and photographers decided that the medium was best discussed by one of their own.

THE MOST vociferous criticism (what little there was of it) came from outside the photographic community. Hilton Kramer, a fledgling art critic and managing editor of the magazine *Arts,* wrote a scathing attack in *Commentary.* What Kramer saw was not a world linked by "essential oneness" but by *political* links, and the pieties expressed in *The Family of Man* as a "self-congratulatory means for obscuring the urgency of real problems under a blanket of ideology which takes for granted the essential goodness, innocence, and moral superiority of the international 'little man,' 'the man in the street,' the active, disembodied hero of a world-view which regards itself as superior to mere politics."

Steichen had shunned "mere politics," focusing on what he considered deeper issues. Yet it was naive to think that an exhibition that was to travel to thirty different countries (and be seen by some nine million people) would not have political import. Surely, it was not for the sake of photography that the United States Information Agency sponsored this ambitious tour. *The Family of Man*, a visual embodiment of "one world" idealism (an idealism turned sour in the politics of the Cold War) was seen by some as a propaganda weapon, a pawn in a worldwide struggle for the "hearts and minds of men."

However one saw it, one thing was clear: *The Family of Man* did as much for photography as it did for diplomacy. As Deschin put it, "You've got to hand it to Steichen. He's put photography on the map."

"IT'S STEICHEN," Queen said, having learned by now who "the Captain" was. She did not look pleased, afraid I'd go running off to the museum again. But this was an invitation to dinner. Was I in the mood for a Chinese meal? Could he pick me up at Limelight so he could see at last what all the talk was about?

We arranged to meet early, before the place filled up. A number of photographers had already arrived, and the moment he appeared he was surrounded. He made no effort to hold them off, and as he walked toward the gallery an entourage followed. I would like to have heard his reaction to the Arnold Newman show, but there was always another photographer, and I didn't get the chance. By the time we left an hour had gone by and Steichen had not even sat down for coffee.

I marveled at his energy. It was not until we walked to Sheridan Square and hailed a cab that I first saw signs of aging. His legs wouldn't cooperate and he had trouble getting inside. He slid on to the seat, heaved in one leg, then the other, and settled back with an embarrassed laugh. I looked out the window, pretending not to notice, and prattled inanely on the way to Chinatown.

Age had not affected his appetite, and at Nom Wah's he ordered a veritable feast. Barbecued spare ribs was the specialty of the house, and since I knew the waiters, having come here with Li-lan ever since she was a toddler, they threw in an extra dish.

Steichen seemed less formidable now that we were alone. He had an easygoing manner, a no-nonsense Yankee directness, and a folksy way of talking, using homespun expression like "by golly" and "gosh."

Conversation came easily, as least what we could manage between mouthfuls of food. I had looked forward to discussing photography, but Steichen was more interested in talking about me: How did I come to marry a Chinese? Was interracial marriage difficult? And what about my daughter? Had she experienced prejudice?

I had a lot to say about that. Li-lan and I had never grown accustomed to being stared at. There were very few Chinese children in New York—Chinese women had only recently gained entry into America—and with her black hair and almond-shaped eyes, there was no mistaking her for anything but "Oriental." My blue eyes and fair coloring made us an unlikely pair, and when people discovered we were mother and daughter, they were often hostile. While I had learned how to deal with it, it was hard on Li-lan. Steichen plied me with questions, so I told him about the time I was pushing Li-lan in her carriage, and a kindly tailor rushed from his shop, offering me the name of a doctor who could "fix her eyes." There were other experiences, less well meant, but I didn't care to spend the evening talking about myself.

I tried to steer the conversation to photography, and finally, halfway through the meal, we got on the subject of women in the field. Steichen was known to be supportive of women. In 1949, he presented the exhibition *Six Women Photographers*—Margaret Bourke-White, Helen Levitt, Dorothea Lange, Tana Hoban, Hazel Frieda Larsen, and Esther Bubley—and he'd shown others over the years. I'd once tried to determine how many women were active in the field compared to men, and came up with a ratio of one to five, a figure that seemed to have changed little in the last twenty years. I wondered why.

"It's because of the way we see women," he said. "We think of them as housewives and don't place value on their work. Personally, I think they're better suited to be photographers than men."

"In what way?"

"They're more intuitive, more open, more in touch with their feelings. The future belongs to women. . . ."

I would have liked to go on. Was there such a thing as a female sensibility? Was a woman's way of seeing different from a man's? But Steichen looked strange. His voice trailed off, and his eyes glazed. A trickle of soy sauce made its way down his chin.

I dropped my chopsticks, alarmed. After a minute or so, Steichen came to. He seemed confused, but I went on talking as if nothing had happened, and after a while he picked up the threads.

He continued to eat, but with far less gusto, and I just nibbled, disconcerted by the lapse. Had he had a small stroke? Momentary amnesia? Or was it simply fatigue? The Family of Man had taken its toll. Steichen was not as well as he would have others believe.

We got through dinner without another lapse and laughed at the messages in our fortune cookies. "Here's one that sounds pretty interesting," he said, holding up a slip and pretending to read. "A certain young woman has agreed to work at a certain museum for a certain curator of photography."

I laughed at what I thought was an attempt at humor, and cracked open another cookie.

"All joking aside, would you consider working as my assistant?" he said. "Wayne Miller is itching to get back to his photography. He set his own work aside just to work on the show."

"I'm flattered, but . . . ." I couldn't find the words.

"You don't have to answer right now," he said. "Why not think about it for a couple of days."

There was nothing to think about, really. Why would I want to give up what I was doing and work in the shadow of the "dean of American photography"?

The answer was no.

I HAD COME to expect the unexpected from Robert Frank. So when he appeared one morning with a flower wrapped in brown paper, I was surprised and touched. But knowing Robert, there had to be a twist. I opened the wrapper and there was a rose, a lovely, long-stemmed American Beauty. He smiled sheepishly. "I didn't have enough money for a real one. I got this one at Woolworth's for a dime." It was paper.

I sensed this was an occasion. Not that Robert needed occasions. He was very generous with people he liked and seldom came empty-handed. His gifts were usually something he owned. He'd given me one of his favorite books, *The End of the Affair* by Graham Greene, and also a painting by his friend San Yu, a Chinese artist who worked in Paris. What I treasured most, of course, were the photographs, the most recent a picture of Pablo asleep, inscribed on the back, "For all the reasons."

Robert looked cheerier than he had in weeks. "Well, I got it!" he said.

"The *Guggenheim?*"

"Yeah. It's not yet official, but Walker Evans called me and told me last night. I guess I shouldn't have worried so much."

Robert had been waiting for this news for months. He'd applied for the fellowship in October and had spent the winter in a state of suspension, growing more miserable by the day. The children were ill, he'd run out of money, and no one, not even John English, was throwing assignments his way. He depended on the grant, completely. He had submitted what he thought was a strong proposal (to photograph America, a sure-fire theme), and he'd lined up five formidable sponsors: Walker Evans, his friend and champion Edward Steichen, the eminent art historian Dr. Meyer Schapiro, and two of the most influential art directors in the country, Alexey Brodovitch of *Harper's Bazaar* and Alexander Liberman of *Vogue*. But it was Walker Evans who was said to have the influence, and though he had assured Robert for months that he'd get the Guggenheim, he'd gone on worrying anyway. The fellowship had never been awarded to a foreign photographer—and what if Walker didn't have the influence he claimed?

I had come to see Walker Evans through Robert's eyes. What I saw was a man of intellect and talent, but also a man with problems—problems with women, problems with booze. Robert had dropped by one day after visiting Walker Evans, and I saw how this troubled him. Walker was the photographer he admired most, and it hurt him to see the shape he was in—sick, hung over, depressed. Their relationship was built on mutual respect, but there was an affinity between them that went beyond the work. They shared certain traits. They were both private men, highly selective of friends, and had no tolerance for those they considered fools. Walker was a loner—he'd become even more reclusive in recent years—and despite Robert's relationship with family and friends, I sensed these same tendencies in him. They also shared certain societal attitudes, and certainly their views on photography.

Although they had known each other for only a year, Robert had become something of a confidant, a role that flattered him or dismayed him, I couldn't tell which. He seemed embarrassed by Walker's revelations of his private life, his stormy relationship with both mistress and wife. He attributed most of Walker's problems, and his drinking in particular, to the decline of interest in his work. Walker was fifty, and in the eyes of many, a has-been. While he still enjoyed a measure of success, both as staff photographer and editorial consultant at *Fortune* magazine, his recent work could in no way compare with the work he did for the Farm Security Administration in the 1930s, or with his work in the 1940s. Photographers respected Walker Evans for his past achievements—and some, like Robert, held him in awe—but for most he was simply another connection, a potential source of assignments.

Robert's attitudes were European. He wasn't caught up in the scramble for success, and he resisted the idea, more prevalent in America, that every success had to be topped with yet another success. He felt that an artist should be honored for a lifetime, regardless of when the work was done.

Robert's relationship with Walker was highly complex, and I didn't pretend to understand it. I'd never met Walker Evans, but Robert promised to arrange a meeting before he left on his trip, which, I was afraid, would be soon. We had become close friends. I would miss him. I put the rose in a vase and placed it on my desk.

QUEEN WAS all eyes and ears, and to escape her surveillance (though we had nothing to hide), Robert and I had been going for walks. He would drop by unexpectedly, and in the short time he had, we'd either stroll around the block or sit in a Third Avenue cafeteria or bar. I enjoyed these breaks because we were free to talk, and it also gave me a chance to watch Robert work. He often carried his camera in a brown paper bag, and if he saw something that interested him, he'd whip it out. One afternoon, as we were picking our way through a crowd of shoppers on West 34th Street, I noticed he was clicking away, holding his camera by his side; it was the first time I'd seen anyone "shooting from the hip." He was just as furtive in restaurants. He kept his camera concealed, and in the middle of a conversation he'd take it out and start snapping away. Wherever he was, and whatever he was doing, he was always observing, always taking pictures with his eyes.

Rather than face Queen and pull me away from my work, Robert dropped in one night after photographing the horse show in Madison Square Garden. He looked neater than usual — same old suit but he'd polished his shoes. And with a gadget bag instead of a paper bag, he looked like any other working professional. He set down his equipment and asked for a drink.

"I botched it," he said. "First job in weeks and I botched it."

I was accustomed to complaints of this kind. Hardly a week went by without some frantic photographer rushing in, clutching a transparency, hoping it could be "saved." Robert worked only in black and white, of course, and had no need of my technical expertise. That was not why he came. What he needed was sympathy.

"How do you know you've botched?" I said. "You haven't even developed your film."

"A photographer knows when he's done a lousy job, and I'm one hundred percent sure that this one's no good."

I asked him what went wrong. Had he used flash and frightened the horses?

No, the lighting was fine.

Something wrong with the film?

No, the film was okay, as far as he knew.

A technical problem?

No, nothing like that.

I could have gone on, covering every contingency, all the reasons photographers give when something goes wrong. But I noticed that Robert was smiling. And I detected a bit of mischief in that smile.

"So what *was* it then?"

"Nothing, really. Just that whenever I looked through the viewfinder I didn't see a horse, I saw *you*."

TIME WAS running short and the Franks were in the throes of preparing for Robert's trip around the country. Their plans were still vague, but they intended to meet somewhere along the route and travel together as a family. Meanwhile, Mary joined an exodus of their artist friends to Provincetown, and Robert stayed behind, free to work without interruption, and to come and go as he pleased.

The Guggenheim had made all the difference; I'd never seen him look so relaxed. The three thousand dollars would not only cover the cost of his trip but provide for the family for the rest of the year. Walker Evans was helping him plan his itinerary, and he'd purchased a car from his friend Ben Schultz.

"How about a ride?" he asked me one night, suggesting a trip across the river to Hoboken to visit the painter Alfred Leslie.

"Can you drive?"

"Of course, I can drive!" he said, reacting like a typical American male, having his prowess at the wheel impugned. "How do you think I'm going to get around the country?"

I was not reassured. When he tried starting the car, it lurched forward, then stopped. Robert muttered the usual expletives, then turned on the ignition and started up again. I braced myself as we veered toward Third Avenue and the El pillars and went bumping over cobblestones on the way downtown. I didn't relax until we reached the pier.

Once on the ferry, we got out of the car, and as the boat chugged its way through the Hudson River toward New Jersey, we stood gazing at the skyline. New York was a city of graceful spires, its harmony unbroken by the architectural tombstones erected later on. A full moon, pasted against the sky, looked like an orange cut-out in an artist's collage.

I'd never been to Hoboken and knew it only as the birthplace of Alfred Stieglitz. (I'd read that famous quote: "I was born in Hoboken. I am an American. Photography is my passion. The search for truth my obsession.") But Hoboken's real claim to fame was On the Waterfront, which had been filmed on the Hoboken docks. It was a working-class town, the kind Robert liked. We stopped at a clam bar on Main Street, a cavern of a place with beat-up tables and sawdust on the floor, and slurped down a couple dozen clams. Robert took in everything—the men in their dungarees and heavy work shoes, the women in house dresses and pink and green hair rollers— almost as if he was already on his trip. Had he brought along his camera, he would have set it on the table, then reached over occasionally and clicked the shutter, catching his subjects off-guard.

Hoboken was not the sort of town where you'd expect to find artists, but a number of painters had migrated there, away from the hassle of the city. Living in lofts in New York was illegal; it meant crawling down fire escapes, concealing stoves and refrigerators behind false walls, and dreaming up ways of evading city inspectors. Hoboken offered fewer problems and lower rents. It also provided more time for work, away from the temptations of the Cedar Tavern.

Like most artists, Alfred Leslie supported himself doing odd jobs. He was presently working as a moving man, and when he came to the door, stripped to the waist, I could see he was suited for the job. He had the well-defined muscles of a body-builder; I would have entrusted him with a piano any day.

"Amigo!" he cried, and from the way he grabbed Robert and hugged him, I thought perhaps living in Hoboken had drawbacks. He brought out a jug of wine, filled three water tumblers, and I watched to see how much Robert would drink, nervous about the trip back home. Word of our visit had apparently spread, and with every knock on the door, another artist appeared. Robert liked talking with painters, but tonight he was content to just sit and listen as they rehashed the usual art world palaver—lofts, "the Club," Bill (de Kooning, of course), and the latest gossip from the Cedar Tavern. Someone mentioned the Guggenheim.

"When do leave you leave on your trip?" Leslie asked.

Robert said soon, then changed the subject, aware of the attitude of painters. Why a photographer when it was the *real* artists who needed the money?

He emptied his glass, then suddenly remembering he had work to do, decided it was time to leave. Maybe it was the wine, or maybe just our thoughts, but neither of us spoke on the way back to New York.

ROBERT KEPT waiting for something to go wrong. "It's not normal for things to run smoothly," he said, and not long afterwards, his fears were confirmed.

We were at his loft and I was watching him work in the dark room (impressed with his scrupulous attention to print quality) when the phone rang. Annoyed at the interruption, he managed a gruff hello.

From the look on his face, I knew it was bad news. "It's this god-damned country," he muttered, then hung up the phone and sunk into a chair. "That was Walker Evans. Jim Agee is dead."

Robert had met James Agee through Walker Evans, and though he'd known him only a few months, he seemed deeply affected. He admired him as a writer, saw eye to eye with him on photography, and shared many of the same iconoclastic political views. He also admired his eloquence. He'd spent several long evenings in Agee's King Street apartment, listening to him hold forth. Agee talked about everything—books, movies, photography, life. Talking came easier than writing, and the novel he'd been struggling to finish, *A Death in the Family*, which was published posthumously and won a Pulitzer Prize, took second place to these monologues. Robert would sit there for hours nursing a scotch while Agee downed a whole bottle, though never seeming to get drunk.

"You should see the way he lives," Robert told me after one of these visits.

"He doesn't give a damn about owning things. He uses orange crates for furniture, and he doesn't give a damn about clothes." Agee had hardly bothered to change in the months before his death, and Robert never saw him in anything but the same old shirt (a surprising observation coming from Robert). Agee was extraordinarily handsome, and I gathered that women were always a problem. Anguished writers held great allure, and one could only commiserate with Agee's wife, Mia, a large, plain woman in practical shoes, for all that she—and the two wives preceding her—had endured.

Robert saw Agee's death as symbolic: This was what America did to its artists. Agee had compromised his talents in order to survive: he was a staff writer for *Time*, a script writer in Hollywood (he'd written the screenplay for *The African Queen*), and film critic for *The Nation*. Yet he was more often than not without money. *Let Us Now Praise Famous Men*, the book on which he'd collaborated with Walker Evans, had sold only six hundred copies. (He had put off writing it year after year, and by the time it was finally published, in 1941, people were no longer concerned with sharecroppers in the South.)

What Robert didn't take into account, in blaming America for all of Agee's ills, was that he had actually fared better than many liberal writers. He had never been questioned by the House Un-American Activities Committee, despite his attack on its policies. Nor had he been drafted during World War II (a war he opposed). If Agee's life seemed less than charmed, neither was it cursed, except, perhaps, by his drinking.

Robert attributed Agee's drinking to his problems as a writer, and the heart attack he'd suffered, dying in a taxi cab at the age of forty-four, to his years of struggle as an artist. If only he hadn't had to sell out to Hollywood and *Time*, if only. . . .

"It's this god-damned country," he muttered, and put his work away for the night.

A COUPLE of weeks later, Robert called and asked me to hurry over. He was expecting Walker Evans. Perhaps if we met and became friends, he might eventually agree to exhibit. "But don't say anything about going to his place last winter. I don't think he'd like that at all."

He was referring to a surreptitious visit to an East Side railroad apartment that Walker Evans kept, both as a *pied-à-terre* and a place to store his

work. Robert had a key so we went in one afternoon and spent hours looking through cartons of photographs. Walker had made no attempt at a filing
system, and as we pulled out the pictures, marveling over each one, I found
myself assembling an exhibition in my mind. We forgot all about time, and
it was only after we heard footsteps in the hall that we became nervous and
decided to leave.

I arrived at Robert's loft before Walker did, and after a cup of coffee
(which I needed were I to bag this lion), I began looking through Robert's
photographs, trying to make it appear I was there for that reason.

"Relax. Just be yourself," Robert said. "I'm sure he'll like you. Just don't
let on that you're after his work."

But I couldn't relax, and when he finally appeared, a small natty man in
a banker's gray suit, I was wooden and ill at ease. I wasn't sure I liked him.
He had cold, unblinking eyes, the kind that could level with a single glance,
and a haughty, turned-up nose.

After acknowledging the introduction, he walked to the other end of the
loft. Robert followed and they talked for some time. They were both sub-
dued, and from the little I could hear, I knew they were talking about Agee.
I kept looking through the photographs, and drew a deep breath when they
finally stopped and walked toward me. But halfway across the floor, Walker
wheeled around, tipped his hat (a smart-looking Stetson) and left.

"I guess this wasn't such a good idea," Robert said. "He's still broken up
about Agee. I'll get you two together another time."

But another meeting never took place, and I never saw Walker Evans
again. And, unfortunately, I never exhibited his work.

ROBERT WAS leaving. He'd made a few short trips around New York, and
now he was heading for Detroit. I rode with him as far as Newark, caution-
ing him about the dangers lurking in the hinterlands. (Having traveled outside of New York with Li-lan a few times, I was aware of people's reactions
to those who look "different.") I wished he'd cut his hair, and I hoped he'd
remember to shave. The "careless look" could pass in New York, but the sight
of a small, grubby-looking young man snooping around with a camera was
bound to arouse suspicions in Podunk. There was also his accent; could he
order a hamburger in a diner without letting on he was foreign? New York

license plates were no advantage in other parts; would he be taken for one of those East Coast "trouble-makers"?

"You've been seeing too many movies," Robert said.

"Movies? When do I get a chance to see movies?" I said. "I'm at Limelight every night of the week."

I doubted that these warnings made any impression, but as we waited for the bus to take me back to New York, he did agree to be careful. "I'll stay out of trouble, stay out of jail, and send you a postcard from somewhere."

The bus pulled up, and we said goodbye.

"WOULD YOU be interested in a Stieglitz show?"

Stieglitz? I pressed the receiver closer to my ear, not quite sure I was hearing right. The caller was Dorothy Norman, who, despite her achievements in several fields, was primarily known in the photography world as having been "the other woman" in Stieglitz's life. "The photographs would not be for sale," she said. "They're part of my private collection."

I told her I'd be honored, that sales didn't matter, and that I'd rearrange my schedule if we could decide on a date. The Arnold Newman exhibition (which included a portrait of Stieglitz and Georgia O'Keeffe) was about to close, followed by Eliot Porter's nature studies in color. Next came Dan Weiner's *Italy*; if I postponed Dan's show for a month or two, I could open with Stieglitz in April.

"Wonderful!" Deschin said, when I called him with the news. "It will give the gallery enormous prestige. But let me warn you about these keepers of the flame. They can be a real pain in the neck."

In preparation, I read everything I could find on Stieglitz, including *America and Alfred Stieglitz: A Collective Portrait*, published in 1934 as a tribute to Stieglitz on his seventieth birthday. Dorothy Norman had helped compile the book, and among the eulogies contributed by various notables in the arts (even, surprisingly, Gertrude Stein) was a piece she herself had composed. She spoke of Stieglitz as if he were a god, and his gallery, An American Place, as if it were a shrine.

Of course, she was young when she wrote this; perhaps the flame no longer burned as bright. She was twenty-one, living on Park Avenue and pregnant with her first child, when she wandered into An Intimate Gallery (the gallery preceding An American Place) and listened, rapt, as Stieglitz held forth. He may have been lecturing some hapless collector on "earning the right to own a work of art" or lamenting the state of American culture, another favorite theme. Whatever the case, she felt compelled to return, and soon became something of a fixture in the gallery, hovering about with notebook in hand, recording Stieglitz's every word. She was not only his Boswell, but model, muse, and business manager; without her efforts at fund raising, the gallery might never have survived the depression years. Though she eventually branched out and made a name for herself—she edited and published *Twice a Year*, a journal devoted to civil liberties and the arts, wrote a column for the *New York Post*, and supported social and political causes—she and Stieglitz remained close. Despite their respective marriages—she to Edward Norman, the Sears-Roebuck heir, and he to Georgia O'Keeffe—their relationship lasted (on one level or another) for fourteen years, until Stieglitz died, in 1946, at the age of eighty-one.

Thrilled at the prospect not only of seeing the Stieglitz prints but of meeting this interesting woman, I arrived at her elegant townhouse on East 70th Street the day after her call. I was ushered upstairs to a spacious living room—simple, modern, all beige and white—and while waiting, I looked at the art. The paintings, most by members of the "Stieglitz circle" (John Marin apparently a favorite) were displayed on a shelf that extended around the room, an ingenious device that made changing the art easy. Interspersed among the paintings were photographs, most by Stieglitz, of course.

While looking at a Stieglitz—a portrait of Dorothy Norman in the 1930s—she suddenly appeared beside me. It was like seeing a photograph come to life. There were the same dark eyes, the same furrowed brow and slightly pained look, and aside from the hair, which was now streaked with gray, she had changed very little. Yet she no longer seemed the same person—no longer the fragile young woman, all vulnerability and tenderness, but a stolid-looking matron, fully in command.

As we talked over tea, I found myself doing the inevitable—comparing her to Georgia O'Keeffe. She did not hold up well. O'Keeffe was twenty years older but much more beautiful. Her face had wrinkled but hadn't sagged, and she still had that impish half-smile, that cool on the surface but smoldering-within quality that must have held Stieglitz in thrall. She had an air of mystery, a woman fascinating at any age.

After I finished my tea, she poured me another, and I wondered how many more cups I would need to consume before she showed me the photographs. Finally she got up and brought out a box, and there on top was a portrait of herself, similar to the one on display. She lifted it out, and there was another. And another and another. I kept waiting for other images to appear—*The Terminal, Steerage, City of Ambition*—but there was always another portrait. By the time she reached the bottom of the box, I had seen about forty or fifty. My hopes were raised when she brought out another box. But out of this came *her* portraits of *him*. While it was a relief to see Stieglitz's great craggy face, by the time she got to the bottom of the box, I knew the kind of show she had in mind.

Though disappointed, I was somewhat intrigued. I liked the idea of a two-person show, as much for the story behind the portraits as for the portraits themselves. But since so many of the poses were so much alike, I suggested we limit the exhibit to sixty prints and left the selection to her. (Who was I, after all, to edit Stieglitz?) I suggested a title, *Portraits of Each Other*, and she readily agreed to it, unperturbed by the implication of intimacy.

Their relationship had always been something of a mystery. No one seemed to know what actually transpired, and Dorothy Norman was discreet and never let on. I was curious, of course, but not wanting to look as if I were prying, I asked, cautiously, "What was it like to photograph Stieglitz?"

"It wasn't easy. Whenever he saw something in me he wanted to record, he'd shout 'Hold it!' and rush for his camera. But when I did the same thing he would burst out laughing. He'd stick out his tongue or make a funny face, and I'd have to wait till he stopped, then catch what I could."

It was hard to imagine Stieglitz sticking out his tongue. He'd been photographed by *everybody*—Steichen, Ansel Adams, Imogen Cunningham, Paul Strand, and who knows how many others—yet he was always the stony-faced pundit. In these by Dorothy Norman, he seemed more relaxed. She had worked up close, searching his face with her camera; you could almost feel Stieglitz breathe.

But his portraits of her lacked that intensity. What seemed to be missing was passion. He had photographed O'Keeffe like a man possessed, exploring her anatomy, her moods, every angle of her remarkable face. These of Dorothy Norman always had the same mood—sad-eyed and brooding. Was it because of his age that he lacked the spark? Or had he lacked the ardor he felt for his wife?

Nevertheless, it would be a fascinating show. With just weeks to work, I plunged right in, tackling the first of the problems. I had agreed to cover the photographs with glass, and since they were matted but weren't framed, I had to find a solution. With the help of Barry, an artist I had hired for the studio and was training to retouch, I devised a way of supporting the photographs on long strips of wood, and covering each row with a single sheet of glass. In addition, there was the usual gallery work—press releases, announcements, invitations, and the like.

So I welcomed Dorothy Norman's participation, at least at first. She called every day, checking and rechecking every detail, and while I understood her concern—this was the first time these photographs were to be shown in this context—I began to feel more harried than helped. Still, she was very effective. Determined to get publicity, she left no contact untapped, and had managed to interest *Life* in running a five-page spread.

Every now and then I thought of O'Keeffe. How would she react when she heard about the show? What *was* the relationship between the two women? And what had it been during those fourteen years? My own guess, based on what little I knew, was that O'Keeffe may have tolerated, and perhaps even welcomed, the presence of the "other woman." It was she, after all, who had gone away, leaving Stieglitz alone a good part of the year. In New Mexico she found the landscape she loved and the solitude she needed to paint. Stieglitz, I imagined, was difficult, and turning him over to an adoring young woman may have relieved her of the burden of an aging man and assuaged any feelings of guilt.

Dorothy Norman had, in fact, appeared at just the right time. In 1926, the year they met, Stieglitz's influence in the art world had already waned. Others had taken up the cudgels. The Museum of Modern Art opened in 1929, the Julien Levy Gallery in 1931, and though Stieglitz was still revered as a pioneer, he'd been relegated to the role of "grand old man."

I found it increasingly difficult, as we worked on the show, to reconcile the idealistic young woman that Stieglitz knew with the imperious woman that I knew. Everything was a problem. Expenses arose that I hadn't anticipated and with Limelight still recovering from the drug fiasco (I was still paying bills out of pocket) I had hoped she would share the additional costs. Since the photographs were rare—the only other set was in the National Gallery in Washington, D.C.—I'd assumed they were adequately insured. Limelight's policy limited the coverage of an exhibition to fifteen hundred dollars (more than adequate for the average show), and I was unprepared for triple the cost. When I explained my predicament, she looked pained and replied, "I'm turning a church in East Hampton into my summer home. It's costing a fortune." I ended up footing the bill.

Then two weeks before the opening, she handed me a list of six hundred names, including notables from all over the world and asked me to send them invitations. Though I thought it unlikely that Indira Gandhi or President Sukarno of Indonesia would arrive for the opening, I sat down and addressed the invitations, fuming. It seemed not to have occurred to her that her secretary might help, or that she might contribute toward the postage. I found myself liking her less and less and didn't look forward to having her present when Barry and I hung the show. But I'd already agreed, and couldn't back out now.

Having agreed to exhibit about sixty prints, I was astonished when she arrived with all ninety-five. From the way she was measuring the walls with her eyes, she intended to hang every one. She immediately took over. She perched on a stool in the middle of the gallery, directing our every move. Barry and I held the photographs in position while she determined the placement, down to the fraction of an inch. "Move to the right . . . no, that's too far . . . a quarter of an inch . . . now down an eighth . . . up a little higher . . . to the left a sixteenth . . . now up a fraction more. . . ." And on and on.

Barry and I exchanged glances. We'd had a difficult day at the studio , and after hours of these minuscule adjustments, I wondered whether he would stick out the night. He was apt to disappear when the going got rough, and though I swore each time that I wouldn't take him back, I always gave in. He was so pale, so thin, so very contrite, and he always had another story: He'd been beaten or mugged, or awakened after an all-night binge to find himself chained to a bed in some flea-bag hotel. I never knew whether to believe him, though an occasional black eye gave his stories credence.

Finally, she announced she was finished. She put on her coat, but returned for another look. "On second thought, drop all the photographs another half-inch."

Barry groaned, and if anything was to drop, I was afraid it would be the glass he was holding. Two of his fingers were bleeding, and I could see he was in no mood to shed any more blood—not for me, for Limelight, or for Stieglitz.

By the time we finished it was morning, and we had seven cut fingers between us. Barry mumbled something about needing sleep and wandered off toward Christopher Street, which was not in the direction of his home.

He didn't show up for the opening, but the gallery was crowded and he wasn't missed. Taxis and limousines kept pulling up out front, and if I were better at spotting celebrities, I would have recognized leaders in several different fields—finance, publishing, politics, and the arts. Dorothy Norman looked grave—this was, after all, a posthumous event—and she responded to their accolades with the shadow of a smile.

She returned the next day, and each time she walked into the gallery, I tightened, afraid she'd remember about that extra half-inch. At one point she asked me to join her at her table, and I did so reluctantly, waiting for the next demand. She leaned toward me, and though there was little chance of our being overheard, she whispered, "O'Keeffe sent her spies."

"Her *what?*"

"Her spies. There was one at the opening, and two here tonight."

"Why would she do that?"

"Why? Because she still can't get over my relationship with Stieglitz. Not even after all these years." She had a cat-ate-the-canary look on her face, and suddenly everything became clear. Now I knew why she arranged for the show—to get back at Georgia O'Keeffe!

My suspicions were confirmed when I learned from visitors during the course of the show that the animosity between the two women did indeed exist. I was told by a painter who had known all three that O'Keeffe had not condoned the relationship, and that it had, in fact, caused her considerable distress. She was in her forties when Dorothy Norman appeared, and she took it as hard as any women faced with a nubile young rival. O'Keeffe had been violently jealous, and, at one point, became ill and was hospitalized, suffering from a nervous disorder.

Yet she always returned to New Mexico; painting always came first. Stieglitz wrote regularly, sometimes three times a day. Whatever their problems and mutual dallyings, O'Keeffe, for Stieglitz, was always number one.

Dorothy Norman may have felt this acutely, for even now, she still seemed to be fighting for her place. She was divorced, her two children were grown, and now that she was no longer in the public eye, she had time to brood on the past. And to renew her rivalry with Georgia O'Keeffe.

Portraits of Each Other did just that. But whatever satisfaction she may have derived was diminished when *Life* canceled the five-page spread. The press still adhered to a "gentlemen's agreement," shielding public figures (politicians, usually) from any hint of adultery.

Even Deschin, who claimed never to have been edited in all the years he'd been with the *Times*, was given the blue-pencil treatment. He'd referred to their "relationship." It was changed to "friendship."

And now I understood what Deschin meant when he warned about the "keepers of the flame."

Li-lan, Mia, and Penny, 1955, by Morris Jaffe.

"I'M NOT ONLY Oriental, I'm underprivileged. All the kids have televisions but me." Li-lan knew how to manipulate me. I felt my resolve turn to jelly.

For years I'd resisted buying a set. Li-lan painted, wrote stories, and put on plays (produced in the living room, Li-lan as the star), and I hated to think of her glued to a set, watching I Love Lucy, and Gunsmoke. But by now I was the last of the hold-outs. Most parents in Li-lan's school—Downtown Community, a private, interracial school where creativity took precedence over the ABCs—had already succumbed. I had hoped to hold out at least another year, but Li-lan's remark (coupled with tears) got under my skin. Three days later, there it sat, a big, shiny Emerson with a nineteen-inch screen, and parked in front of it, slack-jawed and glassy-eyed, was Li-lan.

Determined not to let it take over, I limited her viewing to a half-hour a day, and to programs I'd screened. One of the programs that met my criteria—no shootings, no stabbings, no mayhem—was The Sky's the Limit, a give-away game program geared to parents and children. Two sets of contestants, each made up of a parent and child, competed each night—throwing darts at moving targets, balancing blocks on their heads—and those who defeated each set of contestants on four consecutive nights won a ten-day vacation in Spain, courtesy of Iberia Airlines and the Castellana-Hilton Hotel in Madrid. Before each game, a young actress—Hope Lange before she became a star—would spin a roulette wheel, and if it stopped at the lucky number, the winners of that particular game would win the trip to Spain.

We watched for weeks but no one ever won. Li-lan remained glued but

I gave up, annoyed at myself for having been drawn in. Then, to my astonishment, I got a call from the producer's assistant asking us to appear for a "coordination test."

"A *what?* There must be some mistake."

"I have a letter here from a Li-lan Gee, requesting that you appear as contestants."

The minute I hung up, I laced into Li-lan. "How could you do this to me? Do you expect me to make a fool of myself in front of millions of people? You know I'm not good at games."

"You need a vacation, Mom. Ever since you opened Limelight, you've been such a grouch." She began to cry.

We appeared for the coordination test, which involved nothing more difficult than stacking up kindergarten blocks (even I couldn't flub that) and were given the date to appear. But as the time approached I grew increasingly nervous and made Li-lan promise to keep it secret.

Come the day of our appearance, Li-lan was calm but I was a wreck. On the way to the studio I spotted a bar and thought maybe, just maybe, a drink might help. Li-lan tightened her grip on my hand. "You'll get dizzy and spoil everything. You know you're not used to drinking, Mom."

"I need *something* to help get me through this." I ordered a martini, gulped it down, then ordered another, just to make sure.

Going up the elevator, I felt the effect, but it was not the kind I'd expected. I was woozy, and catching sight of the audience didn't help. There they sat, like Romans at the games, waiting to see me done in.

Also waiting (and for the very same reason), were our fellow-contestants, Mrs. Carp and her ten-year-old son Junior. They had already won three nights in a row; this was the night that would send them to Spain. Mrs. Carp was plump, bursting with confidence, and Junior, though puny, was cocky. His lip curled as he looked Li-lan over, as if to say, "She's only a girl."

Al Collins, the host of the show, led us to the set and told us to "laugh and look happy" should we win a game. In the back of the set behind a screen, a stagehand perched on a ladder, waiting to release a pail of confetti on the winners of the grand prize. He'd been waiting for weeks.

I kept hoping for some major catastrophe, a power failure, at the least. But at the stroke of six, Al Collins bellowed, "The Sky's the Limit!" and after an all-too-brief commercial, the ordeal began. "Will the Gees wrest from the Carps their final chance for a ten-day vacation in sunny Spain?"

I won a temporary reprieve; the first game, he announced, would be played by the children alone. They were each given a jigsaw puzzle, and with a loud blare of music, signaled to start. I watched in the monitor, heart pounding, as Li-lan's fingers flew. I wondered how she could remain so calm—was there something to the myth of "Oriental stoicism," after all? There was a burst of applause as she put the last piece in place. Al Collins shouted, "The winnah, Li-lan Gee!"

Another commercial, and then came a chilling announcement: the next would be played by all four. The children donned Indian headdresses, and Mrs. Carp and I were to toss pingpong balls into the circle of feathers. The music was unnerving, and the martinis didn't help. My first ball went off into the audience, the second hit the floor, and the closest I got after five or six tries was the tip of Li-lan's nose.

The third game was played by the children, and though Li-lan succeeded in throwing several balls into baskets, Junior came out ahead. The score was two to one, in favor of the Carps, and if we tied, winning the fourth (and final) game, we would have to return the following night and undergo this ordeal again.

But we were spared that prospect when Hope Lange turned the roulette wheel and for the first time in weeks, it stopped at the lucky number. The winners of this game would win the trip to Spain!

My hands were shaking, my palms were wet, and I didn't see how I could hold a ball, much less throw one. But this game, luckily, didn't call for balls. The children were seated on kindergarten chairs and given paper cups to hold on their heads. Mrs. Carp and I were also given cups; we were to balance them on our heads, walk several yards to where the children sat, and then stoop and, without using our hands, slip our cups into theirs.

I placed a cup on my head, took a deep breath, and at the first blast of music, sailed forth. Mrs. Carp and I ran nose to nose, arriving at the children at the very same time. I stooped down, slipped my cup into Li-lan's, then turned to go for another. Mrs. Carp stooped down but had trouble getting up, hampered, perhaps, by a girdle. I picked up another cup, and succeeding once again, went gliding back and forth; those ballet lessons as a child were not for naught. I was Anna Pavlova, floating across the stage, while poor Mrs. Carp. . . .

The music stopped, there was wild applause, and confetti rained down on our heads. "The winnahs, the Gees!" shouted Collins. "A ten-day vacation in sunny Spain, courtesy Iberia Airlines and the Castellana-Hilton Hotel in Madrid!"

Stunned, we forgot to laugh and look happy; we just stood there.

Another commercial, and Hope Lange appeared with still other prizes: For Li-lan, a set of oil paints and a two-foot plastic schooner. For me, a string of pearls, two bottles of My Sin perfume, and a set of nine flashlights for the home. More music, more applause, and suddenly, everything was over. The audience filed out, the staff disappeared, and we were left standing in an empty studio.

We wrestled our booty into a taxi, and as I sat peering between the sails of a two-foot plastic schooner, it suddenly hit me — we'd won!

"We won a trip to Spain," I announced to the cabbie. I felt like telling the whole world.

But the world already knew. The telephone was ringing when we walked in the door and rang for the rest of the week — my friends, Li-lan's friends, Limelight customers, retouching clients, and photographers too. Even Leon Levinstein, and he didn't own a set. He'd been photographing on the Bowery, and on wandering into a Skid Row bar, saw us on the screen. He told the winos he knew us, and when we won the grand prize, they got up and cheered.

We were celebrities. Neighbors who never nodded now greeted us, shopkeepers waved as we passed, and Li-lan was a star at Downtown Community School. But most gratifying of all was hearing Li-lan say when I tucked her into bed that night, "Mom, at last I've done something for *you*."

OUR TRIP to Europe was still months off. Prize-winners were limited to traveling off-season, so my much-needed rest had to wait. Barry wasn't much help in the studio; he could only handle the simplest jobs, and he still disappeared when I needed him most. I was tired and overworked; something had to give.

And what was giving, it appeared, was my health. I'd developed arthritis

Helen Gee retouching transparencies, 1955, by Arthur Lavine.

in my shoulder and right arm, and retouching had become very painful. My
doctor advised me to cut down on work—either Limelight or the studio—
I could no longer handle both.

There was no question in my mind as to what that decision would be. I
loved Limelight and believed in what I was doing; retouching was simply
a craft. I couldn't care less about Clairol, De Beers Diamonds, Van Camps
Beans, or, for that matter, any of the products my retouching enhanced.

America was becoming a nation of consumers, and I found little satisfaction in contributing my bit, however insignificant, to the craving for more and more goods. "Built-in obsolescence," a concept developed after World War II, was now a given, and I remembered a time, not that long ago, when nylon stockings lasted for months and appliances didn't break down the day the guarantee expired.

Nor did I care about the fashion magazines. The ideal of the perfect woman—not a mole, a wrinkle, an extra ounce of weight—was one that none of us could possibly attain, however much we spent on make-up and clothes. I hated to think, as I nipped in Dovima's waist or bleached a freckle from Suzy Parker's nose, that I was helping sustain the illusion. No wonder good retouchers were prized. Where would Avedon be without Bob Bishop, his retoucher? His goose-necked women, indeed all of his women in *Harper's Bazaar*, were masterpieces of airbrush retouching, as doctored as the corpses at Whelan's.

Yet there were aspects of retouching I enjoyed. I liked the challenge of each new job, I liked the feeling of work well done, and I liked the people I worked for. And, of course, I liked the money it earned. I particularly liked working for *McCall's*; not only was the magazine a bit more down to earth, but the jobs John English sent me were often unique. I had doctored the Duchess of Windsor's ugly, red hands (in most pictures they were artfully concealed), and I'd turned back the clock for Greta Garbo. She'd been inveigled into posing by Anthony Beauchamp, a photographer whose forte was blonde Hollywood starlets. She hadn't been photographed in so long it was the scoop of the year. Since her face was to appear on the cover of *McCall's*, she wanted to look as young as she had on the screen. I eliminated wrinkles, refined the pores, and took off at least twenty years.

But even at best, the work was a strain. Anything could go wrong at any time, and should I run into trouble, there was no place to turn. There was generally no time for retakes, and whenever I came close to ruining a transparency, I saw myself back painting roses on garbage cans.

One night I came pretty close. I was working on a photograph by Ben Somoroff, an 11×14 transparency of macaroni products for a double-page spread in *McCall's*. The pasta was too dark, and though most corrections were made directly on the transparency with brushes and dyes, this one called for a chemical bath. It was midnight, I was groggy, and not allowing enough time for the chemicals to dissolve, the sediment bit into the emulsion, riddling it with holes. Crying, I called John in the middle of the night, but he said not to worry; he would bypass the editor, send the transparency to the engraver, and have the damage repaired on the plates—no one would ever know. And no one would have known had not Ben Somoroff won the Art Director's Award that year and found that the transparency could not be exhibited. But by that time it no longer mattered.

Losing a transparency was equally disastrous. One weekend, while working on my Dupont account, I discovered one missing. I searched the studio, tore the apartment apart, and finally concluded that it had slipped into the waste paper basket. But the trash had been thrown down the garbage chute, and the only way to retrieve it was to search the incinerator. I covered my hair with a babushka, put on dungarees, gloves, and rubber boots, and went downstairs to the basement. I managed to squeeze through the incinerator door, and crouching knee-deep in garbage, sifted through the refuse of one hundred tenants. I had to keep ducking the garbage that came hurtling down the chute, and watch for the super, who I was afraid would discover me. Or worse, not discover me, and toss in a match. I finally gave up, resigned to the loss of my most lucrative account, and even, perhaps, my career. But on Monday morning, when Queen slunk into BBDO, prepared to confess, there was the "missing" transparency, on the art director's desk.

The strain of the work always had me on edge, reason enough for closing the studio. But could I manage without the income? Bob Borchers estimated that I could start drawing a salary of seventy-five dollars a week by the end of the year, and though this was a pittance compared to my earnings as a retoucher, I decided to take the chance.

Li-lan was overjoyed. "I'm getting back my Mom," she announced to her friends. But I held off telling Queen. She'd been my secretary and representative for the last three years; what would become of her now? Who would hire a seventy-year-old widow with so brief a work history? After agonizing for weeks, I called Tulio Martin, the one retoucher I knew my clients would accept, and offered to give him all of my accounts (except *McCall's*, which I felt I could handle), provided he also took Queen. He agreed, and though losing her was a wrench, I was glad she had a job. (She worked for two years, until she "retired" to a nursing home.)

That settled, I called Romano, the broker who'd shown me the Limelight space, and asked him to perform another miracle: a large apartment with a low rent, within walking distance of Limelight.

"There ain't no such animal," he grumbled. Apartments were at a premium. A shortage had developed after World War II, and for the "privilege" of living in some musty attic or grimy basement, you had to resort to all sorts of devices, from reading the obituaries to paying "key money," or buying ramshackle furniture you didn't need.

Romano went to work, spurred on by my offer of "money under the table," and two days later he called. "I've got exactly what you want, a six-room apartment right near Limelight, and only sixty-six dollars a month."

"I'll take it," I said.

"There's only one hitch. A drunk's been living in it for twenty years, and it will be up to you to clear out the trash."

"I'll take it."

"You better go look at it. The guys in the hall will give you a key."

I dropped my retouching, took a cab downtown, and pulled up in front of a dingy five-story walk-up on the corner of Sheridan Square. Not exactly a show-place but it was opposite Limelight and less than half a block away.

A man was lurking in the doorway. "Looking for somebody, Miss?"

"I've come to see the apartment. Romano told me to ask you for the key."

"There ain't nothin' for rent in this building. You're in the wrong place."

"But this is the right place, 61 Grove Street. I know this neighborhood. I own the Limelight across the street."

"So you're the dame who owns that joint? Wait, I'll see what I can do."

He returned with a key and I followed him down a long, dark hall. At the end, near the mail boxes, were two other men. They looked me over, and I felt them watching as I started up the stairs to Apartment 3B.

I was unprepared for the stench. The rooms all opened on to a long narrow hall, and I peered into each one as I passed. They were all full of junk: dilapidated chairs, broken-down beds, filthy mattresses, heaps of garbage, dirty clothes, and everywhere, bottles and beer cans. The stench seemed to come from the bathroom. The toilet was clogged, and the tub had served as a substitute. Only the living room, with its sagging sofa and overstuffed chairs, looked as if this had once been a home. There was a crucifix over the mantle.

I went downstairs, returned the key, and caught Romano as he was leaving for lunch. "Draw up a lease, and I'll sign it right now."

"Wait, there's one other thing. Those guys in the hall are bookies. But they won't bother you if you don't bother them."

Bookies weren't the problem, money was. The apartment had to be painted and plastered, windows replaced, and new plumbing, new wiring, and kitchen equipment installed. I didn't know how I could swing it, but I signed a lease dated June 1, 1955, hoping somehow to muddle through.

Clearing out the junk was a problem in itself. The junk dealers I called in found nothing worth salvaging, and the new breed of Greenwich Village moving men—Shakespearean actors and aspiring novelists—were particular about what they hauled. Finally, I resorted to the yellow pages and was halfway through the listings before a mover even agreed to look at the place. He'd send his men to make an estimate.

I was working on a rush job and couldn't leave, so I asked Bob Borchers, who was already at work, to give them the key and send them upstairs. They returned with a figure that Bob thought too high. He suggested I keep trying the phone book.

About ten minutes later, he called back. "I think your problem is solved."

"Wonderful. What did you do?"

"I didn't do anything. Flames are shooting out of your living room windows."

I didn't know whether to laugh or cry. I did neither; I went on working. Never having witnessed a fire, I pictured the flames licking their way neatly from room to room, consuming the mattresses, beds, bureaus, chairs, the heaps of garbage, the dirty clothes—and the filth in the bath tub. The fireman had arrived, and I hoped the flames would finish their job before they extinguished the fire.

A little later I called to check. Bob sounded shrill. "The fire's spreading. A woman's threatening to jump off the roof."

"Oh, god! I'm coming right down."

"Don't! Stay home! There's nothing you can do. They're sending up ladders and spreading out nets. I'll call you as soon as I can." After a torturous half-hour, Bob called back. The woman had been rescued, the fire was under control. Two of the firemen had been overcome by smoke, but other than that, no injuries. Still, he insisted I stay home.

"Why? I can't just sit here and do nothing."

"There are some nasty rumors floating around. After all, it does look suspicious. We send up some guys, and a few minutes later the apartment's in flames."

"You mean *arson?* That's crazy!"

"Of course it's crazy. But you'd better stay home until things blow over."

I held off for a while, then went downtown. Sheridan Square was a tangle of crisscrossed hoses, and on every corner of the cordoned-off streets, people stood gazing at the building. Flames had shot through the upper floors, and the windows of my living room (or what had *almost* been my living room) were black, burned-out holes. Several fire trucks were still on the scene, and firemen with pick axes were roaming in and out.

"Firebug! Firebug!" a woman screamed and, darting past the fireman, came running across the street.

I pushed past the crowd, ran up West 4th Street, turned on Barrow, and flew through the kitchen door. Bob hurried me into the basement. "I told you to stay home. Don't come up till I tell you to."

I sat in the storeroom, trembling, and emerged only when Bob said it was safe. He hustled me into a cab, and as it turned up 4th Street, the driver said, "That must have been one helluva fire. How did it start, do you know?"

"I FIND JUST the right place and it goes up in smoke. I'm beginning to think that it's *me* who's jinxed." I was talking to Mr. Sheinfeld, lamenting my luck.

"Did you sign a lease?"

"Yes, but what good is it now?"

"If you signed the lease, the apartment is yours. It's the landlord who's got to fix it up."

This *was* a miracle. But when I thought of the tenants and the losses they'd suffered, it was not a miracle I could enjoy. The tenant in the apartment above ours (who was one of the bookies) claimed to have lost everything, including his wife's three mink coats. The apartment next to ours had been spared the flames, but the smoke had killed a canary.

But when I learned that the neighbors had contacted the landlord, trying to keep us from moving in, my feelings changed. They wanted the apartment for "one of their own kind." Not only was I an arsonist, but a "white" woman with an "Oriental" child—and Limelight a "hangout for Commies and Jews."

Their hostility gave me pause, and I debated moving in. But after I slipped in one day and saw the apartment completed, I found the courage I needed. The rooms were bright and sunny and everything was new—windows, walls, ceiling, floor, and a kitchen with the latest equipment.

Hoping to win over the neighbors, Li-lan and I planned a good will campaign. We would open doors, carry packages for the elderly, inquire about their health, and so on. But most of the time we just peered out the door and scooted downstairs, managing not to run into anyone. Except, of course, the bookies.

WE WERE hardly settled in the apartment when Tony, the bookie who appeared to be the head of the ring, stopped me as I was leaving the building. "Miss Gee, there's one thing you gotta know if we're gonna stay friends. We don't want strangers roaming through the halls. If you're expecting somebody, let us know in advance."

Limelight was my living room, so it didn't really matter. I had very few visitors. Steichen might be one. He'd asked to take me to dinner again, but rather than get waylaid at Limelight, he preferred to pick me up at home. Robert Frank was another. But he was still on his trip, and I didn't know when he'd return.

"But what about my daughter?" I asked. "Her friends visit after school."

"Kids are okay. We just don't want no nosy-bodies snooping around. That's why this building is so safe. You'll never get robbed and you'll never be bothered, not as long as us boys are here."

This was a small price to pay for round-the-clock protection. Tony lived upstairs, and he told me I could call on him anytime, day or night. New

York was a fairly safe city, and Greenwich Village and Chinatown the safest parts. But anyone in the public eye was bound to attract crackpots, and it was comforting to know that Tony was there.

I was curious about the ring. Romano had advised me to look the other way, but it was hard to ignore the presence of three busy bookies, a stream of customers through the hall, and the occasional visits of men in dark suits. It took some time, but I finally figured it out.

Tony handled the money, or so I gathered from the bulges in his pockets and an occasional glimpse of a wad. He was not my idea of a bookie though. He was gray-haired and portly, wore horn-rimmed glasses and cardigan sweaters, and seemed more like an affable grandfather. Caesar was more the type. I'd seen *Guys and Dolls,* and though older than the bookies in the Broadway musical, he fit my picture of a Broadway Joe. He wore pin-striped suits, pointy brown shoes, and with his long, pointy nose and angular jaw, he looked like he'd been cut out with scissors. Caesar apparently did the paper work; he kept darting into a room in the back of the hall, clutching a handful of slips. Vinnie, the youngest of the three, was the lookout. Fat, easygoing, shaped like a pear, he stood leaning against the door, watching for the cops and checking everyone who came in. The customers were mostly from the neighborhood, and I pretended not to notice when some elderly woman crept in to lay a bet, or I recognized a shopkeeper.

Eager to stay in good with the Boys, I decided to bet on a horse. But Tony refused my two dollars. "Nope, I'm not gonna let you play this game. I seen too many restaurant men go broke. They come in with the night's receipts, lay the money on a nag, and before you know it, they're bankrupt. One guy I know lost everything—his restaurant, his home, even his wife. "Nope, you're a very nice girl, and you got a kid. This ain't for you."

Caesar joined in. "This game is for suckers. The only reason we take their dough is because if we don't they'll go lay their bets some other place."

"Just once?" I pleaded, waving my two dollars.

"Nope, not even once. It's like taking a drink. One leads to another and before you know it, you're drunk."

I was touched by their concern. And feeling they had my interest at heart, I thought I'd talk to Tony about a problem we were having at Limelight, a problem that not even Bob Borchers could handle. I'd been approached by a man known as Charlie Small about putting in a jukebox.

"Never," I said, when he proposed the idea.

"It won't cost you a cent, and your customers will enjoy the music."

"Not my customers."

A jukebox was the last thing they wanted. Most preferred classical, some liked folk, and quite a few favored jazz. But whatever their tastes, I was sticking to my original plan, and not supplying music of any kind, much less from a jukebox.

"I'll be back next week. I advise you to change your mind."

The following week he was back. I was sitting with Arthur Lavine and a few other photographers but got up the minute Charlie Small appeared.

"Changed your mind?" he asked.

"No. And that's final."

"I'm giving you three days to think it over. And that's final too."

Bob was alarmed when I mentioned the deadline. "Don't you know that jukeboxes are controlled by the Mafia? We'll have to install one whether you like it or not. It's either that or a brick through the window. Or worse."

Tony knew who I was talking about when I mentioned the name. "Charlie Small? You mean Charlie Piccolo. I'll take care of it, don't worry."

It worked. I never saw or heard from Charlie Piccolo again, and felt lucky to be "in good" with the Boys.

AFTER MY experience with the Dorothy Norman, I was reluctant to get involved with another keeper of the flame. But I was fascinated by the work of Laszlo Moholy-Nagy, and having learned that Sybil, his widow and second wife, lived nearby in the Village, I decided to call.

Moholy-Nagy died in 1946, the same year as Alfred Stieglitz, and though he too had achieved legendary status, he seemed not to have inspired the same idolatry. Except, of course, at the Institute of Design in Chicago, which he founded in 1937, and where he promulgated the concepts he'd taught at the Bauhaus before fleeing Nazi Germany. His name was synonymous with that innovative period between the wars, when new ways of seeing were being explored, and art was pulled from the ivory tower and made a part of everyday life. Moholy drew no distinction between fine and applied art, and he himself worked in various media—painting, sculpture, film, stage design, and industrial design, and, of course, photography. Yet, despite his reputation in these various fields (his book *Vision in Motion* was a bible in the field of modern design), his photographic work was seldom seen. I had not idea how much had survived, and I hoped Mme. Moholy had enough for a show.

"Run over and I'll show you what I have," she said when I called. "But I can't give you much time. I'm a very busy person."

I flew the four blocks to 81 Bedford Street, thrilled at the thought of a treasure trove of Moholys here in the Village, right under my nose.

"Mme. Moholy?" I recognized her the moment she opened the door, having noticed her at Limelight a number of times, as much for her bearing as her understated chic. She was a handsome woman of about fifty or so, with ash-blonde hair pulled back in a chignon, and a manner calling for center stage.

"For heaven's sake, call me Sybil," she said. "I'm not that kind of widow."

What she meant by "that kind" I didn't know, but from the condition of the room—a jumble of modern furniture, surfaces covered with papers and books—she was obviously a busy person, more concerned with her work than her setting.

This she confirmed within minutes: she was a professor of architectural design at Pratt Institute, and when she wasn't teaching, she was lecturing and writing. She handed me her book, *Experiments in Totality*, and I leafed through it, trying to look absorbed, while she rummaged through closets. There were no Moholys on the wall.

She brought out several portfolios. "These have just come back from a European tour, and frankly, I wish they hadn't. I'm hard pressed for space."

Moholy had never considered himself a photographer—he'd referred to himself as a "manipulator of light"—and compared to his work in other areas, his output was relatively small. Much had been lost, some had been sold, but there was still enough here for a good-sized show. There was a large group of photographs, most all of them taken from unusual vantage points, the hallmark of the Moholy style. There was also a small group of photograms, the cameraless images he experimented with in the 1920s, around the same time as Man Ray. But what excited me most were the photomontages—only six, but each one a gem. They were the original mock-ups, made in collaboration with Moholy's first wife, Lucia, using both his own photographs and material culled from newspapers and magazines. They were witty, incisive, surreal.

"Mme. Moholy . . . I mean Sybil . . . your husband was a man of remarkable vision. . . ."

She interrupted. "Let's dispense with the eulogies and get down to business. How much do you think we can ask?"

"You mean, the work is for *sale*?"

"Of course. All it's doing here is cluttering my closets."

Given the historical importance of the work, I had no idea what to charge.

I suggested that she do the pricing. She picked up a pad, scribbled some figures, and handed me a list: photographs, seventy-five; photograms, one hundred and fifty; photomontages, two hundred.

"Aren't the prices too low?" I asked.

"Yes, I think you're right. Let's raise the photographs to one hundred. They're the only ones left, and there aren't any negatives."

"*No negatives?* What happened to them?"

"I threw them out. Glass plates are heavy and take up so much space. I got tired of carting them along every time I moved."

My jaw dropped but I recovered quickly, and we decided on the date, a five-week exhibition opening in mid-October 1955. She agreed to provide me with gallery text, then added, "Don't depend on me for anything else. I'm a very busy person."

The thought of the Moholys thrown into trash cans continued to disturb me, and I began to view Dorothy Norman in a more kindly light. When I told Jack Deschin about my latest experience with a keeper of the flame, he replied. "Sybil? She's no keeper, she's a quencher of the flame."

"**WHAT?** Another *art* photographer? . . . Stieglitz, now Moholy-Nagy? . . . Can't you show work that's more relevant? . . . These men belong to the past."

I had assumed that photographers would share my excitement and was shocked hearing comments of this kind. There was so strong a bias against manipulated work that most could not see beyond it. The photograms were dismissed as antiphotographic, the images seen as nothing more than patterns. New York photographers had little love for the Institute of Design, or for the formalism it espoused. They were even hostile to Aaron Siskind, a former New Yorker now teaching at the institute, who had abandoned social documentary for more abstract work, which they regarded as "pretentious" and "arty." What saved the exhibition in their eyes (aside from the photomontages, which most found intriguing) were the photographs. Yet they were no longer seen as revolutionary. The unusual vantage points that Moholy featured—the bird's-eye view, the worm's-eye view—were now so much a part of a photographer's lexicon that they seemed almost commonplace.

The public was more receptive. It was encouraging to see people gathered in front of the wall text, diligently reading every word. Sybil had contributed a brief biography, along with excerpts from Moholy's lectures and correspondence, including that well-known quote: "Not the person without a knowledge of reading or writing, but the one ignorant of photography will be the illiterate of the future."

Deschin favored the photograms yet gave the exhibition little space. But this was more than made up for (except in terms of readership) by an article by George Wright titled *Moholy: a shaper of your vision and mine* published in a new weekly paper, *The Village Voice*. George lauded Moholy's contribution, not only to photography but all the arts, and suggested as an epitaph one of the most honorable that he felt could be bestowed on any artist: "He changed the way we see the world."

Yet photography had gone in another direction, and while acknowledging the fact (which was beyond dispute), that "the most vigorous photography today is using the camera to isolate what has been called the 'exact instant,'" Wright urged photographers to see the exhibition. "Every few years, photographers should be reminded that there are other models for their work than photojournalism. An evening with this collection might open the eyes of some of our young photographers whose cliches of Hester Street have been cliches for fifty years."

The most vociferous of Moholy's critics was Lisette Model. I ran into her one night while leaving the gallery, but drew to one side, trying to avoid a possible confrontation. Angered by the work, she overlooked her animosity toward me and blasted Moholy instead. She decried what she saw as an overemphasis on superficial elements and the lack of meaningful content. "Bauhaus!" She spit out the word like some ill-tasting food. "Worse thing that's ever happened to the arts!"

I could have pointed out that many of her own attitudes were similar to Moholy's. She too rejected the ivory tower; she too believed that art should be part of everyday life and not the province of an elite. But I was not about to argue, now that we'd finally talked.

For me, the exhibition was a double coup. It was not only one of Limelight's most important shows, but it also led to a reconciliation with Lisette. If, indeed, it was one — you could never tell with Lisette.

For Sybil Moholy-Nagy, it was a disappointment. She came in regularly, checking for sales. There were none. (*The Radio Tower, Berlin,* 1928 almost sold, but the buyer couldn't rustle up the money, and Sybil wouldn't consider an installment plan, not even guaranteed by me.) The Moholys were returned to 81 Bedford, where they continued to clutter up her closets.

THE FIRST time I heard of the *Village Voice* was when Jerry Tallmer announced, earlier in the year, that he'd taken a job as associate editor of what promised to be (provided it got off the ground) a *real* Village newspaper. It was just about time we had one. All we had was *The Villager,* a small-town paper featuring small-town news—births, deaths, tea parties, church socials, cake sales, and a weekly column called *Scoopy Mews,* ostensibly written by the office cat. It was worth a nickel if you were looking for an apartment, though you could generally pick it up for free.

Jerry had been trying to write. He'd been staring out the window watching the pigeons for over a year, but all he could show at the end of a day was a wastebasket full of paper. Then one day he strolled into the office of the *Village Voice,* a shabby loft at 22 Greenwich Street, where the "staff" was struggling to produce the first issue, and from that moment on he was hooked. He shelved the Great American Novel and went to work for the *Voice.*

"That's great," I said. "What will you be doing?"

"Everything." Everything from editing and proofreading to writing theater and movie reviews. The salary wasn't much, only twenty-five a week, which at twelve hours a day, seven days a week, came to about thirty cents an hour. Yet it beat staring at pigeons, and it was all the *Voice* could afford.

The paper was the brainchild of Dan Wolf, a freelance writer, and Edwin Fancher, a psychologist and part-time moving man. Neither knew anything about running a newspaper, but that didn't stand in their way. They had hit on the idea (as stated on the logo) of publishing "A Weekly Paper Designed to be Read." The seed money of five thousand dollars had been drawn against stock that Fancher had inherited, but by the time Jerry Tallmer joined the staff, most was already gone. Norman Mailer was also a partner. He gave them a little money and a lot of trouble, an alliance they would regret (and eventually terminate).

Mailer was going through a difficult period. *Deer Park,* a novel he thought would revive his sagging career, had received poor reviews (the manuscript had been turned down by several publishers) and he also had marital problems. Adele Morales, his second wife, a voluptuous, dark-eyed painter (whom he'd later stab and almost kill) had formerly lived with Ed Fancher, adding to the tensions at the *Voice*. Stoned on pot, his latest kick, he'd show up at the office with "suggestions" and create a scene when his ideas were ignored. "If it's up to Mailer," Jerry complained, "the *Voice* would be a cross between the *New York Inquirer* and the *Police Gazette*."

But Mailer was only one of the problems, and I could feel for Ed Fancher and Dan Wolf, and Jerry too, when they dragged into Limelight night after night, trying to revive after a sixteen-hour day. Fancher, a bland-faced man with a coral red beard, never showed the pressure they were under; nor did Dan Wolf, a short, slender man with hangdog eyes, as he puffed away on a corncob pipe. It was only Jerry, with his nervous laugh, carbon-stained fingers, and rumpled look, who gave a clue to the chaos at the *Village Voice*. Creditors were hot on their trail.

The first issue appeared on October 26, 1955, but instead of celebrating the event, the staff, or what there was of a staff—Ed Fancher, Dan Wolf, Tallmer, John Wilcox (the news editor), and an assortment of volunteers (mostly girl friends and ex-girl friends of Fancher's)—was girding for the next issue. The reception of the public, or what there was of a public—they had printed only 2,500 copies—was mixed. Although purportedly iconoclastic, the tone of the paper was initially conservative, the editors having decided, at least for the time being, to soft-pedal their more progressive views, afraid of scaring off advertisers.

Even so, the paper was lively for there was no dearth of writers willing to contribute articles for free. (If they *insisted* on pay, they were given two dollars). Vance Bourjaily reviewed the current Broadway play, *The Diary of Anne Frank*; Jerry Tallmer wrote a piece on the Off Broadway production of *The Threepenny Opera*; William Murray, a writer for the *New Yorker*, blasted Sloan Wilson's 1955 bestseller, *The Man in the Gray Flannel Suit*; Michael Harrington contributed a piece on Bud Schulberg's book *Waterfront*; Gilbert Seldes wrote a column called *The Lively Arts*, and Peggy Tallmer, a shopping column.

Jerry Tallmer had prevailed on Dan Wolf and Ed Fancher to include articles on photography, and George Wright's review of the Moholy-Nagy show appeared in this first issue. But what pleased me most, besides the review, was that photography now had another voice.

PHOTOGRAPHY had not only another voice, but also another venue. Roy DeCarava, together with his wife Anne, had set aside a room in their apartment at 48 West 84th Street, hoping to make a go of a gallery through sales. A Photographer's Place opened in the spring with an exhibition of Roy's work, and now that photographers had another place to show, I hoped it would take the pressure off me. Running the only gallery in town wasn't easy. In fact, Deschin had anticipated how difficult it would be, and when I first told him plans for opening a gallery, he suggested I hide behind a mythical committee. "You're going to be besieged. It will take you off the hook."

I hadn't listened, wanting to stand behind my judgments, regardless of the cost. But after months of dutifully viewing portfolios, I saw what he meant. Regardless of how carefully I couched my words, rejection was rejection, and it was bound to hurt. Being turned down by a woman was difficult, especially for men. Walking through Limelight was like running the gauntlet—photographers on all sides.

I was also besieged by photographers from out of town. Boxes of unsolicited photographs arrived from as far off as Alaska, and I'd found myself acting as a shipping clerk, repacking the boxes and mailing them back. After plowing through hundreds of sunsets, babies, kittens, and puppy dogs, I'd given up on the idea of finding some undiscovered genius in Peoria. I refused the packages that came in the mail and stopped viewing portfolios altogether. There were few undiscovered geniuses in New York as well. Steichen had unburied them all.

"How do you manage?" he asked me once. "I have a secretary, an office, and a staff. I don't know how I'd manage if I couldn't close the door."

"At times I feel like hiding," I said. "And when it gets too much I stay home."

I hoped that A Photographer's Place would change all this, and that I would no longer need to escape. The gallery had everything in its favor. The exhibition space was nicely designed, the room divided by screens into two separate areas with excellent lighting and fresh white walls. The DeCaravas had taste and judgment and worked very hard; whoever exhibited in their gallery was in very good hands. The hours were short—from 7:30 to 10:00 four nights a week, and 1:00 to 5:00 on weekends—but what it lacked in hours, it made up in quality. I'd gone to the opening and wished them well. But I had one regret, and now it was too late—Roy was a photographer I had wanted to show.

DeCarava was on the upswing. He supported himself as a freelance commercial artist, but he'd won a Guggenheim Fellowship in 1952 (the first for a black photographer) and *The Sweet Flypaper of Life*, a book on which he'd collaborated with the writer Langston Hughes, had been published this year. Most of the photographs in the exhibit were from the book, a tender though stark portrayal of life in a part of the city that most people knew or cared little about. Harlem, for whites, was a playground, a place to hear jazz, to eat soul food, to go "slumming." Even when approached with serious intent, as had several photographers associated with the Photo League, the results were at best superficial. As blacks, DeCarava and Hughes, had no differences to bridge, and in a collaboration eminently successful in combining pictures with words, they expressed the pathos of ghetto life. Some said it went even further, that it expressed the pathos of *all* of life. George Wright spoke of the book in the *Village Voice* as "small enough to put in your pocket and big enough to fill your heart."

I considered competition a very good thing and hoped that others would follow their lead and open galleries too. The DeCaravas planned to concentrate on sales, and the prices they offered were attractive indeed, lower than most at Limelight. Roy priced his own prints at twelve dollars for an 8×10, seventeen dollars for an 11×14, and twenty-five for a 16×20.

Deschin believed that at these prices the work would sell, "if only to a small public of discriminating collectors." In an article celebrating the gallery's debut, he wrote,

> How rapidly such a public can be developed will depend on the frequency and variety of the shows . . . and the willingness of photographers to forget their egos and face the fact: sales resistance for the general public will tighten beyond the $10 and $15 mark. The DeCarava Gallery can become a real testing ground for what the traffic will bear in

the matter of price as well as picture content and quality. This courageous effort deserves support.

Yet despite the modest prices, the gallery did not succeed. But before it closed, in 1957, it presented the work of a number of fine photographers, including Harry Callahan, Sid Grossman, Walter Rosenblum, Eugene Meatyard, and Van Deren Coke. One thing was clear: it was still too early to depend on sales, and a gallery for photography could only survive when subsidized in other ways. As George Wright put it in the *Village Voice*, "There are still not enough collectors in this field to finance a Lord Duveen approach, and there never will be." So it seemed at the time.

ROBERT WAS BACK in New York. He wanted to drop by in the afternoon, but rather than have him tangle with the bookies, I suggested he wait until later in the day. This was his first visit to Grove Street, and I hadn't yet told him about the operation in the hall.

Robert looked tired. Too tired, he said, to talk about the trip; all he wanted to do was relax. He looked even seedier than when he had left. I hated to press him but I was consumed with curiosity; I wondered whether he'd managed to photograph the Ford plant, and whether he'd had any problems en route.

"Problems? I've been in jail."

"Jail? You mean you were actually *arrested?*"

What happened was even worse than I'd feared. He was tooling down a highway in Arkansas, heading for Mississippi, when he was stopped by a patrol car and searched. Everything conspired against him—his accent, his passport, his cameras, his maps, and, of course, his appearance. He was hauled off to jail, fingerprinted and locked in a cell, where he languished for hours without food or drink. He was questioned over and over: What was he doing with those cameras? What was this business about a Guggenheim—wasn't that a Jewish name? And what about those guys he called sponsors? Wasn't Brodovitch a Russian? What about the maps? And what was he doing with a bottle of scotch?

Finally they came to the point. Was he a "commie"? He said no. Did he know what a "commie" was? He said yes.

"I answered everything but I was boiling inside. I was afraid I'd get beat up if I acted like a wise guy. But I did raise a fuss when they got their hands on my film."

The film was returned after they were finally convinced (after being shown some of his work in *Fortune*) that they hadn't corralled a "red."

"So how about your pictures. Did you get anything good?"

"I don't know. I haven't had a chance to develop anything yet."

Robert may have suspected that there was dynamite in those pictures. If he were, in fact, an *agent provocateur*, he could not have more effectively shaken things up. But the book he was to publish was still years off, and all he wanted now was to get back in shape before tackling the rest of the country. But this time he'd be traveling with Mary and the kids, and, I hoped, without incident.

I was happy to see him and sorry he'd be leaving again soon.

AFTER MOHOLY-NAGY I showed Edouard Boubat and not surprisingly sold three prints, one a portrait of Mary and Pablo Frank taken while the Franks were in Paris. The work was charming and very French, and after five weeks of cerebral Moholy-Nagy, most found the change refreshing. Following these two Europeans, I brought the focus closer to home. The first exhibition in 1956 was Leon Levinstein's *New York*, sixty-five prints covering seven years of work by a photographer I considered one of the best of the nonprofessionals. Perhaps, even *the* best.

Leon and I had traveled the same route, via the Sid Grossman workshop. Leon, however, was less thin-skinned than I, and better able to withstand Sid's harsh methods of teaching. He'd studied with him for three years, first at the Photo League, and after the club disbanded, at his Friday night classes in his loft. Leon was no longer a student at the time we met—in 1953, at a *kaffee klatsch* at Sid's—but he still looked to Sid as his mentor. Leon struck me as less zealous than most of Sid's acolytes; he didn't proselytize, nor did he look upon photography as some newfound religion. Yet he was the only one, as far as I could see, who lived up to Sid's frequent exhortation: "Live for photography!"

Leon lived for little else. He worked nine-to-five at a low-level job as a graphic artist, work that required little talent or thought, and made no effort to improve his lot. He never married and, as far as I or anyone else knew, had no romantic attachments of any kind. He lived in run-down furnished apartments, clung to every penny, and except for minimal photographic equipment—a camera, an enlarger, and a few developing trays—had virtually no possessions. Nor did he have many friends. He spent every free hour roaming the streets with his camera, and wherever there were people— Times Square, Coney Island, the Lower East Side—there was Leon Levinstein, a large man with a slow, shuffling gait, skirting the fringes, searching the crowd.

Obsessed with New York—not the turf so much as the people—he concentrated on the anonymous, those faceless people one passes on the street and doesn't notice. He never photographed anyone he knew, or a place without people. Leon was a walker, and though he'd practically covered the entire city, he seemed drawn to the more densely populated, less prosperous parts of town. Yet he denied making social statements, and when asked why he spent so much time on the Lower East Side, he'd reply, "That's where the life is."

Although much of his material was standard fare—women hanging out of tenement windows, lovers nuzzling in the grass—when seen through the eyes of Levinstein, it was all fresh and new. What characterized the work was its powerful use of form; every line, every shape had meaning. Leon was more interested in form than in the "decisive moment," and to catch the shape of a hand, the jut of a jaw, he'd creep perilously close, almost within inches of his subject. He never resorted to a telephoto lens, and it was a mystery to me, and others as well, that a man of his size—he was over six feet—could get so close, yet keep his subject unaware. He never posed anyone, spoke to anyone, or slipped a derelict a dime as a modeling fee. But he did employ a stratagem made possible by the Rolleiflex: he'd turn his camera sideways and pretend to focus elsewhere, throwing his subject off-guard.

What also characterized his work was its feeling, which, though sometimes acerbic, was warm and compassionate. Knowing how Leon lived (or failed to live), I would have expected a certain detachment. But having seen him fly into a rage one day (over something so trivial, I couldn't remember what it was), I realized that under the surface was fire. It was this fire that fueled his work.

Much as I disliked amateur psychologizing (a temptation after years on the couch), I couldn't help but wonder about the circumstances in Leon's past that made him remain a spectator to life. Leon was secretive, and though I'd come to know him better than most others did—he'd been showing me his work for a couple of years—all I ever learned were a couple of facts. He was born in West Virginia, served in the army during World War II, studied painting briefly after coming to New York, and picked up photography when he was almost forty. But he let something drop when we were having coffee one night, and this, I thought, was the clue: His parents were Russian Jews, and in Buckhannon, West Virginia, where Leon was raised, the Levinsteins had the dubious distinction of being the only Jewish family in town.

Having often felt like an outsider myself (which is why I took to "outsiders" like Robert Frank), I could commiserate. But my first real insight into Leon Levinstein came the night we got together to select the prints for his show. He arrived at the apartment with a heavy suitcase, having lugged it through the subway to save the price of a cab, and a process that would ordinarily have taken an hour or two took half the night.

He'd pick up a print, gaze at it lovingly, then talk about the person as if talking about a friend. "See this old lady? She's been sitting on that stoop ever since I started going down to Delancey Street. I'll bet she cooks a good chicken soup." (From the look on his face, he was savoring the soup.)

He'd put it down reluctantly, then pick up another. "Now take this guy. You know why he's happy? He just found that cigarette butt in the gutter. I'll bet it's his first drag of the day." (Leon, meanwhile, was puffing away, scattering ashes all over the prints.)

"Now take this dame." (No, you take her, I thought, seeing it was midnight and we were only half through.) "She's been working Times Square all year. When she's not in a doorway, she's upstairs with a john. That guy on the corner is her pimp."

By the time Leon left, I'd met all his "friends." But they were more than friends, they were family. With a click of the shutter, he made them his own—street vendors, vagrants, sunbathers, whores, rabbis, lovers, teenagers, old men and women, and kids of all ages—they were all part of one large family. And having watched his expression as he gazed at his pictures—he showed amusement, affection, even at times, pride—I suspected that Leon was not as lonely as I thought. He had a family of hundreds, a family that made no demands, didn't argue or fight, needed nothing in the way of financial support, and could be kept under wraps until needed.

Knowing how Leon resisted success, I wasn't quite sure how he'd react to the show. All my previous efforts at promoting his work had failed. I'd once shown a group of his prints to John English. John was so impressed, he wanted to use his work in *McCall's*. But since Leon was nonprofessional and still untried, he thought he'd offer him an assignment (the kind he might have given Robert Frank), and, if he didn't succeed, still pay him a fee. Leon was excited at the prospect of an assignment, but he never showed up for the appointment with John. Yet he was not averse to other kinds of success; Steichen acquired nineteen of his prints for the museum collection and presented his work in several exhibitions, including *The Family of Man*.

Leon seemed pleased at the reaction to his show. We sold four prints (three to people who sent letters inquiring about the one reproduced in the *Times*), and George Wright wrote a glowing review in the *Village Voice*. But what pleased him most was the reaction of young photographers, especially those who had demanding jobs, such as Charles Harbutt, an editor on the magazine *Jubilee*, and Frank Paulin, a successful freelance fashion illustrator. Like Leon himself, they did their personal work on the side.

There was one sad note, and it came as a shock. Leon had written a statement for the gallery acknowledging his debt to Sid Grossman. But what he'd meant as a tribute turned into a memorial. On January 1, 1955, just two days before the opening of the show, Sid died.

ANSEL ADAMS was everything that Leon was not. He was famous, successful, and if his stationery was any indication of his marketing skills — it listed "fine prints, illustration, lectures, instruction" — he was also a master at promoting himself. I was initially put off by the corporate-type logo, finding it at odds with his image as an artist. I was more accustomed to working with photographers like Minor White, whose letters were a crazy quilt of cross-outs and typos, or Edouard Boubat, who, on accepting my invitation to exhibit, had written in hand on blue onionskin paper, "I accept your proposition . . . tell me what you desire."

But I soon came to appreciate Ansel Adams's more businesslike approach.

His exhibition was to follow Leon Levinstein's, and since I was arranging for it to travel to two other venues—the University of Maine and George Eastman House—I was concerned that it arrive on time and be properly packed. (Boubat's loosely wrapped parcel barely made it through the mails.)

I was especially interested in having the show go to Maine. Vincent Hartigan, head of the art department, was incorporating photography into his exhibition program—he'd already taken the Eliot Porter and Arnold Newman shows—and considering how few institutions were interested in the medium, his was a bold step to take. Ansel Adams was more interested, however, in the Limelight show and explained his reasons in a letter:

> Now this exhibit interests me for several reasons, one is that I am erroneously classified as a "landscape photographer," and while I do a lot of work in the Natural Scene, I am still interested in a variety of subject matter. I confess I have been at fault in not properly presenting myself, but I feel now that I should think of my work in more inclusive terms. Two, I would like to take the opportunity in this exhibit to stress the inherent qualities of the photographic image. Of late, there has been such great emphasis on subject alone—to the detriment of the image itself—that I feel compelled to do my bit to help re-establish the qualities of the medium for its own sake. So much contemporary photography reminds me of a great Beethoven Sonata played on an out-of-tune piano!

I could understand his not wanting to be labeled, especially with words that conjured up visions of pictorialism, the very antithesis of his "straight" approach. He had already demonstrated, through his photographs of the Japanese-American Relocation Center, Manzanar, exhibited at the Museum of Modern Art in 1944, that his interests went beyond landscape. But memories being short, I could understand his wanting a more varied presentation. He intended to send what he called his "regular exhibits" to the other two venues, and tailor the Limelight show for New York.

It was not that he loved New York. None of us knew the whole story, but he'd been soured, I heard, by events that occurred at the Museum of Modern Art, causing him to lose both his foothold in New York and his influence at the museum. He and his friend David McAlpin, the museum's trustee chairman, together with Beaumont and Nancy Newhall, had been largely instrumental in establishing the Department of Photography. So one could imagine his anger and disappointment when Newhall, on returning from serving in World War II, was eased out of his position as curator and replaced with Edward Steichen. (Nancy had filled in during his absence.) Steichen took over in 1946, and though Beaumont was subsequently hired by George Eastman House, first as curator and later as director, this was hardly like being at the Museum of Modern Art. And Rochester was hardly New York.

Ansel wanted to include his new Polaroid work. He'd been experimenting with the newly developed (but still unavailable) Professional film and felt that the Polaroids would lend "additional seasoning," and at the same time serve as a "debut of this material in the Gallery world." But the list of photographs he sent was already so long, I saw no way of showing the Polaroids too. And since he wanted the work protected by glass (for which he graciously contributed half the cost), it meant hanging the photographs in single rows. So I was relieved to find when the work arrived — eighty-five photographs plus two portfolios (one with ten prints, the other, fifteen) — that he hadn't included the Polaroids. The photographs were matted, and since this alone took up additional space, I had to exclude about twenty.

Deciding which ones to leave out was difficult, Ansel having left the decision to me. The landscapes were, without question, his finest work, but acquiescing to his wishes, I included a few of the portraits. All together, I hung fifty-three prints, and after making up a price list based on the figures he supplied (ranging from thirty-five dollars for the prints to one hundred for the portfolios), I insured the exhibition for Limelight's usual fifteen hundred dollars.

Ansel had talked about coming to New York, and I'd looked forward to seeing him stride through the door. Was he as impressive in person as in portraits? He looked positively heroic standing on top of a mountain with his tripod, camera, and ten-gallon hat. (Close-ups showed a small elfin face, partially obscured by a woodsman-like beard, and a nose, once broken, that couldn't decide which way to turn.) I admired Ansel's stand on the environment, and I would have wanted to meet him for that reason alone. He'd been active in the Sierra Club since the 1920s, supporting issues which, in this day of superhighways and long-finned cars, were largely ignored.

Li-lan and I were preparing to leave for Spain, prize-winners having to travel in the off-season. So I had little time to listen for reactions after installing the work. But I believed this would be a popular show, particularly with the public. Ansel Adams was an icon, and landscape was a genre that everybody loved.

Photographers, however, were more critical. They admired Ansel Adams's mastery of craft, and they could appreciate the difficulties of photographing nature; the more spectacular the vista, the more likely to end up as "calendar art." They preferred the canyons of Wall Street to the canyons of the West, and as one photographer expressed it, "Forget the hand of God. Give me a bridge or a skyscraper any old time."

Yet despite their admiration, there was no real feeling of excitement. Some found the work overly dramatic, and knowing Ansel Adams's love of music, they equated it in spirit with Wagner, not Bach. Having noticed this same cool reaction when I showed the work of another West Coast photographer, Wynn Bullock, as well as the work of Minor White, I couldn't help but wonder: Were we so influenced by photojournalism here in New York that we couldn't relate to other ways of seeing? Were we so involved in human concerns (as typified by *The Family of Man*) that we'd lost sight of the natural world?

Still, there was no denying the beauty and authority of these images, or the significance of a body of work that went beyond aesthetics. Ansel Adams was one of the last romantics, one of the last to photograph an unspoiled earth, one of the last to see the land as a metaphor for freedom.

Why, then, did his work leave us cold?

EUROPE worked its magic. Instead of spending ten days at the Castellana-Hilton Hotel in Madrid, as provided for in the prize, we went to Rome and Paris, at our own expense, and stayed away a whole month. We had a wonderful time, and I came back refreshed. Limelight had not fallen apart in my absence, and Bob had, in fact, made a sale—one of the Ansel Adams portfolios for one hundred dollars.

"HELEN, have you given up men?" I assured George Wright I had not. But between my daughter's watchful eye (single mothers were not supposed to have personal lives) and the demands on my time at Limelight, sustaining any close relationship was difficult. It took planning and subterfuge and a very patient man.

But George wasn't prying. He was alluding to the next three shows on my exhibition program, each the work of a woman: Esther Bubley, Sabine Weiss, and Imogen Cunningham. Esther Bubley was a freelance photojournalist, active in the field of editorial reportage. She had important corporate accounts, including Standard Oil, and traveled all over the world. She was also active in the relatively new field of documentary-style advertising and was looked upon as a pacesetter. Sabine Weiss lived in Paris, and though active in both photojournalism and fashion, she planned, as did Esther Bubley, to show her personal work. Both were in their twenties, novices compared to Imogen Cunningham, age seventy-four—and a master.

Gender had played no part in these decisions; it was only because of a changes in schedule that the three exhibitions followed one another. Photography was a field—one of the few—in which gender was not a major hurdle. Discrimination against women did indeed exist, yet it was not like it was in the art world, where women generally succeeded by riding on the coattails of men. Would Georgia O'Keeffe have become known without the promotion and support of Alfred Stieglitz? Or Elaine de Kooning without the luster of her husband's name? Though many in the past worked in the shadows of men (Margarethe Mather and Tina Modotti in the very long shadow of Edward Weston), these days women were succeeding on their own. Margaret Bourke-White had helped pave the way, though from what I'd heard, never having met her (she was confined to a wheelchair with Parkinson's disease), she had not been beyond using feminine wiles whenever it served her purpose. Her success at Life was a breakthrough; the first issue appeared with her powerful photograph of Fort Peck Dam on its cover. Yet the field of photojournalism was still dominated by men. (The only woman currently on Life's staff was Nina Leen.) The demands of family kept women close to home, and in order to maintain both professional and domestic lives, many chose fashion as an option. Among the most successful were Louise Dahl-Wolfe, Lillian Bassman, Genevieve Naylor, Toni Frissell, Kathryn Abbe, and her twin Frances McLaughlin (who was as successful as her husband Leslie Gill).

Imogen lived in San Francisco and we'd never met, yet I felt that I knew her; we had been corresponding for several years. She'd written to me at one point asking help in locating a collector who had shown interest in her portrait of Gertrude Stein. She lost his letter but remembered that he lived in Connecticut. I contacted the editor of *The Newtown Bee* and was given the address of Addison Metcalf, a major collector of Stein material. But after Imogen lost his address a second time, I gave up. And so did she, having decided from the tone of Metcalf's letter that he was more interested in Gertrude Stein than photography.

Notwithstanding these lapses, Imogen was well organized, and liked nothing better than to work. "I get so busy immortalizing people for Christmas," she wrote in one of her many letters, "all else is forgotten." In reply to a letter of mine in which I complained of a cold, she said, "I'm really allergic to anything that stops me, from a mosquito bite to flu." While her contemporaries were settling into their "golden years," she was photographing, printing, arranging shows (her exhibit was to travel to the Cincinnati Museum of Art), and enjoying her role as photography's *grande dame*.

It was a role well deserved. Imogen had been working since 1901. She opened a portrait studio in Seattle when she was twenty-eight, and continued to work during the years of her marriage (to the artist Roi Partridge, whom she later divorced) while raising three sons. She was one of the first women to photograph the male nude and created a furor when the pictures were published in 1915. (That the model was her husband didn't quell the outcry.) Imogen went her own way, escaping the influence of both Edward Weston and Ansel Adams, an achievement for anyone working on the West Coast.

Imogen was coming to New York for the opening of her show, so I prepared what I thought were appropriate comforts for a person of her age. I placed a chair in the gallery should she tire and arranged to be free should she need help in getting around the city. But this was before I met her. I was installing the exhibition when in she flew, a small bird of a woman in a billowing black cape, an embroidered beanie perched on her head. She clasped my hands, admired what I'd done (I was always nervous when the photographer appeared), then went scooting around, checking the kitchen, the dining room, even the ladies' room.

Imogen Cunningham, Bodega Bay, 1952, by Consuelo Kanaga.

This was the beginning of a few whirlwind weeks—for Imogen, that is, not me. She was always on the run, always surrounded by friends, none of them strangers to Limelight—the filmmaker Willard Van Dyke, dancer Hanya Holm, photographer Consuelo Kanaga, painter Inokuma, poet Muriel Ruykeyser, sculptor William Zorach, and the painter-photographer Charles Sheeler, all of whom appeared at the opening.

Imogen had been staying at the home of her son Padraic in Fanwood, New Jersey. But New York had attractions that Fanwood did not and, after a few days, she moved into the apartment of a friend a few blocks from Limelight. She popped in regularly. I caught sight of her beanie bobbing around the room, and hoping for a chance to sit down and talk, I invited her together with Padraic for dinner one night. But it was impossible to talk. People kept streaming to our table—friends, friends of friends, and many young photographers, eager to meet her. One, a tall, handsome, sad-eyed young man named Peter Hujar, had brought along work, and when he started slipping prints under her nose, I objected. But Imogen didn't mind. She put down her fork, and after studying the prints, advised him to keep on working. But when he asked for advice about composition, she said crossly, "I *never* think in those terms!" (Years later, when Hujar became known, he attributed that remark to his finding new direction.)

We had just finished dinner when Lisette walked in. Imogen went over to greet her and spent the rest of the evening at her table. She beckoned me to join them, but my relationship with Lisette was fragile, and I thought it best not to intrude. (This happened once before when Minor White appeared, together with a young man named Peter Bunnell; I'd declined then too, and later regretted it, having doubtless missed out on some interesting talk.)

Seeing the two together, I couldn't help but reflect on how different they were, both as photographers and women. Lisette was critical and judgmental, sparing no one; Imogen was outspoken, yet always kind. Lisette was imperious; Imogen self-effacing. Lisette lacked humor; Imogen had wit. Lisette photographed little and her career was petering out; Imogen's was approaching the half-century mark. Lisette's work was hard-hitting, tough, and incisive; Imogen's, tranquil, delicate, and sensuous.

Having made these comparisons, I was surprised when I read a review of Imogen's show in the *Village Voice* and found that the writer, John Barkley

Hart, had made a comparison of his own: "Miss Cunningham's concern with people, reflected in photographs of Negro children on the streets of San Francisco, is at an opposite pole from Lisette Model's intensity of indignation. Miss Cunningham's orientation toward the alienated person is one of quiet sympathy."

Hart favored Imogen's earlier work, the stylized flowers of the 1920s, yet the picture he selected as the finest in the show was the portrait of the artist Morris Graves. In it he found elements of the earlier work — "sensuousness, clarity, fantasy, and patience" — and professed to see in the eyes of the artist "the spirit of creation — cosmic attunement and tragic loss."

The portrait affected others as well. We received three orders for the print, one from the collector Dorothy Meigs Eidlitz. We could have sold several more, but Imogen lost the negative and these were the last ones available. Also popular — and we had orders for two — was the portrait of her white-bearded father, taken when he was ninety, eight years before he died.

Imogen may have inherited her father's stamina. She was still going strong when she left for San Francisco after a whirlwind month, leaving us all feeling tired and old. (She worked until her death at age ninety-three.)

TONY STOPPED ME as I was leaving the house. "Stay upstairs. We're expecting a raid. You don't wanna get caught in the hall."

"A *raid?*"

"Yeah, you gotta expect one now and then. It's the price we gotta pay for running a business."

"But what about Li-lan? She gets back from school around four o'clock."

"Don't worry, it'll all be over by the time she gets home."

We had been coexisting with the Boys quite happily for a year, and I hoped that a raid wouldn't change things. They were not only helpful but protective; it was like having three doormen and body guards to boot. When they weren't busy with customers, I'd stop and chat, and I was beginning to see them as people, not bookies. Each was interesting in his own way. Tony was very much the family man, always pulling snapshots from his wallet and describing the antics of a grandchild. Caesar had a poet son named Dante, but I gathered there was no prospective daughter-in-law in sight. Vinnie was more circumspect. Between watching for the cops and watching the "broads," he was too occupied to talk. But he gave me a reassuring wink now and then, letting me know that his offer of a date still held.

The thought of a raid was disturbing. Would the police rush in, guns drawn? Would the Boys be handcuffed and hauled off to jail?

"Nah, it ain't nothing like that," Tony said. "Just stay upstairs and you won't even know it's going on." He'd been tipped off by informants; the raid was to take place sometime around noon, so he still had time to take a few bets.

I tried to keep busy. Letters had piled up—the usual requests for exhibitions from all over—and this was a good time to respond. I sat down at the typewriter, stared at the paper, but the words wouldn't come. I kept jumping up and listening at the door. In a moment of bravado I opened it and tiptoed out to the landing. I could hear Tony talking. Nothing seemed amiss.

I went back to the typewriter and was eking out a few words when I heard sounds of scuffling in the hall. I ran to the living room and peeped from behind the curtains. Several radio cars had pulled up out front, and from the number of cops I saw milling about, it looked like the entire Sixth Precinct had arrived. People were gathering at the corner of Grove, and the cops were trying to shoo them away. I saw no guns and that was a relief, but I shuddered each time a cop rushed into the building. There was no sign of the Boys, but when they finally emerged—first Tony, then Caesar and Vinnie—they were escorted to radio cars. I couldn't tell whether or not they were handcuffed.

The raid had taken not even a half hour. I stayed in the apartment, and once I was sure the police were gone, I stole downstairs. The hall was quiet, and the only evidence of police having been there was a sign posted on the door: "This is a raided premises."

When Li-lan came home, I told her about the raid, but the only thing that troubled her was the sign. "What if my friends see it? They don't know about the bookies. They think they're just guys hanging around the hall." Rather than wait for the police to remove the sign, I took it down myself. Who would ever know, except Li-lan and me?

Early the next day I heard voices in the hall. They sounded familiar. But taking no chances, I tiptoed down to the landing below, and once I was sure, went all the way down. There were the Boys—Tony was counting money, Caesar was darting in and out of the back "office," and Vinnie was standing at his post out front.

"Didn't I tell you it was nothin'?" Tony looked relaxed, as though nothing had occurred.

"But the police, the radio cars . . ."

"That's just for show. The cops, the judges, they're all in our pocket. Whenever we're nabbed, we're always released. Besides, they ain't got no evidence. They never catch us with the goods."

In walked a customer. Business as usual.

"I WANT so much to see you, I feel like crawling through the wire." This was Steichen's prelude to an invitation to dinner, and I was always glad to accept. We had been meeting from time to time in small out-of-the-way restaurants, places where we were less likely to run into anyone we knew and could talk without interruption. With Steichen I was free to grumble and grouse, knowing that whatever I said wouldn't travel. He would cup an ear and listen attentively, as interested in my travails as in my exhibitions, and he'd sometimes remark when I was having a hard time, "Now if you were working with me. . . ."

Steichen was in much better shape. There were no lapses of speech, no glazing of eyes, and none of the signs of disorientation that I'd noticed in Chinatown. He was still working hard, though not as intensely, and still put in very long hours. He'd gone to Paris and Berlin for the opening of The Family of Man, and to Tokyo, Amsterdam, London, and Munich, in preparation for the openings there. He was also working on two new shows in his Diogenes series: Diogenes with a Camera, III, featuring Manuel Alvarez Bravo, Walker Evans, August Sander, and Paul Strand, and Diogenes, IV, with Gustave Schenk, William Garnett, Marie-Jean Beraud-Villars, and Shirley Burden. A third exhibition, Language of the Wall: Parisian Graffiti by Brassai, was scheduled to open later in the year. But after the monumental Family of Man, these exhibitions, however fine, seemed anticlimactic.

What Steichen liked most was acting as a kind of cultural ambassador on his trips abroad. Millions of people had already seen the show, and judging from reports, the response was overwhelming. In Tokyo people wept, and in Guatemala, whole families of peasants traveled from their villages on foot and by burro and stood spellbound in front of the photographs. Steichen hoped the exhibit would foster understanding among peoples and lead to a better, more peaceful world. (There were other rewards too—honors, medals, and commendations of all kinds.)

Having gone out to dinner with Steichen a number of times, I thought

I should reciprocate and invite him to dinner at home. He was delighted. "En famille? Wonderful! You've told me so much about your daughter, I can hardly wait."

Li-lan and I usually ate at home, and I seldom left for Limelight before nine. I was trying to sustain a feeling of family life, and now that Limelight had a very good cook—Fong was Chinese, but his repertoire was international—I usually had dinner sent over. Since neither of us cared for steaks and chops, Fong generally sent the daily special. Never knowing in advance what the special would be, and we'd had some surprises—tripe with garlic sauce was one—I decided to play it safe and roast a leg of lamb.

I timed the lamb so it would be juicy and pink, and at seven o'clock, when Steichen was due, I waited anxiously for the doorbell to ring. The table was set—candles, flowers, a bottle of wine—and Li-lan was wearing her favorite dress, the white organdy she wore on graduating from elementary school. She was eager to show Steichen her "collection"—the Minor White she'd purchased from the *Great Photographs* show, and the David Vestal she'd bought on the installment plan (five dollars down and fifty cents sent to Vestal each week). Steichen was always prompt, and when he hadn't shown up at half-past seven, I worried that something was wrong.

"I'm sorry," he said, when he finally arrived, "I was held up with last-minute work." His eyes were puffy and he looked a bit dazed. Penny greeted him enthusiastically, yapping at his heels as he walked down the hall toward the living room. Halfway there he stopped and leaned against the wall, and I couldn't tell whether he was holding Penny off or steadying himself.

He sank on to the sofa. I offered him a drink. He took a few sips, then set it aside, ignoring the plate of hors d'oeuvres. He struggled to get up when Li-lan walked in. His voice was weak. "Hello, young lady. . . . Your mother tells me . . . Your mother . . . tells me you're interested . . . in photography. . . ."

Li-lan gave me a questioning look, then took hold of Penny and led her away. Steichen looked ashen, suddenly old.

"Why don't I speak to my doctor," I said, thumbing through my address book.

"Don't! There's nothing wrong. I'm just a bit tired, that's all."

"Would you like another drink?"

"No, I'll just sit here a few minutes, and then we can eat." The lamb grew cold, the salad soggy, Penny looked on with hungry eyes, and Steichen didn't move.

"Are you *sure* you don't want a doctor?"

"Lawd, no! I'm just a little dizzy. I think I'll lie down for a minute of two."

He tried stretching out on the couch but his legs were too long, so I suggested he lie in my bed. He didn't refuse, but resisted my arm, lurching his way to the bedroom.

"What if he dies?" Li-lan whispered.

"He's *not* going to die. All he needs is some rest."

We picked at the lamb, and after Li-lan finished her homework and went to sleep, I tried diverting myself by reading. But I couldn't keep my mind on the book. I kept tiptoeing to the bedroom. Steichen lay on his back, hands folded on his chest, but I couldn't make out his face in the dark, and I listened for sounds of breathing.

Steichen's "few minutes" turned into hours. Watching from the window, I saw Limelight close, saw the last customers leave, saw Bob lock up and walk toward his car. At two, I saw Tim Sheehan, the cop on the beat, check doors as he made the rounds. I looked in again on Steichen, then stretched out on the sofa and tried to sleep. But my mind kept racing, and at four in the morning I was still tossing and turning, brooding on something that had happened to a friend. She had been having an affair with a married man, and for a year they'd been meeting in a house he'd rented in the country. Then one afternoon, while making love, the man had a heart attack and died. Frantic, she dressed him in his three-piece suit, propped him in a rocking chair and set him on the porch, leaving him to be discovered by neighbors.

I got up, tiptoed to the bedroom, and looked in. Dawn, filtering through the curtains, cast an eerie bluish light on Steichen's face. I leaned over and listened, and hearing no breathing, held a finger under his nose and felt for the flow of air. *What if he should die?* Could I ever forgive myself for not getting help? I could already see the headline in the *Daily News:* "Dean of Photography Found Dead in Love Nest." How could I explain it to his wife? And I could hear the neighbors clucking, "Just imagine . . . and with a child in the house!"

Certain he was alive, I went back to the living room and stretched out again. I tossed for a while but finally fell asleep, and was awakened in the morning by Li-lan. "What *are* you doing on the couch, Mom? Why aren't you in bed?"

I ran to the bedroom. Steichen was gone. The covers had been smoothed, the pillows plumped, and there was nothing to indicate that he'd been there at all.

I thought I'd wait and then call the museum. But at around ten o'clock, there was a knock on the door, and there stood Vinnie with a big bunch of flowers. "A florist just delivered these. I guess you got a boyfriend, Miss Gee."

Enclosed was a card. Scrawled in a large familiar hand, it read: "With greetings and all good wishes to Helen from her devoted admirer and friend—Edward Steichen."

He was alive and well.

VYING WITH photographers for seats every night was an army of Off Broadway actors. Limelight was the downtown Sardi's, but unlike its glitzy Times Square counterpart, which catered mostly to the Broadway crowd, Limelight, to the actors, was "home." It was home to the young hopefuls who came from all over, waiting for their one big break; it was a place to chat, to pick up messages and possible leads, and to rest their feet after a hard day making the rounds. It was home to the acolytes studying "the Method" with Lee Strasberg at the Actors Studio, and it was home to the casts of the Off Broadway plays, unwinding after performances.

Kurt Weill's *Threepenny Opera* was in its second year at the Theater de Lys, and its sizable cast (700 actors during its ten-year run), alone took up several tables. Eugene O'Neill's *The Iceman Cometh* was playing to a packed house at the Circle in the Square, Sean O'Casey's *Purple Dust* was a hit at the Cherry Lane, and together with the casts of the Actors Playhouse and the Sheridan Square Theater, the room often looked like a meeting of Actors Equity.

Off Broadway was booming. The cost of producing plays on Broadway was rising, and after Ted Mann made a success at the Circle in the Square with a revival of Tennessee Williams's *Summer and Smoke*, others followed suit, converting small out-of-the-way buildings into Off Broadway theaters. Actors were willing to work for below union wages, using these theaters as a showcase, and the savings in salaries and production costs enabled producers to put on plays considered too risky for Broadway. You could see first-rate productions for two or three dollars, and for a few dollars more, stop in at Limelight for an after-theater snack, and spot some of the actors you've just seen on stage: Ed Asner, Jason Robards, Geraldine Paige, Jerry Orbach, Julie Bovasso, George Segal, Tony Perkins, Telly Savalas, Peter Falk, Earle Hyman, and even, at times, a Hollywood star—Sidney Poitier, Rod Steiger, Claire Bloom.

For most of this activity, we had Jerry Tallmer to thank. Before his reviews appeared in the *Village Voice*, the downtown scene was ignored by the press. It was he who gave Off Broadway an identity and a voice. Jerry was a theater buff, and at every opening night, there he was, a crumpled, bespectacled, Woody Allen type, padding down the aisle in dirty white sneakers with a hole in the toe. (No one would have guessed he was a critic or that he'd win the prestigious George Jean Nathan Award for Drama.) The Broadway crowd was flocking downtown, and if theaters were sold out on a Saturday night, it had much to do with Jerry, rightfully known as "the godfather of Off Broadway."

But while Off Broadway flourished, the *Village Voice* foundered and was on the verge of shutting down every week. Though the staff was working for practically nothing (some even for free), it didn't look like the paper would survive. It won a temporary reprieve when Ed Fancher decided, with its last few dollars, to buy a spot on Jean Shepherd's late-night radio talk program. Shepherd had a following among the young and the hip, and he talked night after night for hours at a time about kite-flying, motorcycling, and his boyhood in Indiana, uninterrupted by music or listeners' calls. He had already demonstrated that he could sell almost anything. When he plugged Sweetheart Soap as a lark one night, it literally walked off the supermarket shelves. And when he plugged *I, Libertine*, a nonexistent book, bookstores were besieged with orders. Shepherd liked the *Village Voice* (he also liked Limelight, and praised the waitresses, if not the photographs) and gave the paper more time on the air than it paid for. Subscriptions poured in and for the time being, at least, the *Voice* was saved.

Faced with continuing crisis, the editors had to keep dreaming up new ways of generating publicity. One idea was the Off Broadway awards, or "Obies." "It's just like the Oscars," Jerry explained, "except we won't be handing out statues." (The *Voice* could hardly pay the printer, much less buy statues.) He asked to hold the ceremony at Limelight, and though I would not ordinarily have agreed to hold any event unrelated to photography, I knew what it was like to teeter on the edge and was glad to help.

My one concern was the air conditioner. I'd recently purchased an enormous unit, and it was not yet in working order. The unit was installed at the front end of the room, and though it was concealed behind a row of louver doors, it made its presence known, not by any appreciable cooling but by a rumbling that sounded like a hurricane sweeping though. The salesman assured me that it would be ready in time for the Obie awards, which were to be held in the middle of June.

What concerned Jerry more than the summer heat was finding a master of ceremonies. If the event was to attract notice and be picked up by the press, the emcee had to be a celebrity. Harvey Jacobs, a budding novelist and space salesman for the *Voice*, suggested Marilyn Monroe. She was here in New York taking classes with Lee Strasberg, and though the idea seemed far-fetched, there was nothing to lose in trying. Harvey called, Marilyn agreed, and using this as part of his sales pitch, he went running around the Village selling advertising space. But the next time he called, she sounded vague, and rather than chance her showing up late — or not at all — the editors contacted Shelley Winters. She was starring on Broadway in *A Hatful of Rain*, and she readily agreed, unaware she was second choice.

June 18 was a very hot day. We had set up the room to accommodate three hundred people, with a table up front for Shelley Winters and the judges — Jerry Tallmer, the actor Earle Hyman, and the drama critic of *Commonweal*, Richard Hayes. People arrived early to ensure getting seats, and by three o'clock the place was filled. But nothing seemed to be going right. Jerry was fiddling with the microphone, testing for sound; I was tinkering with the air conditioner, which was supposed to be working but was emitting hot air; Dan Wolf, the editor of the *Voice*, and Ed Fancher, its publisher, both normally unflappable, were pacing up and down watching the door, waiting for Shelley Winters to arrive.

Then suddenly, out of nowhere, she appeared in the back of the room. Her driver had confused Seventh Avenue with Seventh Avenue South, but had, by some miracle, found Barrow Street and deposited her at the kitchen door. She was smaller than I'd thought, and thinner, too, showing none of the weight that would accumulate with the years. She was in a pale blue suit, nipped in at the waist, and you might even call her petite. Flashbulbs popped and reporters crowded round her, making for another delay.

Despite much mopping of brows and fanning of faces (with copies of the *Voice* placed on each chair), the heat didn't diminish the audience's enthusiasm. Shelley Winters seemed pleased, and with the grittiness and humor that marked her style, she performed as if handing out Oscars at the Academy Awards. There were speeches, and thank yous, and rounds of applause as each winner stepped up and accepted a certificate as an award. Jason Robards was chosen Best Actor for his role in *The Iceman Cometh*, and sharing the award with Robards for his role in Chekhov's *Uncle Vanya*, George Voskovec. Julie Bovasso was chosen Best Actress for her part in Jean Genet's *The Maids* (she would later star in Robert Frank's film, *The Sin of Jesus*) and Jose Quintero as Best Director for *Iceman*. There were several other categories, and I was glad to see that almost everyone who won an Obie was a Limelight regular.

The Obies became an annual event—Geraldine Paige was master of ceremonies in 1957, Kim Stanley in 1958. But by 1959 it had outgrown the room. There was no way of squeezing in six hundred guests, and the presentation moved to Art d'Lugoff's Village Gate. By then Off Broadway was already an institution, and though still a vital force, it was beginning to lose its edge and more and more to resemble Broadway. Prices included.

IN LIGHT OF all the interest in Off Broadway, I arranged for the loan of *Footlights and Spotlights: Theatrical Photographs of the American Stage, 1860–1900*, an exhibition organized by George Eastman House. It included seventy photographs, ranging from postcard-sized cartes-de-visite to modern-day prints, arranged on twenty-four panels together with text. Though most were copies, I was assured by David Pratt, the designer of the show, that the museum had used a new copying process and that you could hardly tell them from the originals. Almost half were by Napoleon Sarony, hailed in the 1870s as "the leading photographer in the Western world"—no modest claim. Sarony, like Napoleon, was pompous and short; a portrait showed him wearing a heavily braided uniform, hand resting on a sword, but looking more like a ringleader in a circus than a military man. Sarony was a pioneer. He posed his sitters in natural light, and this, together with the more natural poses he had them assume, attracted the top performers of the period to his studio—Ellen Terry, Lily Langtry, Lillian Russell, and the most famous Shakespearean actor in America, Edwin Booth. He also photographed Sarah Bernhardt, the Marilyn Monroe of her day. For purposes of comparison, Pratt juxtaposed Sarony's portraits of "the divine Sarah" with those taken by Nadar. Sarony did not hold up well.

Footlights and Spotlights was perfect summer fare. The exodus of New Yorkers for summer retreats was more than made up by an influx of tourists, many of them arriving at Limelight, newspaper clippings in hand. Deschin had run reproductions two weeks apart, and John Barkley Hart wrote a piece for the *Voice*. Even the sleepy old *Villager* came to life, taking note of the fact that Sarony had lived on 12th Street, and that his studio, like those of his competitors—Falk, Mora, and J. Gurney & Son—was nearby, on Broadway, and that he later moved to Union Square, the photo district of the time.

This was the kind of exhibition that appealed to most everyone. Aside from the usual queries about what was coming next, I was able to forget the gallery for a while and concentrate on the place as a whole. Bob Borchers was off on a one-month vacation, and I had to fill in as manager.

MANAGEMENT was not my forte. The kitchen help acted like I wasn't there, and I could hardly wait until Bob returned. Howard Smith, our new part-time coffee man (and later a columnist for the *Village Voice*), was eating his way through a side of beef (a steak at dinner, another for the road) and indulging a sweet tooth with an array of desserts, and when our cream puffs started disappearing and I had to double the orders, I suspected that Howard was also indulging his friends. But I was not good at firing, so I left it to Bob. Neither was I good at paperwork. Every time I tallied the night's receipts, I arrived at another figure. And my efforts at making up the payroll each week always ended up in a jumble of figures that neither I nor the accountant could decipher. Ordering food called for a crystal ball; how else could one determine how many pastries would be consumed during the course of a night? And along with all this, I had to deal with the problems of the staff. I'd had my share that very day. A waitress had informed me that she would be "going to the country." And judging from others who had made the same trip (to Asheville, Pennsylvania, where Dr. John Spencer, a saintly physician, performed abortions in defiance of the law, for the principle rather than money), she would be gone a week. So along with being manager, bookkeeper, and gallery director, I would also be donning an apron.

This was hardly the time to look at portfolios—a practice I'd given up, in any case—and when a young man started pestering me one night about looking at his work, he did not get a pleasant response. I couldn't remember having seen him before. He was tall and burly, wore scruffy dungarees and a shabby leather jacket, and looked a bit down at the heels.

I told him I wasn't looking at work, that the gallery was scheduled for the next three years. (I used to say two, but changed it to three when those I'd put off with that ploy reappeared.)

"I'm not looking for a show. What I need is criticism."

"Look, I'm not a teacher and I don't give critiques. If you need help, take Lisette Model's course at the New School for Social Research."

The following week he was back again. "I told you I wasn't looking at work," I said sharply.

"But all I want is . . ."

"I know . . . criticism. Do you know how often I've heard that?"

But when he returned a third time, and then a fourth, I felt the only way to get rid of him was to look at his work and tell him to come back in five years. "All right, leave your portfolio and I'll look at it when I get a chance."

Rather than leave it at the desk, I brought it home and didn't open it until Bob returned. I was pleasantly surprised. The young man had talent and a fairly good eye. I'd thought I'd include a few of his prints in some future group show.

Footlights and Spotlights was still on the wall, and I was waiting for the work of Manuel Alvarez Bravo to arrive. I'd been corresponding with his English-speaking wife, Doris Leyton, and having heard of the Mexican predilection for *mañana*, I'd asked her to send the work six weeks in advance. She assured me she would, but I became apprehensive when she wrote that her husband had taken a job as a cameraman on a film. "People in Mexico do not buy photographs, so a photographer has to make a living at something else."

Two weeks before the exhibition was to open I was still waiting. Announcements had been printed, the press informed, and after a frantic exchange of telegrams, I learned to my dismay that the photographs had been mailed only days before and were still languishing in the Mexican post office. I was in a spot. I couldn't extend *Footlights and Spotlights* much longer. It had been up since August 1, and it was now mid-September. "We're sick of 'the Divine Sarah,'" a customer complained.

This meant either organizing an exhibition almost overnight, or going through all the complications of switching shows. I went back to the portfolio and took another look. Why not give the young man a break? The work was right here, ready to be shown, and I didn't think he would take umbrage (as others might), being thrown in at the last minute as a substitute.

But then, I couldn't locate him. He'd left no address, and there was no one by the name of Ken Heyman in the phone book. I called Jack Deschin, but he'd met him only once and didn't know where he lived. "All I know is that his folks own a shack somewhere in Westchester."

I was about to give up when Ken walked through the door. He was delighted, of course, when he heard about the show, and after giving him a lecture on professional practices—how was one to find a photographer without a phone number and address?—I invited him to the apartment so we could decide on the prints.

"What's that noise?" he said, hearing the toilet flush. I had been waiting weeks for the landlord to send a plumber.

"I'll fix it," he said. "Have you got a wrench?"

I brought out some tools and he made the repair, emerging from the bathroom covered with grease. I hesitated asking whether he did this for a living; a career as a plumber was not the worst, and could keep him going while he photographed on the side. He looked like he needed the money. But when he arrived for the opening, I hardly recognized him. He was in a well-tailored suit, a shirt, and tie. But he looked ill at ease. He kept watching the door, as if expecting an intruder.

The first to arrive were his parents. They didn't look like the sort that would live in a shack, nor did any of the others who began flocking in. I met a doctor named Menninger and a woman who could double for Margaret Mead. When I looked out front and saw limousines pulling up, I took Ken aside. "What's going on here? Who *are* these people?"

Ken looked sheepish and fumbled for words. "I guess I should have told you . . ."

"Told me *what?*

"That I'm rich. Not just rich, but very rich. My father is a philanthropist and these people are his friends."

David Heyman, it turned out, was an investment banker and a major contributor through a family foundation to medical research, public health, education, and the arts. The doctor I'd met was Dr. Karl Menninger of the renonwned Menninger Clinic, and that was, indeed, Margaret Mead. Ken had been brought up in luxury, and though his father would have preferred that he'd choose Wall Street as a profession, Ken was determined to carve out a career as a working photographer.

"Those old clothes you were wearing, were they camouflage?"

"Not really," Ken said. "I just hate to be reminded of my wealth. Also, I didn't think you would take me seriously if you knew I was the son of a multimillionaire."

And the "shack" in Westchester? A twenty-eight room mansion with French Impressionists on the wall.

TWO WEEKS into the show, a woman stormed over to my table. "I'm going to sue you and Ken Heyman too! You have no right to hang that picture in your gallery."

"What picture?" I said. "I don't know what you're talking about."

"Come, I'll show you." She stalked to the gallery, I followed behind, and she pointed to a picture of an Afghan hound on a city street. "That's my Raymond," she said.

"What makes you think it's your dog?" Afghans were in fashion (having replaced the French poodle), and they all looked alike to me. "There's no collar, no leash . . ."

"I never place restraints on Raymond. I want him to feel free." She flapped her arms like she was about to take flight.

"Is there any one thing that tells you it's Raymond?"

"Yes, I can tell by the look in his eyes."

I telephoned Ken. He got in touch with the woman, offered her a print, and I never saw her again.

This was not the first time I was been threatened with a lawsuit, but it was usually the dining room that inspired these threats. A sliver of glass in a sundae, a splinter of wood in a salad (always "discovered" by strangers) proved nothing more than a nuisance. Whenever we were served, I forwarded the papers to Sheinfeld, and that was usually the end of it.

The first time I was served, I was very upset and saw myself losing everything—Limelight, my studio, my few paintings of Yun's, and whatever else I had of value. I was sued by a young woman who claimed to have suffered both physical injury and emotional trauma after being hit on the head with a tray. Sonya was the one who had wielded the tray, and while I would not have wanted to be on the receiving end of anything wielded by Sonya, the "blow" was merely a tap. She'd swung around after serving a customer and merely brushed the woman's forehead with the edge of the tray. There was no scratch, no bruise, and the woman's only concern was her hairdo. According to the brief, she'd had to postpone her wedding plans, and on top of the one hundred thousand dollars she was seeking in damages, the prospective groom asked an additional ten thousand, having been deprived of a wife's "companionship."

Only once did I come close to what might have been a legitimate lawsuit, and this too involved Sonya. A customer ordered a cannoli, an Italian pastry shaped like an egg roll, filled with delicious sweet cream. The waitresses filled the shells with cream at the beginning of the night, but we'd had a run on cannolis, and Sonya had to prepare one on the spot. She ladled in the cream with a long-handled spoon, set the cannoli on a lovely white dish, and wended her way through the Saturday night crowd. Halfway there, she turned back to the kitchen. She had noted some resistance while filling the shell and thought she had better investigate. When she scooped out the cream, she saw a little black tail, and attached to the tail, a dead mouse.

EUGENE SMITH—at last! I'd been anticipating this visit since the day Lime-light opened. Smith was the first photographer I contacted after conceiving the idea, and he'd responded to my letter with an hour-long phone call, promising his support. And, should my venture succeed, he might even be inveigled into exhibiting.

Photographers sprang up, and within minutes he was surrounded. No one but Smith could create such a stir, not even the elusive Cartier-Bresson (who would probably flee were he noticed). Smith was already a legend, revered by young creative photographers and seasoned professionals alike. He was admired for his artistry, for the passion and conviction he brought to his work, and for his courageous stance in bucking the powers at *Life*. He fought for the right to choose his own assignments (usually those with humanistic concerns), for the right to spend as much time as he needed to explore a story in depth (weeks, sometimes months), and for the right to print his own work, regardless of deadlines. (Most *Life* photographers sent their film to *Life*'s labs, and often saw their work only when the magazine appeared on the stands.) He also insisted on a say in the layout, and even, at times, the accompanying text. The editors resisted but they often complied, not simply because of his reputation as an artist—Smith was one of the few photojournalists who was thought of as an artist—but because of the response of the public to his work. *Nurse-Midwife*, the story of Maude Callem, a black health worker in a backwater of North Carolina, had so moved the readers when it appeared in *Life* that money poured in from all over the country, enabling her to replace her ramshackle clinic with a new, modern facility. *Spanish Village*, a story he worked on during a four-month stay in Fascist Spain, won critical acclaim and was subsequently exhibited at the Museum of Modern Art.

Smith was no longer with *Life*. He'd resigned in 1954, after threatening to many times, and was currently working on a project of his own, a monumental story on the city of Pittsburgh—its social, cultural, and economic life. He was seldom in New York, and now that he'd finally appeared at Limelight, I kept circling his table, hoping to find a way to fend off photographers and pin him down about a show. When one got up another sat down, and Smith, basking in center stage, didn't provide an opening.

He stayed about an hour, and after going to the gallery and looking at the show—this would have been my chance had not others traipsed along—he left. But on saying goodnight, he told me he liked the place and I'd be hearing from him soon. He didn't say anything about our having met once before, and I wondered whether he remembered that night.

It was in 1951, long before opening a gallery had even entered my mind. I'd been invited to a meeting of the American Society of Magazine Photographers at the Hotel Vanderbilt, and afterwards, a group of us, including H. M. (Mike) Kinzer, an editor at *Popular Photography*, drifted off to the bar. Smith had left the meeting early, escaping a slide show by Eliot Elisofon, a fellow photographer at *Life*, and was already ensconced when we arrived. "Want to meet him?" Mike asked.

I'd met Mike Kinzer through his charming Dutch wife Ilona while weekending with Li-lan in Woodstock. She was there for the summer with her infant son Steven, and afterwards we met in New York. Mike and I had spoken about Smith, and knowing how much I admired his work, he led me over to the one empty bar stool, which, luckily, was right next to Smith.

The two made small talk, but I said nothing. Shyness was a problem. Whenever I met anyone I deeply admired, my brain went automatically on hold. But it gave me a chance to look him over, and I liked what I saw. With his steel-rimmed glasses, tweeds, and string tie, he could have been a young professor visiting from the Midwest. He had none of the swagger that went with the trade, and the only clue to his profession—and its hazards—was the taut, pinched skin around his nose and mouth. He was wounded while on assignment in Okinawa during World War II, and fragments of shrap-

W. Eugene Smith, by James Karales.

nel had lodged in his palate, leaving his otherwise regular features looking slightly askew. I heard that he still lived with pain.

I was still groping around for something to say—what *do* you say to a living legend?—when Mike left and joined others at a table, leaving me stranded with Smith. And Smith was no help. He fiddled with a matchbook and kept staring into his drink. Finally, after a long silence, he said. "Let's get out of here. I hate these fancy hotel bars. I know a swell little place on Third Avenue."

I leapt at the chance, hoping a drink would help loosen my tongue. But Paddy's, it turned out, was no place to talk. It was crowded and noisy, and the television, turned on full blast to a wrestling match, drowned out every word. Smith ordered scotch, but the waiter, eyes glued to a stranglehold, brought whiskey sours instead.

I had resigned myself to another stretch of silence when Smith moved closer, muttering what sounded suspiciously like, "I'm going to kill myself."

"You're going to *what?*"

There was no mistaking it now. "I *am going to kill myself.*"

"But you have everything to live . . ." Smith sprang up, cutting me short.

"Wait!" I said, grabbing hold of his arm. "Let's stay and talk." I thought I'd play for time, get him to talk, and meanwhile figure out what to do.

Smith sat down and the words poured out, almost as if they'd been bottled up for years. I strained to hear over the noise of the crowd, but all I could catch was a word now and then—"editors . . . layouts . . . assignments . . . Life. . . ." Soon even these snippets were getting harder to hear, and it wasn't only the television; Smith's voice was beginning to slur. When I could no longer catch a single word, I suggested a walk, hoping it would raise his spirits and help sober him up.

Third Avenue was deserted. The only sound of the city was the rumbling of the trains on the El. We walked arm in arm, like lovers (all I had in mind, though, was keeping him on his feet) and headed for my apartment, some fifteen blocks away. I had promised the babysitter I'd be home by eleven, and it was going on twelve.

We'd gone one or two blocks when Smith spotted a bar, another favorite. A few blocks later he spied another, and we stopped again. We reeled on to Flanagan's, then Molly Malone's, but it was getting harder to steady Smith, and I was having problems myself. At Michael's I called my babysitter, and though I tried to explain that a life was at stake, all she cared about was going home.

By the time we reached the Old Seidelberg, across the street from my apartment, I was no longer sure that I was in a condition to help. And Smith kept moaning, "I wanna die, I wanna die."

I slipped the bartender a dollar bill and asked him to keep an eye on Smith. Then I called Mike Kinzer from a phone in the rear.

"What's wrong?" he mumbled. "It's the middle of the night."

"This is an emergency. Gene Smith is threatening to kill himself."

"*Again?*"

"Can you grab a cab and come to the Old Seidelberg? I don't know what to do."

"I'll tell you what to do," Mike growled. "Put Gene in a cab and go home to bed."

"But what if he goes off and kills himself?"

"He won't. He never does. I guess I should have warned you. We've all been through this with Gene."

So I gave up playing Florence Nightingale. I called a cab, maneuvered Smith into it, and went home to face my babysitter.

THE NEXT time I saw Smith was in 1952, when he gave a talk at the Village Camera Club in conjunction with a small exhibition of his work. It was snowing that night, but the faithful convened. Those who couldn't find seats sat on the floor, cushioning themselves on piles of soggy coats.

Smith arrived late. Smiling, pink-faced, stamping off the snow, he took off his storm coat and Russian-style hat. He motioned to the panels where his work was displayed and announced: "The pictures on these walls were taken with a 35 millimeter camera equipped with a 35 millimeter wide-angle lens. End of technical discussion."

That out of the way, he proceeded with his talk. We sat, enthralled, as he talked about his life—his childhood in Wichita, Kansas, the suicide of his father (a trauma that would haunt him for the rest of his life), his relationship with his mother (a strong woman, who championed his work), and the beginnings of his career in New York. He'd worked for Newsweek, Time, and *Life* before he was twenty-five, and it was only after he developed creatively that his troubles began. He discussed the difficulties he'd faced trying to maintain artistic integrity while working on assignment, and the difficulties he'd encountered on the assignments themselves. We were on the edge of our seats as he described an experience in Fascist Spain while working on *Spanish Village*: He was preparing to leave, after months of work, when he was questioned by the Guardia Civil, Franco's dreaded police. Afraid of having his film seized, he jumped in a car and raced toward the border. But the car broke down, and lugging his heavy equipment, he tried to do the rest on foot. Tired, thirsty, burning in the sun, he collapsed just as he reached the border, and lay there biting the earth.

This ended his talk. Nobody clapped. To clap would have broken the spell. Then someone called out from the back of the room. "Mr. Smith, what kind of lens do you use?"

Out of some one hundred throats came one great groan, and we turned to see who this philistine was.

"Sir," said Smith, eyeing the young man, "I use a 35 millimeter camera equipped with a 35 millimeter wide-angle lens, the same lens used by Van Gogh."

SMITH DROPPED IN at Limelight a couple more times, and at last I was able to catch him alone. He agreed to exhibit but he didn't know when. The Pittsburgh project was consuming all of his time, but he made a tentative date for the following fall.

A few days later he popped in again and handed me a box, the kind that holds photographic paper. "It's your reward for staying on the straight and narrow, and not resorting to a life of crime." I was mystified by the remark, but I took the box, and before I could ask what this was all about, he'd dashed outside and jumped into a cab.

A photograph? It couldn't be. Gene was not known to be generous with prints. He even made it hard to purchase one. He would take the fifty dollars, then forget all about it. Someone I knew had been waiting for years.

I opened the box, and to my surprise, there was a portrait of the renowned humanitarian Dr. Albert Schweitzer, taken in Aspen, Colorado, in 1949. Schweitzer, a devotee of Bach, had been attending a conference of musicologists from all over the world, and though Smith had taken the picture more or less on the run, I preferred it to many of those he'd taken at Schweitzer's medical compound in Labarene, West Africa, in 1953, while working on his photo essay, *Man of Mercy*. The bowed head, silhouetted against a dark mountain range, seemed characteristic of the man—he could be playing the organ, ministering to a patient, or stroking one of the animals that wandered around the hospital grounds.

I had wanted the portrait ever since I first saw it. Dr. Schweitzer was one of my heroes. He had given up a comfortable existence in Europe, established a medical facility in a remote part of Africa, and devoted his life to serving others. Though I loved the portrait and admired the man, I wanted the portrait not for myself, but for another Dr. Schweitzer—this one, Dr. Ernst Schweitzer—the psychoanalyst who had helped me through many dark days after I'd left Yun Gee. He'd given me hope, encouraged my career, and helped with advice on raising my child. And for this he charged only five dollars a session, raising his fee as my income increased. How could I ever repay him? Schweitzer was strict in his observance of doctor-patient relationships and would not even shake hands, much less accept gifts. He too admired Albert Schweitzer, and now that I was no longer a patient, I thought he might accept the portrait as a token of gratitude.

The portrait had been included in the small showing of Smith's work at the Village Camera Club the night of his talk. But the club was crowded and it was hard to see, so I'd asked Morris Jaffe, a member, to take me in when the club was closed. I stood in front of the Schweitzer. "Morris, I've *got* to have this picture," I said.

"You don't stand a chance," he said. "Not for love or money will Smith part with a print."

"But I've *got* to have it. There must be a way."

"The only way is to steal it," Morris said.

What he meant as a joke made sense to me. Morris was a friend; no one would ever know. "You're right. I think I'll take it," I said. (*Steal*, under the circumstance, was too harsh a word.)

"Okay. I'll turn around. I don't want to witness a theft."

Morris turned around and I struggled with my conscience. Honesty had been drummed into me since the day I was born. God, I'd been told, was always watching, recording one's transgressions in a big black book, chalking them up against Judgment Day. But worse than God's wrath was the thought of having to admit to the analyst that I'd "lifted" the portrait. Would I need another session to get rid of the guilt?

"You can turn around now, Morris," I said.

Morris turned around and was relieved to see that Dr. Schweitzer was still on the wall. Just then a fellow member walked in, and I would have been caught red-handed.

I'd told Smith the story during one of his visits, not dreaming, of course, that it would inspire the gift. The next time I saw him I felt it only fair to remind him that I intended to give the photograph away.

"Go ahead," he said. "That's exactly why I gave it to you, so you can give it to the man who helped you."

However egocentric, one had to love Smith.

Dr. Schweitzer accepted the gift. Thirty years later, when he was ill, in his nineties, and approaching death, a group of former analysands got together and helped him during his final illness. To show his gratitude, he gave each of us a gift. Mine was the portrait of Albert Schweitzer.

STEICHEN CALLED and suggested meeting for dinner at a large seafood restaurant on West 47th Street. He was back in town and had lots to tell me.

What he didn't tell me was that he was suffering from gout. He came swinging through the door on crutches, one foot bandaged, too large for a shoe. Brushing aside a solicitous waiter, he made his way to a table for two and, resting his crutches against the wall, lowered himself into a chair. I studied the menu, pretending not to notice as he arranged and rearranged his leg under the table, trying to keep it from protruding into the aisle.

"Gout's a pain-in-the-neck," he said, smiling. Although one would have expected to hear a litany of complaints from a seventy-seven year old man with an ailment as painful as gout, Steichen made light of it. "It's champagne and rich food that brings on these attacks. I guess I have to learn to say no."

Gout had been a life-long problem, and what with all the festivities surrounding *The Family of Man*, small wonder it was recurring now. Wherever Steichen went he was feted, in Paris, Berlin, Munich, Amsterdam, London, Tokyo, and also here in the States.

"How about some lobster?" he said, chuckling. "It's one of the foods I'm supposed to avoid, but I'm tired of watching my diet. Lobster, a salad, a nice bottle of wine . . ."

I knew I shouldn't abet him in this, but I did love lobster. "I'll have mine broiled."

"Good. I've developed a yen for seafood. It must have been that trip to Japan."

Steichen had visited Japan the year before, arranging for the exhibition to be shown at the Takashimaya Department Store in Tokyo (which had museum-like facilities for showing art), and at several other sites in small towns and cities. He'd been concerned about the way it would be received in Japan (he'd removed the picture of the hydrogen bomb) and was thrilled when he heard of its enormous success, and the audience of one million people.

Steichen tackled his lobster with gusto, and between cracking the claws and wiping melted butter from his chin, he talked about nothing except Japan. He'd liked what he'd seen of Japanese photography (it had a coherence and aesthetic he'd found unique), and he was also impressed with the people—their manners, their love of beauty, their feeling for nature. As a horticulturalist, recognized for his crossbreeding of flowering plants, he was delighted with the reverence they showed even the most modest manifestation of nature—a bud, a leaf, a single bloom.

There were aspects of the culture that puzzled him though. He couldn't understand the relationship between the sexes. "I don't know why they keep their women under wraps," he said. "At every dinner, there were only men. Except, of course, for the geishas, and I'm afraid they were wasted on me. I hate being fussed over, though they were a sight to behold in their lacquered wigs and painted faces and gorgeous kimonos. They seemed more like dolls than women."

But there was one night, he said, when he was glad no women were present. He'd been invited to a banquet in his honor, attended by close to one hundred men. After a dozen different dishes and an endless round of toasts ("I found saki more lethal than champagne"), two beautiful geishas minced into the room. They bowed, motioned him to stand, then proceeded to undress him. They took off his jacket and his tie, unbuttoned his shirt, and as they slipped off his braces, he wondered how far this would go. He had visions of himself standing in the buff, one hundred pairs of eyes fixed upon him, a situation not covered in guide books. The geishas opened a box, lifted out two kimonos—one a cotton *yukata*, the other a silk ceremonial robe—and after dressing him in the robe and tying an *obi* around his waist, the men all stood up and bowed.

"I guess the State Department hadn't prepared you for that one," I said laughing, half-choking on a shell. "Are you planning another trip?"

"No, I'd like to go back but I've done so much traveling I want to stay put and get back to my own work."

"You mean, another big show?" I'd heard rumors of his retiring, but didn't want to ask.

"I'm full of beans, and have lots of shows in mind. But what I really want to do is to start photographing again. There's a little shad-blow tree growing on a pond outside my house, and I noticed the other day it's in bloom. Wayne Miller once said it looked like a little girl dancing on one leg. What I'd like to do is photograph it at different times of day and in all kinds of weather."

I was glad to hear he'd been working again. He'd taken few pictures after World War II and had stopped entirely after assuming his position at the Museum of Modern Art, afraid it would influence the way he looked at others' work. Hardly anyone thought of him as a photographer anymore. His early work was considered "pictorial," and though his portraits in *Vanity Fair* were much admired, that was a very long time ago. In this existential world of ours, all that mattered was what you were doing now.

"Will you be working in black and white or color?" I asked.

Steichen was one of the first to use autochrome in the early 1900s, so I wasn't surprised when he said that he might try color. "I was a painter back in the early days, you know, and I've never lost my feeling for color. I destroyed most of my canvases when I decided on photography, but I still have a few left. In fact, just the other day, I came across one of the first pictures I painted. I'd like you to see it."

"I'd love to. When?"

"Right now. It's around the corner, at Esther Bubley's. I've sublet her apartment and use it when I stay in town."

We finished dessert, then set out for Esther's. The building was a walk-up, and I watched with trepidation as Steichen navigated the stairs. He clung to the banister with one hand, clutched his crutches with the other, and pulled himself up, step by step, to the second floor.

The living room was small but comfortably furnished, with a large sofa and overstuffed chairs. A dark, heavily varnished painting stood propped against a wall. Steichen hobbled over, adjusted the shade on a floor lamp, set down his crutches and sunk on to the sofa. "Well, what do you think of it?"

The painting was much like his photographs of the Milwaukee woods, done around the turn of the century. It was romantic, dreamy, with a soft, golden light. "It's lovely," I murmured.

Steichen crossed his arms, cocked his head to one side, and stood there, studying the painting through narrowed eyes. I wasn't sure that he heard me. Was he reliving his days as a young man in Paris? Was he back visiting the ateliers of Rodin and Brancusi? Or was he thinking of all the young women?

Finally he spoke. "I did this before I discovered modern art. Cézanne, Van Gogh—everything was new to me. I sometimes wonder how my work would have changed had I continued to paint."

"Have you ever thought of starting again?"

"As a matter of fact, yes. I'd like to do some sketching, and work with the figure. How would you feel about posing in the nude?" I was too startled to come up with a reason for refusing, and mumbled something about being too shy.

"Don't worry. I'll help you overcome your shyness. As soon as I get over this gosh-darned gout, I'll call and we'll make a date." I was hardly a prude and should have jumped at the chance. But Steichen was sitting on the sofa, and I felt the pressure of a knee.

I was about to stand up when he struggled to his feet, picked up his crutches, and headed for the bedroom. "I've got a surprise for you. Why don't you go to the kitchen and fix some drinks? I'll be back in a couple of minutes."

I prepared two drinks, set them on the coffee table, and waited. What was the surprise—a photograph? He once promised to give me one. I began thinking of some of my favorites—*Apple and Three Pears, Heavy Roses*, the portrait of Garbo. . . .

Whatever it was, he was taking awfully long. When Steichen finally reappeared I saw why. He was wearing a Japanese kimono. It flapped against his crutches as he swung into the room, baring a long white leg.

"Well, what do you think of it?"

"Very nice," I said. "Is that one of the kimonos you were given in Japan?"

"Yep, it's the one they call a *yukata*." Balancing on his crutches, he fingered a sleeve. "Feel. It's only cotton but it's as soft as silk."

I took his word for it, got up from the sofa, and sidled off to the other side of the room. Steichen's foot was bandaged up to the ankle, yet this didn't seem to hamper his movements. A couple of swoops, and he was at my side.

"Nice photograph," I said, pointing to an Esther Bubley on the wall. But Steichen would not be diverted. He pivoted, swooped forward, and we stood face to face. I stepped back a few feet; Steichen stepped back too. I excused myself, went to the bathroom, and after allowing him enough time to calm down, walked back into the room. Steichen was poised on his crutches, prepared to advance. Feigning nonchalance, I sauntered over to an easy chair and positioned myself behind it. He swung forward and soon we were running an obstacle course, circling the sofa and the easy chairs. Each time he swooped toward me I stepped aside, like a matador side-stepping a bull.

"*Ole!*" I shouted and burst out laughing.

"What's so funny?" he said, coming to a halt.

Should I tell him? Should I tell him that I'd experienced every possible male approach—everything from sly innuendo to an outright pass—but that I'd never been pursued by a septuagenarian on crutches, dressed like a Japanese samurai? Laughter is contagious if passion is not, and soon Steichen was laughing too. We sank on to the sofa and laughed till we cried.

Seeing it was late, I got up to go. Steichen picked up his crutches and saw me to the door. "A good laugh is better than a cold shower," he said, and gave me a polite peck on the cheek.

Steichen and I remained friends.

BERENICE ABBOTT was reclusive and seldom came by, and whenever she did, she was with Lisette. They always arrived early, before the place filled up, and settled at a table for two. Whatever they were discussing was not for other ears, and they would even fall silent when the waitress approached. Berenice looked depressed. She had separated from the art critic Elizabeth McCausland, her companion of many years, and considering Lisette's concern about Evsa's roving eye, I doubted they were discussing photography.

I kept my distance, in any case, not knowing how Lisette would react. Her moods were mercurial, and seeing how close the two had become—they were not only friends but colleagues at the New School, Berenice having arranged for Lisette to teach there—I thought it best to see Berenice alone. I wanted to talk to her about putting on a show. I'd known her work for years—she was, in fact, the first photographer I thought of as an artist—yet we had never even talked.

I first saw her work in Yun Gee's studio. I was sixteen years old, cutting school, and while poring through Yun's books, I came across a catalogue of the exhibition *Murals by American Painters and Photographers*, shown at the Museum of Modern Art in 1932. Reproduced in the catalogue was a photomontage by Berenice Abbott, a criss-cross of steel girders and glimpses of city streets. I liked the image, but were it not for the fact that Yun was also in the show, I would not have looked at the catalogue so carefully or read the press clippings stuck between the pages.

Yun talked about the exhibition over a lunch of *dim sum*. Organized by Lincoln Kirstein, chairman of the exhibition committee and well-known patron of the arts, the show proposed to demonstrate to both the public and architects that Americans were as capable of creating murals as were the much sought-after Mexicans. He invited thirty-five painters, including Stuart Davis and Georgia O'Keeffe, and twelve photographers, including Berenice Abbott, Edward Steichen, George Platt Lynes, and painter-photographer Charles Sheeler. Each was given a stipend for expenses (Yun remembered his as three hundred dollars, a tidy sum in the depths of the depression), and asked to create a large-scale work, based on some aspect of the postwar world.

For Yun, age twenty-six and new to New York, this was a dream come true. Exhibiting at the Museum of Modern Art would establish his reputation in New York, and should his work receive notice and lead to commissions, he would finally be able to send for his wife, a poet and dancer named Princess Paule de Reuss, whom he married in Paris in 1929, a few months before the stock market crash. She had since been disowned by her aristocratic family for marrying a poor artist—and Chinese at that.

Yun realized at that time that his chances were slim. *Wheels: Industrial New York*, a panorama of Lower Manhattan, was too modern for American taste. The art world was basically conservative; with the exception of a few, most of the painters in the exhibition were social realists. Yet, to his surprise, *Wheels* was selected by Edward Alden Jewell, art critic of the *New York Times*, as one of the five finest paintings in the show. He referred to it in his review as a "gorgeous fugue," and to Yun as "one of the few to whom I would entrust walls."

On the whole the exhibition was panned, although the photographers fared better than the painters. "Decidedly encouraging," Jewell wrote,

> are the experiments in mural photography worked out under the direction of Julien Levy. One is inclined at once to agree with Mr. Levy, who had selected the photographers and written an essay for the catalogue, that "the photographer is particularly well equipped to meet the problems of mural decoration posed by the modern architect and builder." Not in every instance do the examples on hand score, but there are certain designs so powerful, so brilliant, so arrestingly wrought, that the spectator's response is instant and unreserved.

Among those Jewell singled out were Edward Steichen's oversized photomural of the George Washington Bridge (it exceeded the size limit by several feet) and Berenice Abbot's photomontage of New York. Berenice was also selected by the *New York World Telegram*, together with Yun Gee, as "among those attracting attention."

Other than the fact that photographs were exhibited for the first time at the Museum of Modern Art, little happened as a consequence of the show. The plums still went to the Mexicans. Diego Rivera was commissioned to paint a mural in the RCA building in Rockefeller Center, but the work was stopped when Rivera slipped in his usual bit of Socialist propaganda—a head of Lenin not included in the preliminary sketch—and hastily removed from the wall. Rivera, however, was paid in full.

Yun's failure to obtain commissions despite the fine notice given his work left him deeply depressed. He was never able to send for his wife and after waiting two years, they divorced. I sensed his bitterness as he talked.

There were a number of questions I would liked to have asked: Was photography an art? Did it *really* belong in museums? Was it equal, in his eyes, to painting? But sensing Yun's mood, I didn't ask, and we went on to other things.

Berenice Abbott, 1951, by Peter Pollack. Courtesy of the
Art Institute of Chicago, copyright © 1996 by the Art Institute of Chicago.

BERENICE ABBOTT showed up alone one night and, I hurried over to her table. But before I could get around to discussing a show, she said, "There's something I want to talk to you about."

Whatever it was, she seemed in no hurry. I sat back and waited while she lingered over dessert, marveling all the while at how little she'd changed since she was photographed by Man Ray in Paris in the 1920s. She had worked as his assistant before opening her own studio and returned to America, as did many expatriots, after the start of the depression. The intervening years did not seem to show.

Curiosity won out. I asked what she had in mind. An exhibition, perhaps? "Yes, but not of my work. Atget."

Atget? The great Eugene Atget? "Just tell me when and I'll arrange it."

Why hadn't this occurred to me before? I knew Berenice had a collection of Atget's work, acquired (or "saved," as the story goes) shortly after his death in 1927. I also knew she'd been trying to promote it. Julien Levy held an Atget exhibition in 1932, and another in 1936. Both were financial failures. There had also been a show at the Photo League, but despite these efforts, the work had not yet received the recognition it deserved.

I first heard of Atget in Sid Grossman's class when he passed around a copy of *Atget Photographe de Paris*, a book Berenice had compiled. Sid handled the book like a rabbi with the Torah and spoke about Atget with awe. He'd embodied all the attributes Sid felt essential to greatness — passion, dedication, perseverance, hard work. He'd taken up photography at the age of forty, after a faltering career as an itinerant actor. He made a modest living selling his prints as source material to architects, designers, editors, and painters (Braque and Utrillo were among his customers) and to institutions for their archives. He was obsessed with the city, and until his death at the age of seventy, he trudged through the streets lugging a battered old view camera and heavy glass plates, recording every aspect of his beloved Paris. Now for the first time I would see the work.

Berenice lived a few blocks away, at 50 Commerce Street, in an apartment that served as a studio. The living room showed evidence of on-going work — cameras, tripods, a drafting board, and notebooks. She was involved in a project illustrating scientific principles, but I found it hard to feign interest in pictures of bouncing balls and clusters of soap bubbles with Atgets waiting in the wings.

Berenice moved slowly, but when she finally got around to the Atgets, it wasn't just a treat but a feast. There were some sixty prints, one more marvelous than the next. They were not, however, Atget's own prints, but those she'd made from his plates. Berenice was a meticulous technician, but materials had changed since Atget's day, and compared to the one of his I saw on the wall, they lacked the soft, warm tones. Still, I realized the importance of keeping the collection intact; she was trying to interest museums.

"I've offered it everywhere, but so far, no luck," she complained. "I've shown it to the Museum of Modern Art, George Eastman House, and I don't know how many smaller institutions, but none are interested, regardless of the price. It takes money to restore the plates and keep the collection in shape. I've been carrying Atget on my back for thirty years."

As for the exhibition at Limelight, it didn't matter whether the prints were by Atget or Berenice. People bought images, not rarity or names—the word *vintage* was used primarily for wine. I was sure that the Atgets would sell, if only because they were charming and very French. Everything French was popular these days—fashion, film, literature, and photography. Steichen had purchased several Atgets, if not the collection, and presented two major exhibitions, *The Roots of French Photography* in 1949, and *Five French Photographers: Brassai, Cartier-Bresson, Doisneau, Ronis, Izis* in 1951.

Berenice had printed the images she considered the most saleable—storefronts, street characters, prostitutes, vendors—and though I tried to persuade her to charge more for the prints, she insisted on asking only twenty dollars. "Julien Levy asked only ten," she argued, "and he hadn't sold even one."

"If others respond the way I do," I said (having already decided on six), "the Atgets will walk off the walls."

I was not far wrong. The exhibition opened at the beginning of December, and by the first week of January 1957, two-thirds of the photographs were sold. Most were purchased for their Gallic charm, and it was only the photographers and others "in the know" who recognized their aesthetic and historical value.

It was certainly not lost on either Jack Deschin or George Wright. Deschin spoke of Atget's work in an enthusiastic review as "the symbol of the pure image, the direct statement, and the simple essence of things as they are." George Wright took a more historical approach, and in his article in the *Village Voice* discussed the influence of Atget's work on documentary photography when first shown in America in 1930. It had acted "as a catalyst in the formation of the documentary approach," and the results, he claimed, "were almost immediately visible in the work of the F.S.A. photographers and in the development of photojournalism out of the relatively unimaginative news picture and its dreary cliches."

I appreciated George Wright's perspective, his having been around a lot longer than I. And I agreed wholeheartedly when he concluded, saying, "His work owes nothing to the aesthetics of painting or to any other medium: it is pure photography. He brings the infinite detail of reality—in this case, the streets, interiors, and environs of Paris—to the spectator, isolating it so its significance may be fully understood. He permits us, in Blake's phrase, to 'Hold infinity in the palm of your hand.'"

None but Blake could have expressed it better.

There was no mention at the time of Julien Levy's role in the acquisition of Atget's work, and few people knew that he'd cabled Berenice Abbott one thousand dollars to buy the collection and gave her additional money to work on the plates. This only became known when the collection was sold to the Museum of Modern Art (in 1968, for an undisclosed sum), and Levy claimed his share.

BAD NEWS! Bob Borchers was leaving. I'd always known it was just a matter of time—he was young, ambitious, eager to move on—but faced with it now, I took the news hard. I was surprised that he planned to open a place of his own, having assumed he'd opt for a modeling career. He'd posed for a number of magazine photographers, including Howard Zieff, a Limelight regular (and later, a Hollywood director). Bob's fresh, boyish face had appeared in several magazines, but it hadn't turned his head or tempted him to change his profession.

Replacing him would be difficult, but how very difficult I didn't know until I started interviewing the applicants who answered my ad. It seemed like they were interviewing me.

"What's your weekly gross?" growled the former owner of a fast food joint. And when I told him, he said, "I can double it if you get rid of that gallery. It's only taking up space." Another, a graduate of a prestigious hotel management school, said, "What? No dishwashing machine? No stainless steel?" After inspecting the kitchen, he left. "Work for a woman? Nothing doing," said another. "I got my hands full just dealing with my wife."

After a dozen of these interviews, I began to despair. What Limelight needed was a very special type, someone who accepted the gallery, understood the clientele, and kept the place running just as it was. But it didn't look like this person would appear, and I shuddered at the thought of having to run it myself, even temporarily.

A customer came to the rescue. He had just the man—a Hungarian "freedom fighter," newly arrived and in need of a job. He'd operated a coffee-house in Budapest but took to the streets when the Russians moved in, in 1956, suppressing the anti-Communist uprising. I'd seen pictures in the papers of these courageous young men pitting themselves against Soviet tanks, never imagining that I'd meet one, much less hire one.

Later that evening Mischa strolled in. He was plump and pink-cheeked with smooth, white hands, not exactly my idea of a freedom fighter. I couldn't imagine him hurling a grenade, or firing anything more lethal than a cap pistol. But I was a hiring a manager, not a bodyguard, and he did have a certain European charm. There was no way of checking his refer-ences, of course, but he talked at length about the coffeehouses he'd run, and they sounded pretty much like those in New York. He beamed when he saw Hungarian strudel on the menu and sampled the apple and the cherry as we talked.

"We have very good photographers in Hungary," he said, when I showed him the gallery.

"Most seemed to have come to America," I said, and mentioned the names of several—André Kertész, Martin Munkacsi, Hoyningen-Heuné, Gjon Mili, Moholy-Nagy, Robert Capa, and Cornell Capa. Mischa didn't recognize any of these names, but he jotted them down. I hired him on the spot.

THOUGH IT WAS risky hiring a manager unfamiliar with our ways, Bob had assembled an excellent staff. I was sure we would survive the transition. Mischa was tactful, but even so, he would need to tread carefully when han-dling the help, especially the men in the kitchen. Our current chef, Fong, like most Chinese chefs, had temperament—heaven help the waitress who let an order grow cold. Since I'd been married to a Chinese (who also had "temperament"), I was frequently called upon to help quiet him down. The others in the kitchen were more sanguine. There was Ernie, Fong's assistant, six foot four and the image of Joe Louis; Bernie, the coffee man; Joey, the salad man; and several part-timers who worked the busy hours. Bob had phased out the painters and novelists, and aside from the dishwashers who came and went, they were all professional kitchen workers.

It was only the waitresses who "did things," and this was part of their charm. Clara studied dance; she swept through the room, head held high, and always seemed poised for a leap. Leticia wrote poetry; she was thin, almost bony, and very plain ("sexy as a coat rack," as one customer put it), yet she attracted a large male following, many of them professors at New York University. Naomi was everything that Leticia was not; she was sloe-eyed, curvaceous, and though she professed a number of different talents, the most visible one was her ability to attract men. Men liked to talk to Leticia (she could converse on everything from Kafka to Freud) but liked to look at Naomi (and date her, if possible). There was also Deanna, a convert to Reichean therapy; when she wasn't gracing Limelight with her pale, fragile presence, she was sitting at home in an Orgone Box, building energy or libido or whatever it was those tin-lined telephone booths were supposed to do. Sonya was still with us, riding herd over the others, and there were also a couple of part-time waitresses, waiting to be discovered by a Hollywood scout. Hopes ran high when Susan Harrison, a nineteen year old, was picked up and starred with Burt Lancaster and Tony Curtis in *The Sweet Smell of Success*. (And just in time, for she was moody and difficult, and about to be fired.) Clarence, the porter, rounded out the staff which, together with the part-timers, numbered fourteen. A handful for Mischa, but fortunately they all got along. The question was—could Mischa handle Fong? Could he mediate a crisis when I wasn't around? Fong liked the waitresses, and they liked him, but this didn't stop him from behaving like a mandarin. Having no family in America (like most Chinese immigrants), he treated the waitresses like surrogate daughters. He had something to say about each.

About Naomi: "That girl should get married, have babies. Men too much on her mind. She should not wear tight sweater, and wiggle when she walk. Give men wrong ideas."

About Leticia: "Nice girl, but she don't know food." Leticia was a vegetarian, and though he found her dietary preferences abhorrent, he allowed her to use a corner of the fridge for her yogurt and black strap molasses.

About Clara: "Very nice girl. Don't know why she not married." Clara was not exactly a "girl"; at thirty-five, she was (in Fong's eyes and others') already "on the shelf."

About Deanna: "She get sick sitting in that box. Need a man in her life."

About Mischa, he had no complaints—at least, not yet. He'd prepared Hungarian goulash as the special on Mischa's first night on the job, and this was a very good sign. It could have used more paprika and a little less ginger, but Mischa was so touched he had tears in his eyes. But Fong did not look pleased when after several helpings of goulash, Mischa dug into the strudel with equal zest. "Three pieces too much," Fong grumbled. "Set bad example for the help."

I worked with Mischa the first few weeks, placing orders, checking provisions, arranging schedules, and attending to the dozens of details that went into running the place. But I wasn't much help when it came to the books, and Mischa had to ponder the mysteries of payroll deductions alone. Mischa was slow, and there were times I regretted having hired a European whose tempo was more Budapest than New York. But he got along with the customers and was never without an audience as he recounted his experiences as a freedom fighter, embellishing each version with greater detail. He was seated more often then standing on his feet, but I didn't mind because he seemed to fit in. Everybody liked him, and I did too.

STEICHEN'S WIFE had fallen ill and I saw less of him now. He spent more and more time at his home in West Redding, Connecticut, but continued his work at the museum. We talked on the phone from time to time, and he was enthusiastic about an exhibition he was organizing for the fall — *70 Photographers Look at New York*.

I heard nothing more about the project until I got a call from Grace Mayer, the curator of prints at the Museum of the City of New York, wanting to get together. She needed advice. Steichen had asked her to assist with the New York show, but she wasn't quite sure that she should.

Prior to this call, my contact with Grace had been mostly through the mail. She had the Victorian penchant for hand-written notes, and I already had several, commending me on various shows. She slipped in to see them but always hurried home to her ninety-year-old mother, with whom she shared a suite in the elegant Hotel Carlyle on the Upper East Side. Limelight was about as far downtown as she got. Grace seemed to have emerged from a bygone era, a time when "ladies" were defined by their fine manners and fine hats, both of which she had in abundance.

Not one to sweep into a room, Grace looked around timorously before sitting down. She ordered a lemonade and after an exchange of pleasantries,

Grace Mayer, by Nina Howell Starr.

she got to the point. She liked the idea of working with Steichen, but something seemed to be holding her back. What was it? I asked. Why are you so uncertain?

"Because I'm only a novice," she murmured.

A *novice?* I could think of no one better qualified to assist Steichen than

Grace. She had been working as a curator for many years—just how many she was reluctant to say—and had recently completed a book, *Once Upon a City: New York from 1890 to 1910*, which was to be published in conjunction with an exhibition in the fall of 1958. She was not only experienced in working with photographs, but she'd lived in New York all her life.

But I realized as we talked that her ambivalence had nothing to do with her qualifications, and everything to do with Steichen. Grace was overwhelmed by his reputation and his achievements (particularly the success of *The Family of Man*) and also by Steichen himself. She had known him for some time; he had, in fact, written the preface to her book, and though she found him gracious and easygoing and "oh, so very nice," she was afraid she might disappoint him.

"So you'll give up without even trying?" I was growing impatient with her self-deprecating manner; nothing I said seemed to have any effect. After she returned from telephoning home a second time, I made one final try. "Do you know that Steichen's wife is very ill? He's having a difficult time, and it would help him a lot if you worked on the show."

"Hmmm. Well, in that case, I'll have to give it more thought." From beneath the shadow of her wide-brimmed hat, I detected the flicker of a smile.

A few days later I received a note saying she was taking a leave of absence from her present position and was thrilled at the prospect of working with Steichen. She thanked me for my help, yet I was sure that she would have made the same decision without me. Behind Grace Mayer's demure demeanor, I suspected steel.

Next thing I heard—and from Grace herself—Steichen was giving a lecture at the museum the night of February 19, entitled "Experimental Photography in Color." I was eager to hear what he had to say. Color was a subject rarely discussed, not even at Limelight's talkfests. Creative photographers disdained the use of color, associating it with the advertising world; it was fine for selling cars and deodorants and such, but not for meaningful work. They also associated it with the amateur market and with snapshots in family albums.

I shared these prejudices. Color was seductive. Color tended to glamorize rather than reveal. Color was more literal, less abstract than black and white, lacking its mystery and power. Yet I had once thought of photographing in color. Taking advantage of my skills as a transparency retoucher, I thought of creating a less literal imagery, altering colors and distorting shapes. But I kept all this to myself, knowing these efforts would be met with derision; the current bias against the manipulation of images extended to color as well. I was still interested in the idea, believing these attitudes would someday change. Would Steichen's talk stimulate experimentation and lead to change?

The lecture was sold out, and as I walked through the auditorium looking for a seat, I thought I saw every photographer I knew. There was a ripple of excitement as Steichen appeared, but he moved very slowly, and his face looked drawn. He leaned against the lectern, and when he finally spoke, his voice sounded strained. The words were slurred, the sentences fragmented, and he seemed to be grappling with his thoughts. Was something wrong? Had he had a hard day? Or—I dreaded to think of it—was he on the verge of another lapse?

But after a few minutes, his voice grew stronger, his thoughts more focused, and despite an occasional hesitancy or overly long pause, he succinctly stated his views: Every photograph was an experiment. Every time one lifted a camera, searching for new, effective ways of communicating visual impressions, one was, in effect, experimenting. Color called for no special approach, and experimental photography, whether in color or black and white, need not rely on trick effects. There were as many approaches to color as there were to black and white, and what made a photograph truly experimental was not the content or the approach, but the photographer's thoughtful, emotional, and artistic responsiveness to the material and the subject.

Steichen continued, but each time he hesitated, I grew more apprehensive. I sensed that others were also disturbed, and I was relieved when the lights were lowered and he began to show slides. He showed two hundred images, the work of eighteen photographers using every possible approach. The work had been drawn from all over the country, and except for Ernst Haas, Saul Leiter, Harry Callahan, and Roman Vishniac, few of the photographers were known in New York. I had hoped to discover some unrecognized genius, but between the number of slides—far too many to view in one sitting—and my worry over Steichen, the presentation ended in a kaleidoscopic blur.

Steichen made a faltering attempt at some closing remarks, and it was obvious that the evening had been a great strain. His voice kept drifting off, and it was hard to tell with each new pause, whether or not he was through. It was only when he turned and started walking off the stage that we knew it was time to applaud.

Outside the museum, people gathered in groups. Was Steichen failing? Wasn't it time he retired? Who would replace him when he left?

The speculation continued at Limelight night after night, and not having heard from Steichen for several weeks, I called. He wasn't in his office, but on speaking with Kathleen Haven, I learned what happened. Steichen's wife had taken a turn for the worse. He wanted to cancel the lecture, but the museum preferred it be held. While he was talking, she was rapidly sinking. She died the next day.

ELIOT PORTER and Ellen Auerbach were a most unlikely pair. They had both exhibited at Limelight, Eliot in a one-person show in 1955, and Ellen in the group show *Fourteen Photographers* that same year. Eliot lived in Santa Fe, Ellen in New York, and it was not until I saw a body of work they had done together on a five-month sojourn in Mexico that I realized they were friends. Or, as it appeared, more than friends.

Eliot had made a previous trip to Mexico a couple of years earlier, accompanied by his wife Aline and their friend Georgia O'Keeffe. He became fascinated with Mexican church art, intrigued with its blending of Spanish and Indian cultures and charmed by the decorative touches in the small village churches, fashioned by the peasants themselves. Most of these churches had never been photographed, certainly never in color. What he and Ellen Auerbach planned to do when they left for Mexico in the fall of 1956 was photograph the interiors before the inevitable process of modernization began. It was only a matter of time before the churches would be stripped of their garlands of paper flowers, the hand-carved wooden statues replaced with plastic saints, and the candles with neon lights. They traveled 10,000 miles, by car, train, bus, and plane, photographing markets, pyramids, temples, and ruins, and hundreds of churches. They spent minutes in some, hours in others, often in light so dim their light meters didn't register. Yet they refused to use flash or artificial light, and relied on long exposures, trusting to luck. Getting permission to photograph was often a problem, and once it

Eliot Porter (picking up Ellen Auerbach for the trip to Mexico),
copyright © by Ellen Auerbach, 1956.

was obtained, it was hard to dissuade the astonished villagers who, in their eagerness to please, kept rearranging the interiors.

On their return, Eliot closeted himself in the darkroom, making his own separation negatives and dye transfer prints. From three thousand slides, they selected eighty-five, just enough for a nice-sized show. Fifty were of churches, the altars, niches, crucifixes and statues, including one of the infant Jesus in a homemade baby's dress. The rest were street scenes, marketplaces mostly, and since I intended to exhibit both groups of pictures, I decided to use a thematic umbrella and call the exhibition *Madonnas and Marketplaces.*

They insisted that it be presented as a collaborative effort, neither offering a clue as to who did what. It seemed the work of a single eye, and I was amazed that two people so completely unlike, both in temperament and in photographic style, could create so cohesive a body of work.

Professionally, they were worlds apart. Eliot Porter was well known, despite a late start. He had prepared for a career in science, but in 1931, after Stieglitz showed interest and held an exhibition of his work at An American Place, he gave up teaching microbiology at Harvard and devoted himself to photography. Nature was a passion, and having been blessed with independent means, he was free to spend his days in the woods, observing nature through a lens. He would set up a tripod, focus on a bird's nest, and wait hours, if not days, for the eggs to hatch and the mother to feed her young.

Ellen Auerbach had an early start. She was only twenty-four when she and Grete Stern opened "foto ringl + pit," a studio in Frankfurt famous for its innovative approach to commercial photography, inspired by the Bauhaus aesthetic. The studio closed when Hitler rose to power, and though she'd been in America since the mid-1930s, she had never succeeded in establishing herself. She photographed paintings for a living and did her personal work on the side. She met Eliot while photographing the work of his brother, Fairfield Porter, at the Porter's summer home in Maine.

Seeing the two together, I was struck by how unalike they were. Eliot was reserved and seemed cold. He had a handsome, boyish face and a slim athletic build, but his steel-rimmed spectacles and thin, tight lips gave him a stern, straight-laced look. Ellen was the warmer, more outgoing of the two. She was strong-willed and independent, with a sly, caustic wit. She was very plain, with a beaked nose and gray-brown hair, hardly what you'd think of as the "other woman."

They were as circumspect about their relationship as they were about their work and made every effort to appear less involved. I was curious, of course, but what interested me more than their personal lives were their methods of working together. And since photographers were bound to ask questions, I prepared by asking a few myself.

How did you decide what to photograph?

Eliot was vague. They didn't decide, he said, it just "happened."

So it "happened," and then what? How did you go about composing a picture? Did you agree on the vantage point? The composition? Or did you each take a picture and then decide which to use? Ellen glanced at Eliot, but he continued to look vague and answer in riddles. Getting nowhere, I finally gave up. As the Chinese would say, it was like trying to grasp a cloud.

But when it came to the installation he was not at all vague, though it was Ellen who did most of the talking. They objected to the white walls, claiming the contrast destroyed the subtlety of the colors. And since the prints were trimmed flush and were to be shown without mats, they preferred a background of some soft, neutral color. I offered to paint the panels a pale shade of gray. But Ellen had other ideas. "How about covering the panels with unbleached linen?"

An interesting idea, but I was not about to go shopping for fabric, and take on extra work. I still had my hands full with Mischa. But when they offered to buy the cloth and do all the work, I agreed. And having gone this far, I also agreed to their hanging the prints.

They took measurements of the panels, made copious notes, and two days before the opening arrived in a van, carrying tools, photographs, and several bolts of cloth. They spread out a diagram, arranged the prints in neat piles, and immediately began stapling the cloth to the panels. I was impressed with their efficiency and at how effortlessly they worked. Their movements were synchronized, almost like dance.

My only misgiving was the cloth. Instead of unbleached linen, they'd purchased four different colors—sea-green, rust, beige, and gray. They had spent two weeks laying out the show on the floor of Ellen's apartment, trying each print against each color. And since no one color suited them all, they decided to cover each panel with another color cloth and group the prints accordingly. I was horrified. It sounded like something an interior decorator would dream up.

"Don't worry," Ellen said, "It will look wonderful."

I had my doubts, but it was too late now. I went home, had dinner with Li-lan, and returned later that night, prepared for I didn't know what. But my misgivings vanished the moment I walked in. The gallery was transformed. The linen absorbed the glare of the lights, and the prints looked gem-like against the colors of the cloth. They had created an environment in keeping with the work—it was no longer a gallery but a sanctuary.

"I'm an atheist," one person said, "and though I hate to admit it, seeing this show has been the closest I've come to a religious experience." And another, as he handed me a fifty-dollar check, "I wish I could afford to buy more than one. If I were rich, I'd buy the whole show and install it in my apartment just as it is."

Lew Parrella reviewed the exhibition for the *Village Voice*, taking note of the historical importance of the project. He would have preferred the white walls and a better arrangement of prints, but he spoke glowingly of the work itself.

> There are far too many photographs here to consume fully in one visit; it is almost impossible to fall under their inevitable spell during the Saturday-night din of the adjoining cafe. But it is worth making a few visits (preferably around 7 or 8 o'clock, week nights) because the pleasure, the charm, and the enlightenment to be derived is far more rewarding and satisfying than that sock-in-the-eye treatment we get all too often from photography's brickbat arena.

He judged that the show contained "more than a dozen masterpieces," but rather than list them, he urged the readers to go seek them out for themselves.

Deschin differed with Lew on the installation. He found the photographs "arranged with excellent taste and in appropriate groupings against cloth backgrounds of harmonious color, each serving, though unobtrusively, as a unifying element in the hanging plan." He made much of the fact that Eliot Porter made his own prints, but his praise was reserved for the images themselves and concluded, saying, "The show is one of the most remarkable in the gallery's history, setting a new high standard for the exhibits that will follow."

I saw little of the two during the weeks of the show. Before returning to New Mexico (and married life), Eliot dropped by and gave me a book. "Maybe this will give you some idea of how Ellen and I worked. We didn't aim for the target; the target came to us." It was Eugene Herrigl's *Zen and the Art of Archery*, and I understood now why he talked in riddles.

What little I knew about Zen, I had learned from Yun. I remembered his saying it couldn't be learned from books, that it had to be experienced, and that meditation helped. Nevertheless, I was glad to have the book. Though it brought me no closer to understanding Zen or fathoming "the sound of one hand clapping," it was a lovely memento of a very special show.

AFTER *Madonnas and Marketplaces*, the Elliott Erwitt exhibition was a turnabout, a tweaking of the funnybone, rather than balm for the soul. Elliott was one of the few photographers whose pictures were funny. Occasionally I saw pictures that made me chuckle—the French, particularly, had warmth and wit—but there were few, other than Elliott's, that made me laugh out loud.

Elliott was associated with the cooperative photo agency Magnum, but his humor was reserved for his personal work. Most of these "snaps," as he called them, had been taken on the side while working on assignment in various parts of the world. He carried a camera wherever he went, always on the alert for the absurdities and incongruities of everyday life. Elliott had a sly smile and dark, narrow eyes, and he always seemed to be looking around the bend, eyes twinkling in anticipation of some unexpected event. No dog went by without scrutiny, and they were appearing more and more often in his pictures. He was as obsessed with dogs as with marriage and children—two wives and three kids at last count.

Most found his photographs funny and emerged from the gallery grinning. Some objected to his humor, unable to reconcile it with the sensitivity evidenced in his commercial reportage. They might also have expected more sentimental images, much like the one of his wife and newborn in *The Family of Man*.

Deschin dismissed the exhibition with a short, terse review. He found many of the photographs in questionable taste, and out of the entire fifty, only two or three that revealed "the Erwitt of the legend." He saw Elliott "at his weakest" and wrote in dismay, "To those who have seen Mr. Erwitt's pictures in a kinder, more perceptive light, these come as a shock and disappointment."

In an article in the *Village Voice* headed, "Elliott Erwitt, and the Unbitter Sense of Humor," George Wright responded to those who felt that "Erwitt had fumbled the torch and may even be invited to turn in his card as a sensitive and dedicated artist unless he is prepared to mend his ways and wipe the grin off his face." Unlike Deschin, he found some thirty successful. He saw nothing malicious and a great deal that was penetrating, and commended Erwitt for his depth of understanding and strong opinions about contemporary life.

George spoke of how difficult it was to express humor in any medium, much less photography, and also about how differently photographs were perceived today. "I invite the critics to observe that it would have been almost completely impossible a generation ago for photographs such as these to have been taken at all, let alone be assimilated by the audience, even one as determinedly sophisticated as Limelight's clientele. Photographers are not only discovering the dense net of inter-relationships between persons and the environment and between men and their fellows, they are visually educating an audience to understand the world a little better and to see for themselves. All of us have different eyes now than our grandfathers had."

As I saw it, humor was not taken seriously. Humor was seen as little more than entertainment. Elliott's photographs were indeed entertaining: how could one not be amused by those wonderful mutts with their hangdog expressions? Yet many of his pictures went beyond belly laughs, and made more far-reaching statements. His photograph of a black man drinking water from a sink a few feet away from a fountain labeled "Whites" was more effective than a polemic on segregation.

There was one picture though that I did find offensive and had considered leaving it out. It showed an elderly woman in Nicaragua positioned in such a way that the two melons in the foreground could be construed as breasts. Occasionally, I dropped a picture when hanging a show, but only when I thought it didn't measure up. (To spare the photographer's feelings, I blamed lack of space.) But I had never excluded a picture because of content and was not about to act as a censor now.

A CARD FROM Robert Frank. He regretted not seeing me before leaving for Europe—not that we saw very much of each other these days, his having received a second Guggenheim—but he gave no reason for this trip abroad. Not until he returned did I hear the good news. Robert Delpire had agreed to publish a book of his photographs based on his trip around the country: Les Americains.

Still smarting from his failure to interest publishers here, Robert announced the news with a triumphant smile. Things were looking up. He was beginning to take on occasional assignments; on one of his last trips, he'd photographed the inauguration of Dwight Eisenhower and Richard Nixon. He and Mary had moved to a new loft, on Third Avenue near 10th Street (an area bordering on what was later called the East Village) where they were surrounded by painters. Alfred Leslie lived next door (he'd had his fill of Hoboken and was back among his cronies at the Cedar Bar), and Willem de Kooning lived across the backyard. Robert could look through the window and see de Kooning paint or, more often than not, watch him pace the floor between attacks on the canvas.

Mary was in her element. She had decided to become a sculptor. At first I was skeptical—how with two small children could she find time to work? I was pleasantly surprised when on visiting them one day, I saw a number of plaster figurines lined up on a work table on the side of the room. They were figures of women, earthy yet ethereal, like Mary herself, and so fresh and spontaneous, they could have been tossed in the air and taken shape by themselves. Mary kept gazing at her work as we sat and talked, oblivious even to the cries of the children, and I felt like an intruder, interrupting her reverie.

Nowhere did I see a single photograph, nor did Robert ever mention his work. But he did say something about wanting to make a film. Rudy Burckhardt had lent him a camera, and he was more fascinated with the prospect every day. Was he, like Mary, on to something new?

GENE SMITH dropped in one night as we were about to close and invited me out for a drink. I went reluctantly, not wanting a repeat of his "suicide" performance, but this, at last, was the chance I'd been waiting for. We went to the Short Stop, a bar grungy enough to meet with his approval, and I was relieved to find him in a very good mood.

Smith's fortunes had changed now that he was no longer with *Life*. The break had come over the Schweitzer story, an assignment he considered the high point of his career. He'd spent months in Lambarene, photographing the doctor in his medical compound, and on returning to New York (late as usual), he buried himself in the darkroom, emerging weeks later with hundreds of prints. (Smith never felt satisfied unless he worked till he dropped.) But they were not what the editors wanted. Instead of concentrating on Dr. Schweitzer (who'd been awarded the Nobel Peace Prize the previous year), Smith had spent as much time, or more, photographing the patients, the villagers, and the animals, all in the name of what he considered "truth." Smith suggested they run a special issue or, if not one, then two. Meanwhile, *Look* scooped *Life* with a story on Schweitzer, and by the time "A Man of Mercy" was published in *Life* (in 1954, with twenty-five reproductions), Smith had already resigned.

He'd won the freedom he yearned for, but now he was paying the price. He lost not only a nationwide audience, but financial security as well. A Guggenheim helped—Smith was the first photographer to be awarded two —but it was hardly enough to support a wife and four children. And now there was a fifth. Margery Lewis, a young woman he'd been "seeing" (an affair known to everyone except his wife), had given birth to a son. She had moved to Philadelphia, escaping the onus of an out-of-wedlock birth, and managed somehow to fend for herself. Between working on the Pittsburgh story and visiting his new son, he was seldom in New York. Never knowing when he'd reappear, I asked about a show the minute we sat down.

"Oh yes, a show," he said. "How about October?"

I agreed, even though October was just weeks away. I also agreed to his hanging the show, the one condition he imposed. Smith had a theory about hanging shows, which was somehow related to music. "It's like this," he said, waving his arms as though wielding a baton. "Each photograph strikes a certain note and when you hang a group of them together, they strike a certain chord. It's like composing a symphony. You develop allegros, andantes, crescendos, just like on a musical score. The music rises and falls, and as people walk through the exhibition they experience the same swells of emotion, just like they were listening to Beethoven or Bach."

It sounded a bit strange, and as October approached, I grew increasingly apprehensive. It wasn't only Smith's theory that was worrying me now but whether he'd arrive on time. Or whether he would arrive at all. The whole world of photography seemed to be waiting for this show, Smith's first major exhibition in over ten years.

The day before he was due, I took down *Lyrical and Accurate*, an exhibition on loan from George Eastman House, and gave the gallery a fresh coat of paint. This had not been a popular show, and I could almost hear the sighs of relief when customers looked in and saw me packing the crates. Minor White had designed the show, trying to make a point. What he intended to do by drawing on the work of photographers as removed in time and diverse in style as Peter Henry Emerson, Eugene Atget, Alfred Stieglitz, Walter Rosenblum, and W. Eugene Smith, was to redefine the terms "pure photography" and "straight photography." He had hoped to create controversy, but none developed. Not everyone shared Minor's passion for ideas.

Smith surprised me. He arrived at midnight, only four hours late, and I was glad that he'd brought along help. Trailing behind him carrying several large cases were his assistant, Jim Karales, and an attractive young woman Jim introduced as "Ellie, my new bride." They planned to work straight through till morning, allowing Smith enough time to catch some sleep before the opening that night at six.

I resisted going into the gallery, having learned from past experience that the way to avoid Smith's problems was to avoid Smith. I showed them around the kitchen in case they got hungry, and left. I looked forward to soaking in the tub, catching up on reading, and attending to some long-neglected beauty rituals, on this, my one night of freedom.

It was one o'clock, and I was creaming my face when the phone rang. "It's me, Gene Smith. We've run into a snag. We left some important photographs back at the house. But don't worry, Jim's driving there to get them. It'll give me time to think." Croton-on-Hudson was fifty miles away.

I finished my face and went on to a book. Half an hour later the phone rang. "It's me, Gene Smith. Do you happen to have any booze in the house? I need something to keep me going."

I offered to bring what was left of my liquor supply—some vodka, scotch, a jigger or two of rye—enough to keep him going but not enough to get him drunk. I filled a shopping bag, threw a coat over my nightgown, and hurried across the street. Smith was sitting on the gallery floor, surrounded by photographs. So far, he'd hung only three.

"Don't worry," he said, catching me eyeing the empty walls. "As soon as Jim and Ellie return, we'll start rolling along."

I was back in bed and had just dozed off when the phone rang. "It's me, Gene Smith. They're back and we're ready to start work. By the way, where do you keep the ketchup?" I directed him to the ketchup, the mustard, and the mayonnaise. There was soy sauce, too, if he wished.

I was still tossing about when the phone rang. "It's me, Gene Smith. I've got to catch some shut-eye. Do you happen to have a cot?"

I did have a camp cot, but it would take time to dig out. It was stored in an upper closet in Li-lan's room, along with a tent and her gear for summer camp. Balancing on a ladder, I lowered the tent and a tarpaulin and was reaching for the cot when an axe went clattering to the floor. Li-lan woke with a start. "*What* are you doing with my axe, Mom?"

"It's that damned Gene Smith," I muttered, too tired to explain. Li-lan took it in stride; she'd grown accustomed to strange goings-on.

Seventh Avenue South was deserted except for the newsdealer on Sheridan Square. He waved, surprised to see me at six in the morning; I rarely emerged before noon. Smith was sitting where I'd left him—on the gallery floor. But now there were many more photographs—two hundred, maybe, or more.

"Where are Jim and Ellie?" I asked.

"They left," Smith grumbled. "Off on their honeymoon, I guess."

The three photographs had been taken down and five others hung in their place. They were arranged on the wall in a kind of spiral design, like notes on a musical score. I had expected a symphony; this was hardly a tune.

I set up the cot, Smith stretched out, and before I could remind him that the opening was at six, he'd fallen asleep.

At noon I went back to check on his progress, but he was still snoring away on the cot. I barricaded the gallery with a stack of chairs, draped a curtain across the entrance, and tacked up a sign: "Smith exhibition postponed until tomorrow."

"Aren't you being optimistic?" Deschin asked when he came early to review the show. "Do you *really* think Gene will be finished by tomorrow?"

"Of course, he will. All he needs is another night."

Exactly at six the crowd arrived. I had doubled the number of invitations, and the exhibition had been announced in Deschin's column in the *Times*. Some looked annoyed, others perplexed, but the photographers were hardly surprised. Not easily put off, they parted the curtain and peered inside. There was Smith, asleep on the cot, and scattered all over the gallery floor were photographs, coffee cups, beer cans, and half-eaten pieces of strudel.

At midnight he emerged. "What day is it?" he said, rubbing his eyes. Controlling myself as best I could, I told him that hundreds of people had been turned away and that this would be the first time a Limelight show opened late.

"Don't worry," he said. "I'll finish tonight. But I'll need something to keep me going." Benzedrine headed the list. The liquor was no problem, but the benzedrine was. "Try Times Square," Smith advised. "Just slip a clerk a five-spot and he'll give you a couple of bennies."

That night, in a sleazy all-night drugstore, I negotiated my first under-the-counter deal. "I guess you need this stuff, Miss," the clerk said, "but don't come back for no more."

The next night I searched out a clerk in another store. Smith had added sleeping pills to his list, and this complicated things even more. Two days later, he added a razor, shaving cream, and double-edged blades.

Progress was slow. Smith always seemed to be striking the wrong note. He hung a new group of photographs every night, taking down those from the night before. And every night a crowd showed up, only to be turned away. But Smith was enjoying his role as artist-in-residence, and it looked like he'd never leave.

Smith's wife, Carmen, had been phoning all week, and all week I'd been explaining, "Gene's working. . . . Gene's sleeping. . . . Gene's almost done. . . ." After six days of this, she finally blew. "What the devil are you running down there, a gallery or a rooming house? Tell Gene he's got to come home!"

To make matters worse, I'd made my usual pilgrimage up to Times Square and came back empty-handed. "I guess it's about time I got going," Smith said.

"But what about the exhibition?"

"Don't worry," he said. "I'll be back in a couple of days."

The minute he left, I took down the fifteen prints he'd hung on the wall and started over. I kept the installation simple—just sixty photographs in single, formal rows. It wasn't exactly a symphony, but it was a resoundingly beautiful show.

LISETTE HAD become my ally. I had been trying, without success, to get Berenice Abbott to exhibit, but each time I asked, she refused. "No one cares about my work anymore. People think I'm old hat."

"What do you mean, old hat?" Lisette snapped. I had gone to their table to say hello, and it was Lisette herself who raised the question of a show. "No great photographer is ever old hat! And besides, Berenice, you might make some money."

"*Money?*" Berenice was always in need of money, or so she said every time we talked. Teaching at the New School was hardly a living, and whatever she made on her scientific photography, she funneled back into the work. As a documentary photographer, she was out of the swim; photojournalists were the ones in demand.

Much of what she said was true. Berenice was admired for her work in the past, particularly *Changing New York*, a project she began in the 1930s and completed under the auspices of the WPA. Inspired by Atget, she'd trudged through the streets with a large view camera, recording the changes in the city. New York had been photographed by everyone—there was hardly a photographer who hadn't at some point trained a camera on our skyscrapers. But had any produced an image as enduring as *Exchange Place*, her timeless picture of the canyon of Wall Street? Or the glittering panorama of *New York at Night?*

Berenice was also admired for her technical expertise. Unlike Lisette, whose distaste for things mechanical was all too well known, she enjoyed tinkering with equipment, always looking for ways to improve things. She accused manufacturers of producing "antiquated" equipment, and in a talk at the Village Camera Club in 1952, charged them with being behind the times, back in the "model-T stage." She also lashed out at the photography establishment—publishers, editors, and museum directors—for their neglect of serious work. In calling the serious photographer the "forgotten man," she may have been talking about herself.

I liked her feistiness and looked forward to seeing more of her, now that she had agreed to exhibit. At Lisette's urging, we made an appointment for the following day, allowing plenty of time to look at the work.

Berenice was her usual charming, languid self, but today she was slower than ever. She kept on talking about other things. She had developed a few ideas that she believed would make money and thought I would want to know about them. One was a way of hanging pictures without the use of nails. She showed me a piece of some rubbery stuff. "This solves the problem of holes in the wall. You put a strip of this material on the back of the frame, press it against the wall, and voilá—it holds." It was a wonderful idea and certainly saleable (a similar product appeared on the market years later); I made the mistake of telling her so.

Berenice perked up. "How about becoming my agent? If you can find a company to produce it, we can both make a fortune."

I told her I was trying to run a gallery and had no time for anything else. But Berenice was not easily dissuaded. She left the room and returned with a jacket she had designed for photographers. It had some twenty pockets for carrying small items—cigarettes, keys, extra rolls of film. Another good idea, but not for me. Next she showed me a tripod she'd developed. Whatever its features, they were lost on me, as were her experiments to reduce the silver content in film. It was hard to convince her that salesmanship was not my forte.

"If you can sell photographs, you can sell anything," she said.

Not wanting to mislead her, I thought she should know that except for an occasional flurry, the sale of a photograph was still an event. The Atgets were an exception. Despite all the attention given the gallery in the past three years—the attendance, the reviews, the increasing interest of the public in creative photography—collecting was not even in its infancy. It was more like a fetus waiting to be born.

Giving up on me as an agent, Berenice got around to the show. She brought out a portfolio of recent work, taken along Route 1 while driving from Maine to Florida. I was not impressed. But how do you tell a photographer—a *great* one, no less—that the work was not up to par? Never having encountered this problem, I was at a loss.

I tried to get around it by telling her that I had my heart set on her New York work, but she was adamant about Route 1. "Otherwise people will think I've given up. Or that I'm dead." It was sad, hearing her talk this way, and for a moment I wished that Lisette were here. We had reached an impasse and the show was in doubt. Then I remembered her portrait of James Joyce and asked to buy it. I loved the portrait (as well as Joyce), and if all else failed, at least I'd come away with the picture.

She climbed on a stepladder and lowered a box from an upper shelf. Out of it came not only James Joyce, but his daughter Lucia (before she went mad) and several other portraits I'd never seen before. She started to identify them. "André Gide, Jean Cocteau, Marie Laurencin. . . ."

"These are marvelous!" I said. "How about making it a portrait show?"

"But I did these back in the 1920s. People will think I'm ancient."

"But think of how interested everyone will be, seeing all these great names together."

"Hmmm." Berenice sat down and considered the idea. "Do you think it would lead to portrait commissions?"

I couldn't promise but thought it worth a try.

She picked up the ladder, left the room, and returned with another box. Out of this one came others—Djuna Barnes, François Mauriac, Princess Eugène Murat, and a touching portrait of Eugène Atget, taken shortly before he died. I counted thirty-five, enough for a show.

But Berenice wasn't through. She left the room again and came back with yet another box. Out came two portraits of smiling G.I.'s, the kind taken in department stores during World War II. "These are the ones that will get me commissions," she said.

I didn't argue. Getting Berenice to exhibit had been difficult enough, and

I was not going to risk her backing out now. But I had no intention of including the G.I.'s, and to make sure she wouldn't insist on slipping them in, I titled the exhibition *Portraits of the Twenties* and immediately sent out press releases.

After mounting the show, I braced myself for a scene with Berenice. It never happened. She was pleased with the exhibition, pleased with the review, and pleased with the reaction of the public to her work. Not once did she allude to the missing G.I.'s. She was disappointed, of course, that there were no sales, except for the James Joyce — to me.

MY FREEDOM fighter hadn't worked out. Mischa was no more effective as a manager than the day he started; the only change was in his girth. He'd consumed a mountain of strudel over the past eight months and gained at least twenty pounds. Whatever experience he may have had in coffeehouses in Budapest was probably as a customer, I concluded, not a manager. I had to make a change.

I mentioned this to Lathrop, the scion of a wealthy New York restaurant clan, who had been dropping in for the past six months. His family owned several tearoom-type operations, and he'd been regaling me with his experiences managing one of their Upper East Side locations. I thought he might have some leads. But he was out of touch, having embarked on a career as a photographer's agent. However, he proposed an idea. "Let Mischa go, and I'll run the place until you find the right person. I like Limelight, and I want to help."

"Won't that interfere with your work as an agent?"

"Not at all. My time is my own. I can run around Madison Avenue and see clients during the day, and still put in a full night here. Let's take a look at your kitchen."

Eyeing our latest Bowery recruit, he decided we needed a dishwashing machine. I told him I couldn't afford one. "Don't worry. I'll get you one and it won't cost a cent. The dishwashing machines in my family's restaurants are replaced regularly, even when they're in good condition. The next time one's available, I'll see that you get it."

Lathrop also suggested making changes in the menu. He asked his brother, Marshall, the head of the family firm, to come look it over. But we waited until Fong left on his mid-winter vacation, knowing he'd resist any change. The first thing to go was my rose petal sundae, a concoction I created after reading a book on flower cookery. It was popular with couples but not with the kitchen men. Less romantically inclined, they groaned each time they got an order. They had to chop up a rose, blend the petals with whipped cream, and if they ran short of roses and Aphrodite's was closed, they had to run around the Village and find another florist. Marshall offered to return and study the operation as a whole, but I held him off, not knowing what these suggestions might be. The waitresses in his restaurants wore frilly white aprons and organdy caps, a far cry from Limelight's black stockings and blue denim skirts.

The day Lathrop started work I came down with the flu, and though I would have liked to be on hand to help ease the transition, I couldn't pull myself out of bed or even talk on the phone. But to stay in touch, and to check the receipts, I arranged for Clarence to pick up the deposit slips at the bank each morning and drop them in my mailbox.

The first few nights the receipts were as usual, but toward the end of the week they climbed. On the weekend, they climbed even higher, unusual for a cold week in January. The following week the receipts rose still higher, and while I would have liked to see what Lathrop was doing to have increased the take by almost a third, I decided not to make my usual mistake and get out of bed too soon.

The flu hung on, and on my ninth day in bed, Sonya called. Lathrop hadn't shown up, and it was almost six. The help was standing out front in the cold. I sent Li-lan over with a key.

Was Lathrop ill? Had the subway stalled? I phoned several times and when he hadn't arrived by ten, I was afraid something awful had happened. "I doubt it," Sonya said, the next time I called. "As soon as you're feeling better, we've got to have a talk."

Rather than wait, I got up the next morning and dragged across the street. I put the key in the door, and as I stepped into the vestibule I heard an explosion and felt the building shake under my feet. A cloud of black smoke billowed from the back, and walking toward me through the smoke came Clarence, his woolly gray hair covered with soot.

"It's the furnace, Miss Gee. It's been out of order all week."

"*All week?* Why didn't someone call the repair man?"

"Mr. Lathrop wouldn't like that. He said he could fix it himself."

"The photographs!" I ran to the back. The gallery had been spared, but everything in the kitchen was covered with soot. Even the cat, cowering under the sink, looked a deeper shade of gray. I called the emergency service, and, while the furnace was being repaired, I telephoned the staff. Those I reached came to help. Lathrop didn't appear, but if he had, they would have dropped their mops and left. Two part-time waitresses had already quit, and the others had simply been biding their time, waiting for me to return.

Lathrop, it turned out, was a martinet. He was demanding and abusive, and I listened in disbelief as they told me what happened. He'd come to work only a few hours each night and had failed to order provisions. By the end of the week they had nothing to serve except coffee and tea.

"Why in the world didn't you call me?" I said.

"Lathrop told us you were critically ill and he warned us not to disturb you," Sonya said. "He made it sound like you were on your death bed. And on top of all this we were freezing. Lathrop kept tinkering with the furnace, and we had no heat for a week. The only customers who came were the diehards, and they sat around in their mufflers and overcoats. Some of them drank coffee with their gloves on."

"That's impossible," I said. "The receipts . . ."

I went to the desk, opened the cash drawer, but all I found were a few dollars in change. But stuffed in the back were several notices from the bank together with bounced checks. Then I realized what Lathrop had done. To increase the receipts, while dipping into the till, he'd inflated the figures and added checks of his own. And these were the ones that had bounced.

I picked up the phone and called Marshall. "Your brother Lathrop has wrecked my place! I've lost money, I've lost customers. . . ."

"I'll come right down. I'm sure we can straighten this out," he said, and in no time at all he was at the door. "I guess I should have known. It's not the first time I've had to pull Lathrop out of a scrape. But I assure you, it's the last."

"So he's been in trouble before?"

"Lathrop is erratic. That's why we never let him work in any of our restaurants."

"Then why did you encourage him to work for me? Why did you come here and offer advice?"

"I thought that Limelight was Lathrop's last chance. He's never succeeded at anything he's tried, and I thought this would be a fresh start."

"At my expense . . ."

Marshall offered to make up the losses. After checking the receipts of the previous year, I gave him a figure reflecting the difference. He whipped out his wallet and paid me in cash, relieved no doubt by the modesty of my claim and for not turning this into a cause célèbre; Limelight might have made Winchell's column again.

"You were right about Lathrop," I told Li-lan that night. "He *is* crazy." She was interested in graphology, and after buying her a book on the subject for Christmas, I'd gone around Limelight collecting samples of handwriting. Her analysis of character was amazingly accurate, but I dismissed it when she said, "That man Lathrop, he's crazy."

I continued my quest for a manager, collecting references and samples of handwriting too.

"QUICK, open up! It's me!" I recognized the voice. It was Vinnie.

Still half-asleep, I threw on a kimono and opened the door. Vinnie flew in and raced down the hall, Tony and Caesar behind him. Halfway to the living room, Tony stopped and ducked into the bathroom. I heard him flushing the toilet, over and over, and when he emerged, he was mopping his brow. "Whew, that was a close call. Lucky you was home."

The raid had come without warning. There hadn't been the usual tip-off, and he'd had no time to dispose of the receipts. Vinnie posted himself at the window and peered through the curtains; Caesar paced around the living room, jaw clenched tight; and Tony plopped down on the sofa, his face a dark scowl.

Penny gave a few welcoming yaps, then ran to the door, sniffing and barking. "Can't you get your mutt to shut up?" Tony hissed. I tiptoed down the hall, dragged her to the bathroom and locked her in. My heart was pounding, and I was beginning to shake. What if the cops broke down the door? Would I be jailed as an accomplice?

"Don't worry," Tony whispered. "They need a search warrant to get in, and anyway, they ain't got no evidence. I flushed the slips down the toilet."

What the cops *would* find, besides three bookies, was one terrified female in a faded kimono, trembling uncontrollably. Wasn't that evidence enough?

Tony tapped my arm. "You got any beer?"

Beer? How could he think of beer with cops in the hall, and for all I knew, about to break in? I went to the kitchen and brought out a six-pack.

Caesar refused. "I don't drink, not even beer."

"You don't drink, you don't smoke, you don't do nothin,'" Vinnie muttered.

Caesar stopped pacing and glared at Vinnie. "I'm a family man. I got a good wife and a good son."

"We're all family men," Vinnie said. "But that don't mean you can't have some fun."

"Shut up, you guys," Tony growled. "Can't you wait till the cops go?"

I was sorry that I'd thrown out the Miltowns. They were prescribed by a doctor when I was giving up smoking, but I preferred the jitters to a dull vegetable state. I could use them now.

Vinnie kept checking the windows, and after what seemed like hours, the police cars drove off. But Tony was taking no chances though. "Let's wait a while, I wanna make sure they're gone."

Finally, Vinnie tiptoed to the door and crept downstairs. "Okay!" he yelled, and Caesar and Tony got up and left.

I put the chain on the door and took off my kimono. It was drenched in sweat.

I WAS AT Limelight talking to Charles Rado, the New York representative of the French photo agency, Rapho-Guillumette, when Tony appeared at the door. He could not have arrived at a more inappropriate time. I was talking to Rado about a Brassaï show, which I was planning to put on next year. Tony had never shown up at Limelight before, and I was afraid he was bringing bad news. There hadn't been a raid for several weeks, and I dreaded that another was due.

Tony marched over, so I had no choice except to introduce them. Tony grunted. Rado, a courtly Hungarian with impeccable manners, made a futile attempt at conversation. He was frail and hypersensitive and had a facial tic. I could tell from the way he was twitching that he was uneasy and wanted to go. He took my hand and brought it to his lips, a gesture, though gallant, that I always found embarrassing.

Tony looked glum. "I gotta talk to you. But not in here. Let's go to Jack Delaney's."

He ordered two beers and came right to the point. "I got a proposition, and I think you're gonna like it. How about opening another coffeehouse?"

"Why would I want to do that?" I said. "My hands are full just running one. I'm still trying to find a good manager."

"Stick with us, and you got no more problems. We'll rent a nice place, get you a good manager, and with me as a partner, you won't need to worry about nothin'."

"You're joking," I said, but I knew he was not. This *was* bad news. I'd heard about Mafia "partnerships." First you were approached with what looked on the surface like an attractive offer. If you showed no interest, you were encouraged to "cooperate," either with a brick through the window, a broken arm, or worse. After you agreed—one had no choice—your "partners" would stay in the background, and in the eyes of the clientele, nothing had changed. But gradually they took over and you were eased out the door.

But what would Tony want with a coffeehouse? What would he want with a place where people sat all night and the average bill was a dollar and a half?

"Limelight doesn't make any money," I said. "I opened it because of the gallery."

"That's okay. You can hang on to Limelight if you want. You'll have a second joint, and you can hang pitchers on the wall there, too. You see, things are kind of tight. I don't how long we can hold out in the hall, and besides there ain't no telephone there. We need a place where we can work in the back."

Now it was clear—they wanted me as a front. "Thanks for the offer," I said. "I'll have to think about it for a couple of days."

"Let me know soon. We gotta make plans."

Tony left, and I trudged back to Limelight, feeling drained of all blood.

TONY APPROACHED me several more times about opening another place, but by playing the part of the indecisive female—a little scattered, a little daft—I managed to hold him at bay. In the meantime, I found a new manager, a young Norwegian named Pehr Danielson, and it looked as if he might work out. Now I was able to set Limelight's problems aside, and deal with this latest threat. The last time we met, Tony mentioned the Limelight lease, saying, "It ain't worth the paper its printed on." Legalities meant nothing when dealing with the mob. All Big Ben needed was a word from the Boys, and in thirty days I'd be out on the street with my tables and chairs — and photographs.

Mayor Wagner had appointed a new police commissioner, and according to Caesar, who kept feeding me information when Tony wasn't around, he was determined to crack the ring. The raids were now being conducted by a special squad from police headquarters, and Tony's payoffs ("two thousand bucks a month") no longer helped.

"Don't let nobody in your apartment," Tony warned, after a man who claimed to be from the phone company went roaming through the hall, a coil of cable wire dangling from his shoulder. "He ain't a repairman. He's a dick."

"But there is something wrong with my phone." I'd noticed some strange clicking sounds.

"Be careful what you talk about. Somebody could be listening."

"My telephone's being *tapped?*" I was horrified at the thought of surveillance, yet at the same time amused, thinking of what they would hear. Li-lan spent hours talking to her friends.

I hadn't told her of the trouble I was in. I had not, in fact, told *anyone*. Not Deschin, not Steichen, not even Kevin Sullivan, the man I'd been seeing for the past few months. And I certainly wouldn't tell Mr. Sheinfeld, knowing that he'd say, "Get rid of the place. It's been a headache from the start."

Tony said not to worry. "Play along with us and everything will be okay." But his assurances didn't help. I was caught in a snare and, short of giving up Limelight, saw no way of disentangling myself. Why, oh why, had I moved to the Village? And why, of all places, to 61 Grove Street?

One afternoon, as I was leaving the house, Vinnie pointed to two men walking across the street, one wearing a beret, the other an artist's smock (the kind that went out with Whistler). "Don't let them fool you. They ain't artists," he whispered. "They're cops."

I suggested to Tony that he shut down for a while and wait until the heat was off.

"What? And risk losing my business?" he said. "I got a nice neighborhood clientele, and once your customers start laying bets with other guys, they don't always come back. I built this business from scratch, and I ain't gonna take any chances losing it now."

"But aren't you taking chances running from the cops?"

"Nah, it's just a nuisance, that's all. So long as we can run up to your apartment and get rid of the goods, they can't pin nothin' on us. But there's one thing got me worried. What if you ain't home and we can't get in?"

"I'm always home during the day," I said.

"What if you're taking a shower and don't hear us knock? Gimme your key and we won't have no problems."

I had to think fast. "I'm sorry," I said. "I don't have an extra one."

"That's no problem. Just give me your key and I'll go have one made."

"On second thought, I may have another. I'll go upstairs and get it."

I rummaged through a drawer, found a key, brought it downstairs, and handed it to Tony.

"Thanks," he said. "You're a livin' doll."

But it wasn't the key to the apartment. I hoped he'd never find out.

I LIVED in fear of another raid. What if Tony discovered I'd given him the wrong key? What if he were caught while fumbling with the lock? I lay awake nights, visions of Mafia vengeance running through my mind: men encased in concrete and dumped in the river, men taken for rides and pumped full of bullets, men squashed like bugs in car-crushing machines. Being a woman made no difference; their code of honor applied only to their own.

I stayed home, ready to rush to the door at the first sign of a raid, and left the house only at night. The timing could not have been worse. I was assembling an exhibition for the *Village Voice* and was swamped with work. The *Voice* was sponsoring a photographic competition based on the theme "Greenwich Village—the Living Tradition," and I'd agreed to exhibit fifty or sixty of the more interesting entries. I'd been worried about the quality of the work and was annoyed with myself for having agreed to the show simply out of loyalty to my friends at the *Voice*. But as it turned out, I was not disappointed, thanks in large part to their fine choice of judges: Grace Mayer, Cora Wright, Mike Kinzer, and Irving Desfor, photo editor of the Associated Press. First prize was won by Kenneth Van Sickle, a young photographer and filmmaker, and the presentation of the awards—photographic equipment and photography books—was to be held at Limelight on a Sunday afternoon. The bookies weren't working, so I was free to attend.

I'd been housebound two weeks when the next raid took place, and I managed, luckily, to reach the door in time. Tony flew in, panting and puffing, but this time, barely made it to the bathroom. After flushing away the slips, he staggered into the living room and collapsed into a chair. His face was purple, and I quaked when I thought: What if he has a heart attack? Who would I summon—the *police?*

The cops pounded on the door, and I stood numb with fear, certain they were about to crash in. Penny kept yapping and running back and forth, and once again I had to grab her and lock her up. Tony stretched out on the couch and loosened his tie while Caesar and Vinnie looked on apprehensively. Caesar's hands were trembling, and even Vinnie, fat, easy-going Vinnie, seemed shaken. I regretted not having taken a resuscitation course, though in my present state, I could not have administered it even if I tried.

After the usual eternity, things quieted down. I tiptoed to the bathroom, let Penny out, and waited to see if she'd start barking again. But she was focusing her attention on Tony, sniffing at something interesting on his shoes. He had revived and was breathing more easily, but seemed in no hurry to leave.

"Vinnie, get away from those windows," Tony snapped. "Ain't we got trouble enough?"

"But I see a camera poking from those curtains in that apartment across the street."

"Shut up!" Tony growled. "You talk too much."

Cameras? Curtains? I turned to Tony, but he didn't respond, and after another half hour, they left.

I thought of Vinnie's remarks, and a couple days later when I caught him alone, I asked what he'd meant. Vinnie seemed to have developed a crush one me—he'd been asking me out for a couple of months—and I knew I could count on him.

"I'm not supposed to say nothin', so make sure you keep it under your hat," he said. "The cops are holed up in an apartment across the sheet, and they're taking pitchers of everybody who goes in and outa the house. Not just pitchers, but movies too."

"*Movies?*"

"Don't worry. Pitchers don't mean nothin.' You gotta be caught with the goods."

I left the house reluctantly that night, appalled at the thought of appearing in a film, co-starring with neighborhood bookies.

THIS DOUBLE LIFE was getting me down. I had developed a deceptively calm demeanor, and when I went weaving my way through Limelight every night, no one, not even Pehr Danielson, our new manager, had any inkling of what was going on. I'd arranged a few shows, but I was feeling overwhelmed, and I was afraid that 1958 would not be a good year.

It had started out fairly well. *Chim's Children*, a posthumous exhibition by David "Chim" Seymour, who had been killed while covering the Suez crisis in 1956, was a testament to his love of children and his concern for their plight in a war-torn world. He was known for his photographs of the Spanish Civil War and for his subsequent work with UNESCO documenting the effects of war on children throughout Europe. He was one of the founders of Magnum, and like Robert Capa, who had been killed in Indochina two years earlier, he was president of the agency when he died. A fitting tribute, the exhibition had originated at the Art Institute of Chicago, one of the few museums with a department of photography, which was established in 1945 by its curator, Peter Pollack. *Chim's Children* went beyond sentiment, striking a much deeper chord.

I'd also shown the work of an advertising photographer, Bert Stern. Madison Avenue was encouraging a more innovative approach, and Bert, its wunderkind, was known for his interpretive use of color. He'd made a splash with his striking Smirnoff Vodka ads (which helped replace gin in the ever-popular martini), and he'd won the Art Directors Award for three consecutive years. Bert Stern's attitude toward color was that anything goes — off-color, out-of-focus, overexposure — as long as it worked. Since the exhibition was to include both prints and transparencies, I left the installation to him. His assistants built light boxes for the display of the transparencies and painted the gallery charcoal gray. The effect was dramatic. But I wasn't pleased when at the end of the show they left without repainting the panels. It took three coats of white paint to cover the gray.

After Bert Stern, I showed *Rendville, USA*, James Karales's picture story of a small mining town in Ohio, unique for its integration policy. Karales, a young up-and-coming photojournalist (later on the staff of *Look*), had spent a summer in the town, getting to know the inhabitants. Like Eugene Smith, for whom he'd worked as an assistant for several years, he had to know his subject before taking a single shot. Rendville had incorporated right after the Civil War, its constitution providing for equal rule. The office of mayor rotated between blacks and whites, and other municipal offices were equally shared. This arrangement, buttressed by the moral authority of the local church, appeared to have worked. But the town was dying. The exhaustion of the mines had impoverished the inhabitants, and most were forced to leave. Those who remained were demoralized, yet despite the shabbiness and decay of their once proud town, the principles it embodied were still alive. Karales's documentation was both touching and timely. The Civil Rights movement was gaining strength in the South, and the town of Rendville, regardless of its plight, was a model that others might follow.

TONY CHASED after me as I was leaving the house. "We gotta talk. Let's go to the Short Stop."

More bad news? Tony ordered two beers, then started right in. "Business is lousy. You gotta help me out. I need five hundred bucks right away, and another hundred a week till I get on my feet."

I didn't have five hundred, and even if I had, I wasn't going to hand it to Tony. "I can't," I said. "I have a payroll to meet, and there's hardly anything left after the help is paid."

Tony persisted. "Look at it this way. It's a business expense, just like paying rent. Everybody in the Village pays somebody off. Why should you be any different?"

So far, I'd been lucky. Most restaurants and bars paid for "protection," but perhaps because of my relationship with the Boys, Limelight had been spared the weekly squeeze.

Tony looked grim, no longer the affable grandfather but a hood defending his turf. Playing the helpless female would no longer work. "It depends on how much money we take in on the weekend," I said, "I'll do the best I can."

"Make sure it's five hundred. I'll pick it up Sunday night, right after you close."

Money was short. Several small buildings around the corner were being razed to make way for an apartment house, and since Louis' and the Circle in the Square had occupied these buildings, with them went part of the after-theater trade. The theater was moving east, about ten blocks away, and other coffeehouses, like the popular Figaro and the Gaslight, were closer. The turnover of managers hadn't helped—I'd tried two others before hiring Pehr—and for the first time in years, the receipts were low.

I gave Pehr the night off, not wanting him to know about my problems with the Mafia. He was happy for the break, having been working since morning, preparing the dishes for our Sunday buffet, a sumptuous spread he'd recently introduced. Among the dishes, all beautifully arranged by Pehr himself were smoked salmon, quiche, chicken in aspic, salads, casseroles, and a variety of rich desserts. A food columnist referred to Pehr as a latent interior decorator and *artiste extraordinaire*.

After closing for the night, I tallied the receipts, trying to determine how much to give Tony. Rather than dip into the till and leave Pehr short, I decided to use the money I'd earned retouching transparencies for the latest issue of *McCall's* (the one account I'd kept after closing the studio). But all I could spare after paying my rent was two hundred and twenty-five dollars, less than half of what Tony demanded, and I hoped it would placate him until I was able to raise more.

Sitting alone in the dark, empty room, I brooded on my latest predicament. What if Tony kept raising the ante? How long could I go on before Limelight was forced to close? How many more exhibitions should I plan? But the real question was: How long could I go on leading this double life?

I heard a rap on the window, and looking up I saw Tim Sheehan, the cop on the beat. Surprised to see me sitting there alone, he knocked on the door and asked if I needed help. Tim looked drawn. He was grieving over the loss of his four-year-old son Michael, who had been swept into an open manhole during a flash flood in Queens. Everyone in the neighborhood loved and respected Tim, and I hated for him to see me consorting with the likes of Tony. I told him I was fine, just checking the books.

The longer I waited, the gloomier my thoughts. And when Tony hadn't arrived by three in the morning, I decided to go home, get some sleep, and slip him the money when I saw him in the hall.

But when I got up in the morning and went downstairs, there was no sign of Tony or the Boys. I assumed he'd decided to shut down for the day, perhaps expecting another raid. There had already been five in the past few months, each more frightening than the last. But when he didn't appear for the rest of the week, I knew that something was amiss. Had the police caught up with him? Had he been eliminated by the mob?

I heard nothing for weeks, and there was no one I could ask. Then one afternoon, while shopping on Bleecker Street, who should I see, buying tomatoes at a vegetable stand, but Caesar. He looked older and thinner than when I saw him last, and though attired, as always, in his natty pin-striped suit, he seemed to have lost that cocky Broadway look.

"I'm glad to see you, Miss Gee," he said. "I sure miss them days in the hall."

"What happened? Where's Tony?"

"He ran off with a lot of dough in the middle of the night. I hear he's livin' in Florida."

"Do you think he'll come back?"

"He better not. Too many guys are lookin' for him."

"And what are you doing, Caesar?"

"Nothin.' I ain't got a job, and I'm sick of hangin' around the house. I don't know what to do with my time."

I liked Caesar and asked him to drop in for coffee some night. But, of course, I knew that he wouldn't. The bookies were gone—and gone for good. Yet I couldn't quite believe it. I kept expecting to wake up one morning and find them in the hall. Business as usual.

Weegee at Limelight, copyright © by Paul Seligman.

WEEGEE WAS a pest. He didn't appear often, but when he did, there were complaints. He would roam around the room, popping off flashguns in customer's faces, and scowl and mutter when they protested. He'd go from table to table handing out greasy name cards, rubber-stamped with his logo, Weegee the Famous.

But Weegee the Famous was no longer so famous, and not everyone knew who he was. What they saw was a short, paunchy man in a large, baggy suit, with fleshy lips and hang-dog eyes, chewing on a cold cigar. He looked—and smelled—like he slept in his clothes, a habit he no doubt developed during his years as a press photographer, on call twenty-four hours a day. Though past his prime and down on his luck, he still behaved like he was back in the 1930s and 1940s, cruising the city in a radio car, beating the cops to the scene of a crime (often rearranging the scene for the sake of a shot). Fires, car crashes, gangland killings—these were his stock in trade. But his real fame came after the publication of his book, *Naked City*, followed by the sale of the film and television rights. After five years in Hollywood, where he worked as a consultant and acted in bit parts, his career foundered. It never revived. Yet, if he was scrounging for a living, you would never know it. He was brash, abrasive, and never failed to remind you that he was Weegee the Famous, his alias for Arthur Fellig.

My own dislike of Weegee went back several years. I'd run into him one day while I was out walking with Li-lan, and I'd noticed as we talked that he kept looking her over, a lecherous gleam in his eye. He called a few days later, asking to photograph her in the nude. I hung up and hadn't spoken to him since.

I was willing to let bygones be bygones, and after Limelight opened and he started coming around, I treated him just as I would anybody else. But there were continuing complaints, not only from celebrities, for whom Limelight was an oasis—Rod Steiger and Claire Bloom weren't keen on having their hand-holding publicized—but from others too. They claimed invasion of privacy, and I had to agree. Limelight's advocacy of photography gave no one the license to shoot indiscriminately, and after a customer threatened to smash Weegee's camera, I banned all picture-taking, except with permission.

Weegee was warned and appeared to comply. But on a night when Bob Borchers was off and I was in Europe, he stole in with a young woman who was acting as a model. He was trying to sell a story on the seamy side of life in Greenwich Village, so he'd gone to raunchy parties, photographed transvestites, drunks, junkies, and whoever else he thought would titillate the readers of some trashy magazine. Since Limelight offered no such attractions, he posed his model with a crow perched on her head. The picture itself was innocuous enough, but it was run as the lead in a sleazy magazine called Night and Day.

I was furious, afraid it would attract an equally sleazy crowd, the kind that came to the Village looking for excitement, and not finding it, created its own (like beating up "queers" on a Saturday night). For a while we noticed some unsavory types, like the one who ordered coffee but then never touched it, his hands too busy under the table. Or the flasher who whipped open his coat, treated a waitress to the sight of his genitals, then fled. Others looked in but turned and left, not finding Limelight their kind of place.

"Out!" I said, when Weegee reappeared. "And don't ever come back." He stayed away for a year, but then one night I saw him peering through the window, and he looked so forlorn I invited him in, not because I had a change of heart, but because I wanted to exhibit his work.

Tabloid photography was seldom taken seriously. Yet I found Weegee's work superior to most of what I saw in Life. It had passion and wit, and lacked the sentimentality of so much current work. Weegee looked at what others refused to see. He reveled (some might say wallowed) in the rawness, the grittiness, the underbelly of city life. Along with his shots of bloodied corpses of gangsters, there were images that lingered in the mind long after the daily papers were thrown out. Was there a photograph more harrowing than the one of a woman screaming in horror, her children trapped in a tenement fire? Or a more powerful social statement than the shabbily dressed woman ogling two mink-clad dowagers arriving at the opera?

Weegee looked pleased when I asked him to exhibit, but within minutes he reverted to his usual gruff self, his smile giving way to a scowl. "I got to think about it. Come to my studio and we'll talk it over."

The "studio" was a hovel on West 47th Street, littered with newspapers and boxes and files. There was a rumpled cot with dirty sheets, empty coffee containers on every surface, and what looked like the accumulated detritus of a lifetime spilling from shelves and piled on the floor. I refused his offer of a seat (on the bed) and stood while he showed me his work. He'd been experimenting with a trick lens, and proudly displayed his "art"—a woman with five breasts, others with multiple limbs.

"When do you want to show them, next month?" he asked.

"These aren't exactly what I have in mind," I said. "I'd like to exhibit your newspaper work."

He shook his head. "You're missing the boat. These broads with five tits will be a sensation. Nobody's done anything like it."

I couldn't convince Weegee that sensation was not my aim, and after a frustrating hour, I left. I thought he'd change his mind, but he never called, and I never saw him at Limelight again.

I WAS AT the desk, filling in for Pehr, when a man in a business suit, a typical Madison Avenue type, came up to pay his check. Stuck in his breast pocket, waving as he walked, was a beautiful, iridescent peacock feather. He handed me a card. "I'm Phil Mikoda, head of public relations at Ansco."

And the feather? I didn't ask. It took more than a peacock feather to cause comment in the Village. But he told me anyway. "My hobby is breeding peacocks. I own a farm in Binghamton, near the Ansco plant, and I also breed palomino ponies and black swans." A few days later, he was back again, feather in hand, proposal in mind. "How would you feel about hosting a peacock dinner and inviting all the camera editors who write for the newspapers?"

"*Peacock?*"

"Actually, pea*hen*. It's the males who have the beautiful plumage. The females are mousy and drab."

"That's no reason to *eat* them," I snapped, appalled at the thought of eating such birds, regardless of gender. Furthermore, I was not about to get involved in a public relations scheme for a manufacturer of film.

Deschin thought it was a great idea. "It would take nothing less than a Roman feast to bring all these writers together. Why don't you think about it? It might be fun."

The more I thought of it, the less awful it seemed. After all, hadn't I eaten all sorts of strange dishes while I was living with Yun? We ate bear's paw at one banquet, sea slug at another, and at another, a dish called wildcat stew. Peacock, by comparison, was as exotic as chicken.

I agreed to the dinner, but Fong was upset. "Peacock no good. We give them roast pork."

"But everyone's been invited. I can't back out now."

Roast pork was Fong's forte; peacock was not. I was afraid he'd quit rather than lose face. But after hours of cajolery and many "high hats" (which, Fong said, was what the Chinese called flattery), he finally agreed.

The dinner was on a Monday, the night we were closed, and I steered clear of the kitchen while setting up the tables, leaving the fate of five peahens to Fong. Phil Mikoda arrived with a beautiful stuffed peacock under his arm, which he said he'd purchased from a defunct whorehouse in Texas. It had a long, sweeping tail, and I would liked to have used it as a centerpiece, draping the tail between the rows of plates. But I was afraid the feathers might tangle with the forks.

Everyone showed up except Mabel Scacheri, the camera editor of the *World Telegram*, having decided at the last minute that eating peacock was barbaric. There was Deschin, of course, John Adam Knight of the *New York Post*, Seymour "Sy" Spector of the *Journal-American*, Don Langer of the *Herald Tribune*, Ralph "Skip" Miller of the *World Telegram*, Irving "Doc" Desfor of the Associated Press, and freelance writers Norman Rothschild, George Wright, and Cora Alsberg Wright. I'd also invited a few personal friends—the radio personality Jean Shepherd, his fiancee, the actress Lois Nettleton, and my date Kevin Sullivan.

We started with cocktails, and after a couple of rounds, it hardly mattered what we ate. There was a burst of applause when the peahens appeared, five beautifully browned birds on five silver platters. Fong did not disappoint. He'd prepared the peahens as he would Chinese duck, with honey, garlic, ginger, and soy sauce, turning an otherwise dull bird into a culinary experience. I pulled Fong out of the kitchen at the end of the meal, and he was given another round of applause.

Peacock under arm, Phil Mikoda went reeling up to Times Square, where he was spotted by a talent scout and invited to appear on the popular *Tex and Jinx* television show. Ansco decided to make the dinner an annual affair, but once was enough for me. The dinner was held elsewhere in subsequent years, but it was never as exciting—or as tasty—without Fong's Chinese touch.

MY UNIVERSE was made up of a triangle—my apartment on the corner of Grove, the Chemical Bank diagonally across on West Fourth, and Limelight midway down the block. I seldom went as far as Fourteenth Street, but I accepted Virginia Admiral's invitation to the De Niro exhibition at the Zabriskie Gallery uptown. I'd known Virginia for several years. She had been married to De Niro, a figurative painter of considerable talent, and though they'd divorced shortly after their son Bobby was born, they still remained friends.

"Bobby will be there," Virginia said, "but you may not recognize him. He's a big boy now."

Bobby was a toddler when I saw him last, and he was not a child whose company I enjoyed. He was hyperactive, hard to reach, a rambunctious rolypoly with small, close-together eyes. Virginia lived a few doors away on West Fourteenth Street, and having discovered that I, too, was alone with a small child, she thought it would be nice if the children could play together. We were both freelancers, working at home. Virginia was running a manuscript typing service, and I was beginning my retouching career. We both had the same problem—what to do with the children when we had to pick up and deliver work. So whenever one of us had to go out, we dropped

a) Peacock dinner. b) Helen Gee. c) John Adam Knight, George Wright, Jacob Deschin. d) Jean Shepherd, Helen Gee, Kevin Sullivan, Lois Nettleton (back to the camera).

our child at the other's house, an arrangement that pleased us both. But since Virginia's business was more active than mine, Bobby was more often at our house.

I dreaded his visits. He would charge around the apartment, chasing our new puppy Penny, and in minutes the place was a shambles. He always managed to arrive when I was in the middle of a job, and I could feel the drawing board shake as he ran around the room on his short, sturdy legs, leveling everything in his path. When the scene grew too wild, I would scoop up Penny and hold her in my lap, and try to go on with my work. But this didn't slow Bobby down. He'd keep on whirling, not even stopping for cookies and milk. Li-lan watched wide-eyed as Bobby performed, serving more as audience than playmate.

Virginia's visits to clients grew longer and longer, and I often found myself feeding Bobby supper and bathing him too. I put the children in the tub together, and once when I left the bathroom to fetch clean towels, I returned to find Bobby straddling the tub, a foot on each side, and Li-lan studiously engaged in what was known in army parlance as "short-arm inspection." Not having come across this in the child-rearing books, I didn't know what to do. Rather than make the wrong move (and set the stage for life-long neurosis), I did nothing. Li-lan was entranced with her discovery, and that night, while I was tucking her in bed, she said in the voice she used when confiding secrets, "Mommy, did you know that little boys have udders?"

Zabriskie's was crowded, and after greeting the artist and viewing his work, I scanned the room, looking for a chubby teenager with close-together eyes. There were several teen-age boys, but none that fit the bill.

"Is Bobby here?" I asked Virginia. "I don't see him."

"Over there," she said, pointing to a slim young fellow about fifteen years old.

"*That's Bobby?* Why, he's so attractive . . ."

"Yes, and he has his heart set on becoming an actor," she said.

And so do half the kids in the Village, I thought, unaware that I was looking at the young Robert De Niro, a future star.

NINETEEN FIFTY-NINE started out well. The first exhibition was by Robert Doisneau, a good beginning to what I'd hoped would be a less difficult year,

Dan Weiner, by Sandra Weiner.

now that the bookies were gone. I hadn't quite recovered from the trauma of the raids, but putting on this exhibition helped. Doisneau's warm Gallic wit was like a glass of good wine; whenever I walked into the gallery, I came out refreshed. How could one not but be delighted with his picture of lovers kissing on a crowded street? Or his tattooed sailor stretched out on a bed contentedly viewing a wall of pin-ups?

But this respite was cut short with a sad piece of news: Dan Weiner had been killed in a plane crash. He was in Kentucky working on a story for a medical magazine when the subject of the story—a psychiatrist who visited his patients piloting his own plane from town to town—got lost in a snowstorm. All four men on board died.

I felt the loss keenly, both personally and professionally. Dan was one of the few photojournalists with a strong point of view, never reluctant to say what he thought. He had none of the dash or swagger of a Robert Capa or the romantic aura of a Eugene Smith; his appeal was of a gentler, more down-to-earth sort. He wore tweeds, smoked a pipe, and had an air of calm purpose. He would sit at a table puffing away, and if he appeared to be pondering the state of the world, in all likelihood, he was. Dan had been active in the Photo League, and despite the lingering effects of McCarthyism, he remained committed to social issues. While working for mainstream publications such as Fortune, Collier's, Life, and Look, he angled for assignments he believed socially relevant. He went down south for Collier's in 1956, covered the bus boycott in Montgomery, Alabama, and photographed Dr. Martin Luther King, Jr. He collaborated with Alan Paton on the book South Africa in Transition, and he traveled to the Soviet Union and its satellites in Eastern Europe for Fortune, an unusual assignment in light of the Cold War.

Like Eugene Smith, whom he deeply admired, Dan tried to see beneath the surface of things to arrive at what he saw as "truth." Rather than focus on the drama of large events, he sought out those seemingly insignificant moments that illuminated the large events. His picture of a lone white woman riding in an empty bus in Montgomery, Alabama, testified to the success of the bus boycott and the triggering of the Civil Rights movement.

But unlike Smith, Dan was easy to work with—no hassles, no tantrums, no need to star. Though he decried the superficiality of most of the work published in the big picture magazines, he got along well with editors, referring to them, jokingly, as plumbers: "Wherever they see a hole, they fill it with a picture."

Dan's work was cool rather than impassioned, not the kind that swept you away, but the kind you couldn't forget. I'd shown his Italian work in 1955 and hadn't thought at the time of another Weiner show. But sharing his feelings about apartheid, a subject largely ignored by the press, I showed his South African work in 1956. Though the photographs barely touched on the horrors of the system—Dan had been hampered by governmental restrictions—they offered a glimpse into a racist society, thus opening the door, if only a crack.

Russia was Dan's last major assignment. Having faced governmental restrictions there as well, he gave us a view of the everyday life, offering us yet another glimpse into a country about which we, in America, knew little—and feared. I presented Russia and Eastern Europe in the spring of the year as a memorial to Dan.

I HADN'T heard from Steichen for some time. The Millers had become his surrogate family, their having grown close while working on *The Family of Man*. Steichen was eighty and thinking of retirement. When it came to choosing a successor, Wayne, his assistant, was the likely choice. But Wayne wanted to get back to his own photography; he and Joan packed up the family and moved to the West Coast. Steichen visited them often, trying to fill the void in his life. He'd suffered a slight stroke shortly after his wife died, but as soon as he recovered he was back at work, organizing an exhibition of five hundred prints drawn from the five thousand in the museum collection, most of them acquired during his eleven years at the helm. His criteria were excellence, and though he hadn't intended it as an historical survey, the exhibition covered most of the important developments in photography from its beginnings to the present day.

Photographs from the Museum Collection was Steichen's only exhibition during this personally difficult year, and though it won little of the acclaim given *The Family of Man*, Deschin seemed to prefer it, calling it "a brilliant definition of photography as an art." Deschin also took note of the exploratory, almost abstract, nature of some of the work, particularly that of the contemporary Japanese, which Steichen had recently acquired for the collection. Aline Saarinen praised the show, and I could almost see Steichen smile when she wrote, "The camera is no more a mechanical and passive tool for the photographer-artist than the brush and chisel for painter and sculptor."

Steichen had also traveled in 1958. Accompanied by his brother-in-law, Carl Sandburg, he attended the opening of *The Family of Man* in Moscow, and on his own, visited photographers in Stockholm, Paris, and London. Instead of presenting a few small shows each year as he had in the past, he now seemed to favor one large exhibition of hundreds of prints. Though nothing like the scale of *The Family of Man*, the shows reflected a much broader point of view. With the help of Grace Mayer, who had finally quit the Museum of the City of New York and was now his full-time assistant, he was working on *The Sense of Abstraction*, a large exhibition scheduled to open in 1960.

We had seen less of each other in the past year and a half, but we still met for dinner when he returned from his trips. He looked quite attractive with his new shaggy beard, but grief had left its mark. His eyes had lost their twinkle, and the only time he brightened and seemed his old self was when

he talked about the California redwoods. He had joined a movement to save the trees; for one hundred dollars you could keep a tree from being felled by loggers. "I've adopted a redwood," he said proudly one night. "I've saved a tree from the axe."

Steichen was like a redwood himself—tall, old, and virtually indestructible; it would take nothing less than lightning to cut him down. He'd recovered from every ailment—strokes, the gout, spells of disorientation—and I was confident he'd weather this period of bereavement too.

He spent more time at home in Connecticut, continuing his work with the shad-blow tree which, at the suggestion of the filmmaker Pare Lorenz, he was filming in color. I'd been meaning to visit him, but kept putting it off, immersed in the problems at Limelight. We spoke on the phone from time to time, and I kept abreast of his activities through Grace Mayer and a couple of friends.

Ken Heyman visited him now and then, and after one of these visits, he dropped in at Limelight. I asked about Steichen, of course.

"He seems lonely," Ken said. "You ought to go see him. He's crazy about you, you know."

"That's nonsense," I said. "Steichen adores women. I'm just one of many."

"You're wrong. He asks about you every time I see him, and I think he'd marry you in a minute if you gave him the chance."

"Marry Steichen? He's more than double my age."

"Look at Picasso, Charlie Chaplin . . . this wouldn't be the first May-December romance. Steichen is well off and your life would be simpler. It can't be easy running this place."

Ken nattered on, and I was getting annoyed. He had a complex about his money, never quite sure he was being loved for himself, yet here he was, urging me to marry for security. Getting nowhere, he tried another tack.

"Tell me, Helen, have you ever held a Rodin in your hand?"

"No, I haven't. And what's that got to do with Steichen?"

"He has quite a few in his collection. If you married Steichen you could hold a Rodin in your hand."

"Yes, and I'd also have to hold Steichen," I snapped.

That put an end to it. Ken gave up acting as a marriage broker, and I forgave him for trying, knowing he had my interest at heart.

Edward Steichen, by Ken Heyman.

WHO ARE *the world's ten greatest photographers?*

Popular Photography had conducted an international poll, inviting "243 eminent critics, teachers, editors, art directors, consultants, and working photographers" to participate. I had little faith in polls, but I was glad to be asked, if for no other reason than to submit the names of a few dark horses —Robert Frank for one—not that any stood a chance.

The magazine imposed only one condition: "The photographers you nominate must be *working photographers*—men who are currently producing pictures. They need not be professionals." That nonprofessionals were eligible spoke well for the editors, for even if none was chosen, it acknowledged the importance of the work being done outside the commercial arena. Taking note of the word *men*, I submitted the names of several women—Berenice Abbott, Lisette Model, Imogen Cunningham, Dorothea Lange, and though she was currently involved in making films, Helen Levitt.

The results were published in the May 1959 issue of the magazine, and there wasn't a surprise in the lot. *The World's Ten Greatest Photographers*, according to the poll, were Ansel Adams, Richard Avedon, Henri Cartier-Bresson, Alfred Eisenstaedt, Ernst Haas, Philippe Halsman, Yousuf Karsh, Gjon Mili, Irving Penn, and W. Eugene Smith. Of these ten, I would not have chosen even half.

I would not have chosen Gjon Mili. Technically his work was interesting. He was the first to use electronic flash and stroboscopic lights, techniques he'd picked up from his friend and sometime collaborator, Harold Edgerton, while working at Westinghouse as an engineer. His "light drawings" were intriguing, particularly the one of Picasso wielding a flashlight, drawing a picture in the air. But I found his work in *Life* mediocre. More impressive than his photographs were the parties he gave, large sprawling affairs with hundreds of guests, most culled from the magazine world.

Nor would I have selected Ernst Haas. He was one of the first to use color for street photography, and for this he deserved credit. His *Magic Images of New York*, a twenty-four page spread published in *Life* in 1953, was still his finest work. He was already leaning toward the saccharine and the trite. Haas had dash, good looks, and European charm (he'd arrived from Austria in 1951) but his reputation, like his ego, I believed was overblown.

I would not have chosen Alfred Eisenstaedt. Eisie, as he was called by his associates at *Life* (and by those who could abide this penurious little man) was an industry in himself. His output was prodigious. He covered the world and took mountains of pictures, and though he was considered by many the quintessential photojournalist, I had yet to see an image I found memorable.

I would not have chosen Philippe Halsman. Halsman shared the distinction with his colleague Eisenstaedt of having done close to a hundred covers for *Life*. He was a charming man, courtly and kind; I preferred the person to the work. His attempts at humor were heavy-handed; his Mona Lisa with a moustache more depressing than amusing, and his Salvador Dali with objects flying around the room silly rather than funny.

I would not have chosen Yousuf Karsh. Karsh worked in the tradition of fashionable portrait painters, depicting celebrities as they wished to be seen. His oeuvre was a roster of the world's *Who's Who*, everyone from Winston Churchill to Georgia O'Keeffe. But the results were predictable—always the same lighting, always the same poses—and though many of these portraits were strong, they lacked insight.

I was ambivalent about Richard Avedon, and also Irving Penn. Avedon was, without question, one of the finest fashion photographers of our time. He was innovative, interesting, and though his work was limited to the field of fashion, I believed he belonged on the list. Penn was a close second. His range was broader; he looked beyond fashion—his portraits of Peruvian Indians were already considered classics—but I found his work more tasteful than "great."

"Great" could certainly be applied to Ansel Adams—there was no finer landscape photographer anywhere—and, of course, Eugene Smith. Of all ten photographers, the one who I was sure was on everyone's list, and rightfully so, was Henri Cartier-Bresson.

Tastes change, in photography as in everything, and I wondered how this list would hold up in ten or twenty years.

GOOD NEWS from Robert Frank! Barney Rosset, the iconoclastic publisher of Grove Press, had decided to publish an American edition of his book. But with changes. Robert had reservations about the French edition. He disliked having pictures interspersed with text, and he also disliked the text itself, finding the selections too dry and sociological. Walker Evans had offered to write a new text but Robert held off, preferring a writer whose work he admired, someone say, like William Faulkner. But when he met Jack Kerouac at a party one night, he knew that he was the one. Robert happened to have a copy of *Les Americains* with him, and the two went outside and sat on the curb as Kerouac leafed through the pages, "digging" the images.

On the Road was creating a stir, largely because of interest in the Beats. (Being denounced by the literary establishment—"typing, not writing," as one critic put it—had not hurt sales.) A raid on Lawrence Ferlinghetti's City Lights Bookstore by the San Francisco police and the seizure of several "obscene" publications—one of them Alan Ginsberg's *Howl*—drew attention to the Beats, and the trial that followed (which subsequently led to the vindication of *Howl*) was a *cause célèbre*. But it was an article in *Life* that brought the Beats fame. They made good copy. Though treated as a curiosity (in New York, you could "rent-a-beatnik" for a party), the movement caught on. Kerouac's *On the Road*, the bible of the Beats, appealed to something deep in the American psyche: traveling the open road, whether by foot or motorcycle or fin-tailed car, spelled freedom.

But the Beats, it turned out, were more than a curiosity, more than a bunch of scruffy malcontents, exploited by the media for entertainment value. Their attack on the establishment and middle-class mores was coming

Henri Cartier-Bresson, by Frank Paulin.

to be seen as a threat, another manifestation of a growing need for change. The Civil Rights movement, though still in its beginnings, was shaking the nation. The sight of jeering whites trying to prevent black students from entering a school was a disturbing picture on dinnertime television. It was a picture out of sync with the way we saw ourselves—the greatest, the richest, the most powerful nation in the world, and the most democratic and humane.

What Robert saw was another side. He was appalled by the intolerance he'd witnessed (and experienced) and by the violence he sensed beneath the surface. Yet his book was not a polemic; it went beyond the economic, the political, and the social. Robert saw not a land of "togetherness," but of loneliness and spiritual malaise.

This was not a picture one cared to see. When *The Americans* was published in 1959 Robert came under attack. He was "sick," a "liar," his view of America a total distortion. A few young photographers defended the book, but their voices were lost in the uproar. In an article titled "An Off-Beat View of the U.S.A.," *Popular Photography* published reviews by several of its editors. Les Barry saw the book as an attack on the country; James Zanutto accused Robert of a "desire to shock and provide cheap thrills"; and John Durniak, finding Robert's picture of the country "one-sided," wrote, "If this is America (the United States) then we should burn it down completely and start all over again."

The most virulent attack came from the magazines's publisher and editor-in-chief Bruce Downes. "There is no pity in these images. They are images of hate and hopelessness, of desolation and preoccupation with death. They are images of an America seen by a joyless man who hates the country of his adoption. Is he a poet as his friend Kerouac says he is? Maybe, but he is also a liar, perversely basking in the kind of misery he is perpetually seeing and persistently creating. It is a world shrouded in an immense gray tragic boredom. This is Robert Frank's America. God help him. For him there is, there can be, no other."

Charles Reynolds, the magazine's picture editor, was kinder. He credited Robert with several powerful, moving images, and though he found "none of the love and enthusiasm of his hipster friend," he conceded that, "an artist with a strong viewpoint, however limited, is better than no viewpoint at all."

Only Mike Kinzer, the managing editor, accepted the book wholeheartedly. In response to the criticism of its "one-sided" view, he wrote, "It is useless to argue that Robert Frank should have devoted a part of his book to the vast and smiling American middle class, another to the champagne-and-jaguar stratum, and so on. The fact is that he feels strongly about some of the things he sees in his adopted country and wants to call them to our attention." In defense of the book's title, he said, "As for the title seeming to imply *all* Americans, it is quite clearly intended as tongue-in-cheek, but the intention was perhaps too subtle." (Robert's original title, *America, America*, which I would have preferred — it sounded more like a cry than a condemnation — got lost somewhere along the publishing route.)

While I could understand the reaction to Robert's point of view — the underbelly of America having been hidden so long — I was puzzled by the attacks on his technique. The "meaningless blurs, muddy exposure, and drunken horizons" that Arthur Goldsmith complained about in his review were nothing new. Many young photographers — Gary Winogrand, for one — were playing with these same techniques. William Klein, a photographer who made a brief flurry (before leaving to live in Paris) with his abrasive, hard-hitting photographs in a self-published book with the unwieldy title, *Life is good and good for you in New York William Klein trance witness reveals*, was far more radical in approach. Compared to Klein, Robert was almost conservative. But unlike Klein, whose subsequent work in Tokyo and Rome showed him to be a one-note player, always sounding the same harsh tones, Robert's genius (and I was convinced it was genius) lay in his ability to capture the spirit and atmosphere of wherever he happened to be — the romantic aura of Paris, the gray melancholy of London, the grittiness and energy of American cities.

Not having seen him for quite a while, I wondered how he was holding up. The criticism was some of the most fierce I'd heard leveled at anyone, other than politicians. I expected to find him deeply depressed, but Robert was perverse; he sounded almost cheerful. He had been working on a film with his new Beat friends and having cut his eyeteeth on *Pull My Daisy*, he was ready to start another, *The Sin of Jesus*, based on a story by Isaac Babel.

When I mentioned the criticism, all he had to say was, "Well, at least they'll stop calling me the poet of the camera. How I hate that!"

LIMELIGHT had a large bookish following. There were always a few novelists scribbling away (I discouraged the use of typewriters because of the clatter of the keys) as well as a playwright or two. One, a beautiful young black woman, Lorraine Hansberry, seemed to be filling an entire notebook; her Raisin in the Sun was a hit on Broadway, and I wondered whether she was at work on another play. William Cole, a prolific anthologist and publicity director at Knopf, usually appeared with a writer friend, and whenever he beckoned me to his table, I never knew what literary luminary I'd meet. The large man with the white moustache and black-rimmed glasses was Frank O'Connor, and the dour man with hang-dog eyes, the humorist S. J. Perelman. The intense young fellow with a neatly trimmed beard was the cartoonist Shel Silverstein, and the mild-looking chap with the egg-shaped head and horn-rims, the cartoonist and social satirist Jules Feiffer. (His Sick, Sick, Sick, Sick was appearing in the Village Voice, for which he was paid five dollars a week.)

It was through Bill Cole that I met James Baldwin. He had just returned from France where he'd lived for seven years, escaping the racial tensions he found here at home. He'd rented a small apartment on Horatio Street, a few blocks from the White Horse, and was busy revisiting his old Village haunts. Limelight, of course, was new to him, and though he liked the place and enjoyed the gallery, he was not one to sit around over coffee. He suggested we "do" the West Village, which meant stopping at every bar. Expecting a long evening, I stayed with soda, while he and Bill downed scotch. Being small and thin didn't limit his capacity, while Bill, over six feet and a seasoned drinker, was reeling after several of these stops. Jimmy talked endlessly — about Paris, New York, and the reason for his return; he'd felt guilty and estranged enjoying the good life in France while reading about the troubled situation in the South. Jimmy was homely. He had bulging eyes and sunken cheeks, and a tense, nervous manner. But when he talked he became radiant, almost beautiful. His language was precise, as elegant as his prose, and his face lit up when he made a point, and he punctuated the air with his thin, graceful hands.

We ended up at the White Horse, and it was only then, as we stood on the corner of Hudson and West 11th, that we realized he was drunk and might need help getting home. We started toward Horatio, but halfway up the block Jimmy broke away and headed toward the river.

"Bill, you've got to stop him," I said. "It's dangerous down there at the docks."

"Stop Jimmy? Not a chance. Not when he's out looking for guys."

He looked so small and so vulnerable, and we watched as he disappeared into the dark.

NORMAN MAILER showed up from time to time, but I was never too happy to see him, not knowing what he'd do next. He'd stand on the stairs scanning the room then go weaving his way through, sometimes drunk, sometimes stoned, but always in great fighting form. He'd raise his fists ad shadow-box in the aisle while I stood guard at the gallery, afraid he might find it a good place to spar. He was generally accompanied by his voluptuous wife Adele, who was suspicious (with good reason) of every woman within yards of Norman. ("You mean you've *never* slept with him?" she'd say, unable to believe that one's only interest in Norman might be his writing.) The Mailers lived nearby, on Perry Street, and I was often invited to their parties. The one time I went I couldn't believe that the meek little man sitting in a corner was the same belligerent Norman. He looked like nothing so much as the bored, weary owner of a secondhand store. While this may have had to do with whatever he'd imbibed, I only wished he were that benign when he appeared at Limelight, and spared me the Joe Louis routine.

BECAUSE OF the gallery and the kind of clientele, Limelight had become known as the "intellectual's coffeehouse." Contributing to the reputation were the many academicians who came in every night, most of them from the New School and NYU. The New School was a bastion of philosophical thought, and having served as a sanctuary for Jewish intellectuals, there were many refugees on the staff. You could tell them by their accents, their earnestness, and their prodigious consumption of *kaffee mit schlag*. There were also a number of professors from Columbia, many of whom lived in the Village.

Meyer Schapiro, one of the scholars I admired most, lived nearby, on West 4th Street, and though he came in only now and then, I was always delighted to see him. Schapiro's lectures at Columbia were legendary. He was typical of a generation of intellectuals of modest background, among them the art critics Harold Rosenberg and Clement Greenberg, who were educated during the depression. He was shaped by those years, and when he analyzed a painting he went beyond the brush strokes and discussed it in relevance to society. He was unique for his understanding of and respect for photography; most in art circles had little or none. (Harold Rosenberg's appreciation of Aaron Siskind was based on the semiabstract nature of the work and a presumed relationship to Abstract Expressionism, the movement with which he, as a critic, was allied.) Schapiro had been an influence on Minor White, who had studied with him at Columbia, and he was one of Robert Frank's sponsors for the Guggenheim Fellowship.

I REGRETTED that I had so little time to talk. Surrounded by hundreds of people every night, there were few I got to know well. Celebrity, as such, didn't interest me, but there were several in the public eye with whom I would have liked to spend time: Alger Hiss (who was more infamous than famous, having just been released from prison); the actor-comedian Zero Mostel; the folk singer Freddy Hellerman of the Weavers; the sculptor Isamu Noguchi; the poet May Swenson; the "mother of experimental films," Maya Deren; the director John Houseman (otherwise known as Mr. Theater, who, in fact, bought a photograph); and, of course, Cartier-Bresson, who was just as elusive as ever.

But being constantly on call, either in the kitchen or on the floor, I had little time to socialize. And now that I was once again faced with finding a manager, Pehr having been offered a better-paying job, I had no time at all to talk.

SONYA CAME PADDING down the aisle in her space shoes. She had invested a week's wages on these orthopedic clod-hoppers, and was in the process of breaking them in. "Those two men in the back want to see you," she said, pointing to a table near the gallery.

"About a photograph?"

"No, but it sounds important." She handed me a card. It read Michael Rothman, Business Manager, Local No. 1, Dining Room & Restaurant Employees Union, AFL-CIO.

Not again! I was forever being approached by representatives of organizations of all kinds—animal rescue leagues, homes for the handicapped, societies in support of banning the bomb—all proposing exhibitions illustrating their activities, 8×10 glossies in hand. It was hard to refuse when I believed in the cause, and I hoped this wasn't yet another request. I'd recently turned down the garment workers' union, and was not about to accommodate the AFL-CIO. I went to their table reluctantly.

"Sit down," Rothman said, motioning to a chair. It sounded like an order, I remained standing. "This is Gomez, one of our organizers. Your restaurant is being unionized, so you'll be seeing a lot of us. We want you to sign an agreement acknowledging the union so we can set up a meeting and negotiate a contract."

"That's ridiculous!" I said. "This isn't a restaurant. It's a coffeehouse . . . a photography gallery. . . ."

"As soon as you sign, we'll start the ball rolling." Rothman handed me some papers. I handed them back.

"*None* of the coffeehouses are organized. How can you organize painters . . . dancers. . . ."

"We'll give you three days to think it over. If you don't sign, we'll throw pickets out front." Rothman pushed the papers at me and left.

I ran home, tears flowing. How could this happen to me? Hadn't I always sided with labor, supported unions? Hadn't I always respected picket lines? Never had I crossed one. *Never.*

What would happen to Limelight if the union took over? Would the character of the place change? Would we have to hire the waitresses through the union hall—hash-slingers in uniforms instead of actresses and dancers? I felt betrayed. I had prided myself on offering benefits to the help that no other coffeehouse did—two days sick leave, vacations with pay—I had even thought of instituting a profit-sharing plan, but when I mentioned the idea to Sam, my accountant, he'd laughed. "Profits? What profits? They're making more money than you."

Business was still off. The construction around the corner was an ongoing problem. Part of Fourth Street was cordoned off, creating a road block around Sheridan Square. Many of the small shops around Christopher Street were feeling the pinch.

Sam had seen the handwriting on the wall, and for months had been urging me to sell. Finding a buyer would be no problem, of course. *Everybody* wanted to own a coffeehouse, it seemed, enticed by the lure of the social life. Few seemed to realize how difficult it was; they might have been surprised (and changed their minds) if they knew how often I looked around the room and wished I were a customer, not the owner.

"You should have listened," Sam said. "It's too late now. No one will buy a place that's being organized. It's a miserable thing to go through."

"What should I do?"

"There's nothing you can do except trust to luck."

RATHER THAN trust to luck, I spoke to Jesse Simon, a labor negotiator who came in for dinner almost every night (even more often than Ed Koch, the future mayor of New York, who dined on steak three nights a week). Jesse was outraged. "What's wrong with those guys! Everybody knows there's no money in coffeehouses. I'll talk to a friend high up in the local and see if she can help."

I went back home, too upset to face the customers, too angry to face the help. I paced the apartment, going over and over the same ground. Who *was* it who called in the union? Sonya? No, not Sonya. She'd been working for me for years and seemed content. Leticia? No, not Leticia. Right now she was "in the country" (visiting Dr. Spencer) and had other things on her mind besides unions. Shelley? No, not Shelley. I'd been her confidant, always lending a shoulder when her romances fizzled.

I went down the list and finally settled on Carlos, the only dishwasher who stayed on the job for months. Was he a union plant? Or was it one of the part-time waitresses?

Jesse phoned; he had good news and bad. The president of the local had promised to "go easy" on Limelight, but it was too late to call off the organizers; they were planning to unionize all the coffeehouses in the city, starting with Limelight, the biggest and the busiest. The field looked ripe. In the Village alone, there were close to forty, but all were small, owner-run businesses, with profits (if any) in pennies. If Limelight couldn't afford a union, how could the others?

"Don't they realize that they'll destroy the coffeehouses? There's no way we can meet their demands."

"The organizers couldn't care less about coffeehouses," Jesse said. "The more members, the more dues."

"How depressing. What do I do now?"

"There's nothing you can do except sign the agreement, meet with the organizers, and try to negotiate the best possible deal. Let's hope the president of the local keeps his word."

I GIRDED myself for the meeting, which was being held in the morning, when I was generally not at my best. The furnace had conked out the night before, and Rothman and Gomez sat huddled in their coats, waiting for Florence, the employees' representative, to appear. (Florence had been slated to be fired for chronic lateness, but was now, apparently, assured of a job.) I heated some left-over coffee and trembled as I filled four cups.

Jesse had given me pointers the night before. "Keep cool. Don't let them rile you. They'll probably make outrageous demands, but remember, it's only a tactic. It's part of the game."

The first demand was a raise in pay—50 percent, across the board.

"But I can't afford even a 10 percent raise. Business is slow. . . ." I went to the desk and brought out the books. "Here, see for yourselves."

Rothman pushed the books aside. "We're on to these tricks. Every boss keeps a double set of books."

The next demand was for vacations with pay.

"But I already give one week with pay after a year of work. No other coffeehouse . . ."

"I don't give a damn about other coffeehouses . . . one week's vacation after six months of work."

The next demand was for five days sick leave.

"But I already give two. How can I afford five?"

Rothman did most of the talking, mouthing his words as though by rote —"profits . . . workers . . . exploitation. . . ." It sounded like a playback of the 1930s, delivered on a soap box in Union Square. But regardless of the rhetoric, I couldn't quite see myself as a capitalist pig. Florence spoke up with a demand of her own. "Why can't we have a pastry cooler in the gallery? It would save us trips to the kitchen." I was finding it hard to control my rage.

"We'll deal with that later. Let's get back to salaries," Rothman said. "A 50 percent raise or we'll call a strike."

I offered ten. "Anything more and I'll be forced to close. Fourteen people will lose their jobs."

Gomez smirked. "So we'll get them new ones. And as for you, just come down to the union hall. We can always get you a job as a bus girl."

That did it. I lost control. I grabbed my cup and threw the coffee. It slopped all over his overcoat.

Gomez sprang up. "You bitch! "If you wasn't a dame I'd knock your block off."

"Easy." Rothman grabbed hold of his arm. "Come on, let's go."

"You'll pay for this," Gomez yelled. "There'll be pickets out front tomorrow."

I stared at the empty cup in my hand. I couldn't believe what I'd done.

How could I tell Jesse? He'd been trying to help and I blew it. If only I'd kept calm, if only . . .

I was about to go home when the phone rang. I hated to answer, afraid it was Jesse checking on the outcome of the meeting.

It was Rothman. "That was a pretty dumb thing you did. Gomez is a very tough guy. You better not pull any more stunts like that."

"I was very upset. Did he mean what he said about pickets out front?"

"Not unless I agree. We better talk it over. How about lunch tomorrow?"

WE MET in a midtown restaurant, a union shop. Rothman was quick to tell me he paid for his own meals and refused to accept favors from bosses. He chose a seat behind a potted palm. "We're not supposed to be meeting, so keep this under your hat."

I apologized for having lost my temper. "How would *you* feel if you were faced with losing your business?"

"Listen, I spent some time last night checking out your place and I see there's very little turnover. How do you expect to make money when people sit around all night?"

"I didn't open Limelight with the idea of getting rich."

"Let's talk about it while we eat. How about a nice juicy steak?"

"Thanks, but I haven't eaten much the last few days. I'm too upset."

"Then try a bowl of chicken soup. It'll do you good."

Why this sudden concern, I wondered. My experience with the bookies made me wary of "protectors." But Rothman seemed nice enough; perhaps I'd misjudged him. He was fiftyish, gray-haired, and actually quite mild, not nearly as bombastic as he'd seemed before. Over soup, I poured out my problems—the incompetence of managers, the demolition on 4th Street, the drop in receipts. Rothman nodded sympathetically. "It must be hard for a woman alone."

"And now I'm faced with the union. I feel I'm being penalized for what I've already done. If I hadn't given the help any benefits at all, I wouldn't be expected to double them now. It's unfair."

"That's not how Gomez sees it. He's mad, and he's still talking about throwing pickets out front. I'll hold him off as long as I can. But don't do anything crazy at the next meeting. You'll only make it hard for yourself."

I nodded, saying I'd stay calm next time.

"Good. How about lunch next week? We'll try another one of our union shops."

SAM'S LATEST financial statement confirmed my fears. The receipts were down, we were just breaking even, and if the union took over, Limelight would go under. It was no longer a matter of hiring actors and dancers, but survival. Sam suggested I apply for a liquor license; the profit on liquor was very high and would help Limelight weather whatever occurred. I resisted at first, afraid it would change the character of the place, but finally agreed to wine and beer only.

I applied for a loan, hired an attorney who had clout with the State Liquor Authority, and was assured by the bureaucrats (whose palms I greased) that despite the premise's shady past (prior to its occupancy by Limelight), I would have no trouble having my application approved. But it would take a few months; the wheels of government moved slowly, even when lubricated with oil.

Lunch with Rothman became a weekly affair. I smiled at every quip, hung on to every word, and forced myself through four-course meals. He briefed me before each meeting, telling me what to expect, how to handle Gomez, and how to counter the union's demands. But most of the time he talked about himself. And his garden. Rothman cultivated roses, and soon I knew everything there was to know about roses — types, fertilizers, diseases, pests.

What I really wanted to know about was the union itself. I'd been disturbed by reports of union corruption, goon squads, and ties to the underworld. Rothman evaded the subject, but he did admit that he was no longer starry-eyed, and that the idealism he'd felt when he first worked for the union had died. Now it was only a job.

The "negotiations" were a charade. We continued to hold meetings — the prospect of a wine and beer license kept Gomez in check — but we kept on covering the same ground. Rothman played tough, Gomez barked threats, and after a few weeks Florence no longer appeared. I remained calm, but watched with apprehension as the staff fell apart. Three of the waitresses, including Sonya, had quit, and the kitchen help, knowing that no one could be fired while negotiations were under way, grew lax. Fong, no longer able

Lew Parrella installing an exhibition, by Frank Paulin.

to maintain control, was talking about going home to Jamaica; I suspected he was looking for a job. Clarence went on working just as always—where could an elderly black man with a game leg find a job? I saw that he was afraid when Gomez held out his hands and said one day, "See these fingers? Every one of them's been broken in a union fight." What would be left of my staff when the union was through?

SOMETHING had to give. Pressured for time and not feeling well, I turned to Lew Parrella for help. He had assisted in the gallery when I first started out, but I'd seen very little of him in the past five years. He was now the American editor of the international, trilingual magazine *Camera*, and this, together with his own photography and the demands of a nine-to-five job with an advertising agency, kept him busy. I offered him a free hand and he jumped at the chance.

I had already scheduled a couple of shows—Brassaï in the fall, Edward Weston the coming year, and the current exhibition, *The History of Photography* from George Eastman House, I was planning to run for a full six weeks and give Lew time to get organized. This was longer than most Limelight shows, but the subject, I believed, would sustain interest. There were 190 facsimile prints mounted on twenty-four panels. An explanatory text divided the history into three distinct periods: the early period, from 1839 to mid-century, dealing with the daguerreotype and talbotype; the middle period, relating to the wet collodion plate; and the contemporary period, beginning in 1888, with the invention of the "Kodak" and transparent flexible film. The text included commentaries on the social, political, and cultural developments, placing the photographs within the context of the times.

I thought surely by the time the exhibition was over, my problem with the union would also be over. We'd been "negotiating" for months, yet nothing had changed. The wine and beer license had still not come through, and I was still having lunch with Rothman, still listening to him go on about roses. But what was beginning to worry me was Rothman himself. I was afraid he was growing too fond of me.

"Do you have a boyfriend?" he asked one day.

No, I said, I was too busy, and furthermore, what man would put up with my endless travails?

"Don't you miss male company?"

Yes, I did. But that would have to wait. (I was certainly not going to tell him about Kevin.)

This seemed to satisfy him. But I felt that something was afoot when he invited me for lunch at the Governor Clinton Hotel. The manager was overly solicitous. He shook Rothman's hand, escorted us to a table, and sent over a bottle of champagne. Rothman seemed preoccupied. He kept tugging at his moustache and straightening his tie. Finally, he spoke. "I've got bad news. The union is launching a new campaign. We're planning to organize the Stouffer's chain, and we won't be able to meet for lunch for a while."

I feigned disappointment. "That's too bad. But don't worry, we'll keep in touch."

Rothman reached into his pocket, then held out a fist. "Guess what I have in my hand."

"I can't imagine." (Not a ring, I hoped.)

He opened his hand and in his palm lay a key, engraved with the number 1929.

I played dumb. "Wasn't that the year of the stock market crash?"

"Oh, yeah . . . the depression. Well, this has nothing to with the stock market. It's for a room on the nineteenth floor."

"Whatever for?"

"Well, ah . . . the manager slipped it to me when we were shaking hands. . . ."

"You mean to tell me, it's a *pay-off*? Doesn't he know you can't be bought? Why, you told me yourself, you even pay for your meals."

"Yeah, well, ah . . ."

"Does he think I'm *that* kind of girl?"

"Look, Helen, it wasn't my idea. . . ."

"Then give it back. How dare he!"

Rothman slipped the key back in his pocket and stared down into his plate.

No sooner had I congratulated myself on this clever ploy than I started to worry about the union again. How would this affect Limelight? Would Gomez return after the Stouffer campaign? The food turned cold on my plate.

"No," I told the waiter, "I don't want dessert."

I was through. I was through with this whole charade. Whatever happened, happened. I was tired of playing games. I thanked Rothman for the lunch, wished him luck with the Stouffer campaign, and left.

Two weeks later, the letter from the New York State Liquor Authority finally arrived. My application for a license was denied.

MY PORT in the storm during these harrowing months was Kevin Sullivan, the attractive (and elusive) bachelor I'd been seeing on and off—mostly off—for the past year and a half. Kevin spent most of his evenings at Chumley's or the White Horse, tippling and talking with his writer friends, hard-drinking poets like Delmore Schwartz and John Berryman, and his bright, literate, politically ambitious friend, Pat Moynihan, on those nights when Pat was in town. Kevin was not about to switch from scotch to cappuccino, but he often dropped in around eleven o'clock and listened as I reported the day's events—and disasters.

Kevin was a good listener. He'd studied for the priesthood and, having spent ten years in the Jesuit Order, listened to my laments with the patience and forbearance of a priest in the confessional. Kevin had left the order, not because of a loss of faith but because he could no longer live up to his vows. He could accept the vow of poverty (the order supplied all his material needs, including hearty breakfasts of steaks and chops) and he could accept the vow of chastity (though considering his proclivities, I wondered how), but what he couldn't accept was the vow of obedience. Being in the order was like being in the army, and when he was told to teach chemistry and his field was literature, he decided it was time to leave.

Besides, he'd discovered the world of women. He had officiated at a wake, and seeing a beautiful young woman kneeling at the casket, he began to long for the less spiritual side of life. He wasted no time after leaving the order, and his success with women was due as much to his ability to listen, as it was to his wit, his eloquence, and his very good looks. He was six-foot-two, with grayish-blonde hair, and resembled the young senator from Massachusetts, Jack Kennedy.

I did my share of listening, too. Kevin had job problems. He'd taught in the English Department at Columbia for several years, but had recently been "kicked upstairs." He held the impressive title of assistant dean of graduate faculties, but he hadn't a clue as to what he was supposed to do. He spent most of his time trying to look busy, shuffling papers, walking briskly through the halls, and devising ways to elude his boss, the eminent scholar Dr. Jacques Barzun. I clucked sympathetically; Kevin loved teaching, and it seemed such a waste. His field was the Irish Literary Movement, and his book, *Joyce Among the Jesuits*, had won Columbia University's prestigious Bollingen Award.

"A Jesuit should not be let loose among women," Jerry Tallmer warned when he heard we were dating. Jean Shepherd, a nonstop talker, told me much the same thing but in many more words. But I was not about to listen to anyone. I knew that Kevin was difficult—we had problems from the start—but the attraction was irresistible, and our break-ups and reconciliations merely strengthened the bond. We blamed our difficulties on living apart. I believed in testing the waters before getting in deep, but considering the social climate and our own set of circumstances, living together was out of the question. I had a daughter to consider, and Kevin a job.

Marrying was a risk, but a chance worth taking. Kevin was undergoing psychoanalysis, and he appeared to have changed. He'd given up women, cut down on drink, and developed a yen for the creature comforts of marriage, for slippers and a hearth—we already had the dog. I had similar yearnings, but less for the comforts than for the stability of married life, and for someone to help me guide Li-lan through adolescence. (She was now sixteen.) Li-lan liked Kevin and looked forward to having a live-in father (which she hadn't had since she was two years old), and one with whom she could discuss poetry and books.

Yet we went on vacillating, and were it not for Louis Guss, an Off Broadway actor who was in between roles, we might have gone on as we were. Lou was peddling jewelry to make ends meet, and seeing us together at Limelight one night, he came to our table and spread out his wares. What caught my eye—and Kevin's too—was a wide gold band with a filigree design, one that could easily serve as a wedding ring. Kevin picked it up and slipped it on my finger. "Well," he said, "how about it?"

A few days later, we left for Maine. It was the beginning of September, the weather was beautiful, and now that the labor union was gone and Lew was helping in the gallery, this was the ideal time. We left with Li-lan's blessing, promising to return as man and wife.

We rented a cottage by the sea, and after a romantic first night, complete with full moon, we tracked down a doctor in Wiscasset and made an appointment for Wassermans, the blood test required by law. The tests came through after a three-day wait, and next we went searching for a justice of the peace. The only one in Wiscasset was a barber, and when we arrived for the ceremony, he was in the middle of a shave. He asked the customer to stand up, jaw covered with foam, removed the towels from another whose face was being steamed, and the two served as witnesses. The barber picked up a Bible, mumbled a few lines, and in less than two minutes, we were man and wife.

We got in the car and drove around looking for a liquor store—one town was "wet," another "dry"—and after buying a magnum of champagne, we returned to our honeymoon cottage.

Kevin lifted his glass. "I don't feel very married, do you?" he said.

I had to agree. I did not.

WE RENTED a duplex apartment in a brownstone on Van Dam Street in the Village, and while I stoked the home fires, adjusting to married life, Lew Parrella kept the gallery going. He'd organized two exhibitions and was working on a third. In gathering the work for *Seven Young Europeans,* the first of these shows, he was assisted by Romeo E. Martinez, the esteemed editor of *Camera.* The photographers Lew selected were Jean Mounicq and Jean Marquis of France, Fulvio Roiter of Italy, Fernand Rausser and Rob Gnant of Switzerland, and Tadeusz Rolke and Rozena Michalik of Poland.

The Poles attracted most of the attention. Work from behind the Iron Curtain was seldom seen, and we were surprised to find that it was not the dreary, propaganda-tinged work we had expected. Rolke adhered to the documentary tradition, providing us with a glimpse of gypsy life, while

Michalik used abstract, "photogrammic" forms, creating an effect both mystical and surreal. We could only speculate—had Michalik escaped the eye of the cultural watchdogs? Or were Polish artists less programmed than we'd thought?

Images of Love, Lew's second show, presented variations on this currently popular theme by thirty American photographers. Lew had asked them to select their own work, and besides the usual plethora of men and women in loving embrace, there were mothers and children, several pregnancies, and a birth. A few had submitted pictures without people: Ansel Adams sent his well-known *Birches*, Eliot Porter and Ellen Auerbach, a wreath of flowers (taken during their Mexican sojourn), and Imogen Cunningham (one of the only three women in the show), an empty bed with crumpled sheets (the image I found the most erotic). I'd expected to see the John F. Kennedys on the wall, but Jacques Lowe, the Kennedy's family photographer, had sent a picture of a couple kissing instead. Most in the show were already well known, but several, among them Bruce Davidson and Jay Maisel, were just beginning to come into their own.

Images of Love was a pleasant exhibition, and I was sorry that Deschin had given it little space, if only for the sake of Lew. But Deschin had grown weary, as many of us had, of anything smacking of *The Family of Man*.

USING THE weather as a pretext, I telephoned Elizabeth Brooks, the woman who'd been cleaning my apartment for ten years, and suggested she stay home. It had been snowing all day, and according to the radio, would continue all night.

But Elizabeth protested. "You need me, Miss Gee. I'll see you in the morning."

As usual, I weakened. Whenever she said, 'You need me, Miss Gee"—she still called me Miss Gee though I'd been married four months—I gave in. Yet I knew it meant another quarrel with Kevin. He'd taken on a wife, a child, and a dog, he argued; he hadn't married a cleaning woman too.

Kevin may have had reason to complain. Elizabeth had never been much good at cleaning out corners, but now that she had rheumatism and failing sight, having her clean even the one day a week, was more of a hazard than a help. She had thrown out my contact lenses, used Kevin's boxer shorts as dust rags, and invariably mismatched his socks. I could understand his rage when she misplaced his annotated copy of *Ulysses* (which he used teaching Joyce at the New School) and when she threw out the first few chapters of an aborted novel (though he himself said it belonged in the waste basket).

What I couldn't understand was his indifference to her plight. How would she survive if I fired her—or, as he put it, "retired" her? Elizabeth was proud, and I knew she'd prefer to go hungry rather than apply for welfare. She'd worn the same old housedress year in, year out, and the same threadbare coat fastened at the neck with a safety pin.

The minute Elizabeth arrived I knew something was wrong. She leaned against the door jamb, wavered as she walked, and when she stooped to unhook her galoshes, I was afraid she was going to faint. Ignoring her protests, I led her to our guest room. (The only "guest," so far, had been Kevin; it was where he slept after one too many.) Elizabeth lowered herself gingerly to the edge of the bed. "Ain't nothin'," she said. "Just a little headache."

I went searching for an aspirin, but finding none—Kevin had apparently exhausted the supply—I threw on my coat and hurried down the block to the drugstore. On my return I thought it strange when Penny wasn't there to greet me. She stood cowering at the top of the duplex stairs and refused to come down when I called.

Elizabeth! I ran to the guest room. She was still on the bed, but she'd fallen backwards and her eyes were closed. Was she asleep? Had she fainted? Was she *dead?*

I ran downstairs and pounded on the landlord's door. Bob Conley worked nights in the newsroom of the *New York Times*, and he'd just come home. He dashed upstairs, took one look, and picked up the phone. Within minutes the apartment was swarming with cops.

I called Kevin at Columbia; he sounded upset. "Elizabeth died in the *apartment? Where* in the apartment?"

"The living room." Kevin was superstitious and had a horror of death. He said he couldn't return home; he was having lunch with graduate students and had a meeting with Jacques Barzun at four.

Bob offered to stay until the coroner arrived. A cop was assigned to stand vigil, to be replaced every two hours by another. ("The only way to get police protection is to be dead," Bob remarked.) At three we were still waiting. I called Li-lan at school and suggested she stay overnight with a friend. Bob went downstairs and brought up a six-pack and a platter of cold cuts. He and Mary Jane were planning a party that night, the first since they purchased the brownstone.

I found it hard to eat. I kept thinking of Elizabeth lying there, and the shock of her death gave way to grief. What would happen to her? Would she be buried in a pauper's grave? As far as I knew, she had no family. She married at fifteen, lost a child in the fifth month, and hadn't seen her husband in forty years. Her life was all work, going to church, and scraping by as best she could.

I kept listening for Kevin, but by eight o'clock I'd quite given up. The guests were arriving for the Conleys' party, but Bob stayed on, refusing to leave until the coroner arrived. At around ten o'clock the doorbell rang, but I groaned when I saw an attractive young woman mounting the stairs. I directed her to the party down below.

"Party? I'm the coroner." She stepped inside, unzipped a black bag, and asked us to witness the examination of the body.

What with the shock of the death and the ten-hour wait, I was hardly in shape for a viewing. The room smelled foul. Elizabeth's lips were purple and her golden-brown skin looked gray. The coroner took scissors from her case and slit open her dress, exposing several layers of underclothes—a slip, a camisole, two long-sleeved shirts. When she came to the corset, the old-fashioned kind with metal stays, she tried cutting through but the scissors snapped. I brought poultry shears from the kitchen.

"Ah, a money belt!" Lying on her crotch was a leather pouch. The coroner opened it and pulled out a wedding ring and five gold coins. Next she pulled out something shiny and brown, the size and shape of a shrimp. "Ah, a fetus! And very well preserved." I swallowed hard and turned away— was this the child that Elizabeth lost? Next came bankbooks, six in all. She handed them to the cop. "When you take an inventory, make sure you list each one separately." She completed her examination, wrote a report, and swept out of the house, as cool and unruffled as when she came.

"Five gold coins, one wedding ring, one fetus, six bankbooks. . . ." While the cop took the inventory, I studied the bank books, astonished to find that Elizabeth had never made a withdrawal and continued to make deposits until the week before she died. She had accumulated nearly thirty thousand dollars.

"I wonder why she went on working," Bob said. "She could have re-tired years ago." I wondered too. I thought of all the years I'd put up with unswept corners and half-mopped floors. I thought of my contact lenses, Kevin's socks and his boxer shorts, and all the quarrels we had about Eliza-beth during these past four months. I felt duped.

But when the morgue wagon arrived, when Elizabeth was stuffed in a body bag and thumped down the stairs, I felt a deep sense of loss. The Con-leys' party was breaking up, and the guests stood in the hall, watching as she was carried out. I ran upstairs, threw open the windows and started to clean. I swept and mopped, turned over the mattress and stripped the bed. The cold winter air cleared away the smell, and it also helped clear my mind. I began to see Elizabeth in another light, not as a miser hoarding a bit of wealth, but as someone needing to feel like a person. If she'd gone on working long past her time, it was probably not for the money. I could still hear her say, "You need me, Miss Gee."

I was on my knees scrubbing when Kevin walked in. Seeing the bed stripped and the mattress turned over, he yelled, "So! She died in our bed!" He left and didn't return for two days. It was hard to accept, but now I knew that whenever I needed him he would not be there. The marriage would go on, at least for a time—there would be the usual recriminations, tears and regret—yet I knew, down deep, it was over. It died that day with Elizabeth.

DURING THESE months of travail, there had been several fine shows: *The Eye of Paris*, Brassaï's first one-person exhibition in New York; *Louis Faurer*, his per-sonal rather than his fashion work; and *Photographs by Professors*, an exhibition Lew arranged to coincide with a meeting of the College Art Association in New York in 1960. He built the show around the work of seven teachers: Lou Block of the University of Louisville, Van Deren Coke of the University of Florida, Allen Downes of the University of Michigan, Walter Rosenblum of Brooklyn College, Aaron Siskind of the Institute of Design, Henry Holmes Smith of the University of Indiana, and Minor White of the Rochester In-stitute of Technology.

The exhibition called attention to the growing acceptance of the medium by colleges and universities, and in presenting the work of such disparate photographers, it also drew attention to the diversity of approach. Over thirty colleges and universities had added courses in photography to their fine arts curriculum. Not everyone saw this as progress, however. Many photographers were suspicious of the trend and though pleased that the medium was gaining wide acceptance (for which they credited Steichen and *The Family of Man*), they doubted that it would thrive in the halls of academia. Working for grades, they believed, would stifle the creative spirit.

Lisette expressed these same doubts, quoting one of her favorite aphorisms: "Only the truly creative student can survive school." She exempted her own class at the New School, which was part of the adult education program and "free of grades and degrees and all that nonsense." When Lisette wasn't conducting a vendetta, or sounding off on her latest enthusiasm—the most recent was parapsychology—she was sharp and to the point. I was always interested in her views, regardless of how extreme. Now that I was "safely married," she invited me to sit at her table, even when Evsa was there. It had taken six years.

BEING MARRIED TO Kevin was like riding the cyclone in Coney Island—it might not kill you, but it was a frightening ride. Every upswing in mood was followed by a fall, and I never knew what lay ahead, how steep the climb, how deep the drop. Our quarrels often took place after an enjoyable evening when we'd had friends in for dinner. I liked to cook, and since we no longer availed ourselves of Limelight food, I immersed myself in cookbooks and made a different dish every night. Kevin was picky. I did my best, trying to rival not only L'Escoffier but also the chefs in the Jesuit Order. (I still heard about those breakfasts of steaks and chops.) Actually, though, Kevin knew little about food, having eaten in pubs most of the time. But now that he had a wife, he was a tyrant, demanding only the finest—flowers, candlelight, five-course meals. It took many dinners and many fights (during which I wept out of frustration and rage, unable to match his facility with words) before I realized that this was not what Kevin wanted at all. He didn't want home life, slippers, and a hearth—or, for that matter, a wife. What he wanted was Chumley's and the White Horse. Even a hamburger would do.

STEICHEN SUFFERED another stroke, leaving him partially paralyzed and unable to speak. For a man of his energy to be made helpless was sad, and my first reaction when I heard the news was that rather than live out his days in a vegetative state, it might have been better if he had been felled, just like one of his redwood trees.

We hadn't talked since I married, and now, more than ever, I regretted the lapse. Grace Mayer had kept us informed of each other's activities, but when she told Steichen I'd married, he didn't believe it, calling her an "incurable romantic." I meant to keep in touch and to see him now and then, but between fixing up the apartment and dealing with the unending problems at Limelight, I was busier than ever. Steichen was far from my mind.

I was also involved in a time-consuming project, thanks to Steichen himself. *America's Many Faces*, a project sponsored by the Urban League, was conducting a nationwide search for photographs dramatizing the multiracial character of the country. Having lent his name, if not his presence, Steichen had recommended me as a judge on the screening committee, together with Kathleen Haven and Roy DeCarava. Photographers were asked to submit pictures depicting cooperation and friendship across racial lines, religion, and national origin, as well as ones showing the difficulties, prejudices, and open conflict that result from these differences in background. Inspired no doubt by *The Family of Man*, the league was planning both an exhibition and a book. Steichen's book was selling in the millions, rivaling that bestseller of all time, the Bible. We met regularly and screened hundreds of prints, but the time was largely wasted. The project never got off the ground.

From Kathleen, I learned that Steichen was improving. He was slowly regaining the use of his limbs and had even begun to talk. I wanted to go see him, rather than depend on secondhand reports, but knowing how sensitive he was to appearing infirm, I thought I'd wait until he was up and about.

Then one afternoon I answered the phone, and heard what sounded like Steichen's voice. The words were slurred but I managed to make them out. "I've got good news. . . . Try and guess what it is."

"You've recovered!" I said cheerfully, not wanting to let on that my marriage was in trouble.

"Not yet. It'll take some time before I'm back in the pink."

"It's the shad-blow tree. You've started photographing again."

"Nope, guess again."

Now what could make a man of eighty recovering from a stroke so happy? I couldn't imagine.

"I've gotten married!"

"*Married?*"

"Yep, and I'm as happy as a hound dog."

I wasn't too surprised, though the timing seemed strange. Grace was so proper; I would have thought she'd wait until he had fully recovered. Perhaps she'd been overeager, never having married before. She worshipped Steichen, and I could think of nothing nicer for the two of them than to spend their "golden years" together. "I'm happy for Grace, and I wish you both well," I said.

"Grace? I didn't marry Grace. I married Joanna."

"Joanna? *Who* is Joanna?"

"She's a young woman who came to interview me in the hospital. We fell in love."

"A *young* woman? How young?"

"Twenty-six."

"Good God!" This was not even a May-December romance; it was more like January-December.

"Congratulations," I said, weakly.

I was not the only one who was shocked. Despite the efforts of Steichen's family to keep the marriage quiet (his daughters were double his bride's age), word got around and there was all sorts of speculation: Who *was* this Joanna? A gold-digger? An opportunist? Was she one of those groupies who pursue men with names? Or, was it possible (I hoped) that she loved him? I worried about Steichen. What would happen once the bloom was off the peach and Joanna discovered that living with an eighty-year-old man had its problems? How would Steichen hold up when she finally left? Would that be the blow that would fell this great tree?

Grace held up bravely and went on working at the museum. But she no longer acted as informant, and my best source was still Kathleen Haven. She visited the Steichens at their estate now and then, and after one of these visits I asked her how he was. "Wonderful," she said. "Steichen looks great. But Joanna has aged considerably."

He rested a great deal, nodded frequently, but awakened often enough to keep an eye on his attractive young wife. The marriage lasted for fourteen years, until Steichen died at the age of ninety-four.

KEVIN KEPT our marriage from his family. His mother was living in a nursing home and should she learn that her "baby"—the youngest of her seven sons—had married a divorced woman, and outside of the faith, he was afraid the blow might kill her. She was crushed when he left the Jesuit Order, her dream of having a priest in the family shattered. The marriage, on top of this, might prove too much. To keep her from finding out, Kevin installed a separate phone in his study, and each time it rang he poured himself a drink, resigned to a litany of complaints.

Not having to meet the clan was a relief. If the Sullivans were anything like the people I grew up with in Washington Heights, an Irish-Catholic enclave where we were the outsiders and prejudice was rife, I didn't think they would welcome either Li-lan or me. Kevin claimed to feel like an outsider himself, and with the exception of his niece Susan, who was interested in acting (and eventually became a television star), his contact with his family was mostly by phone—cordial, but distant.

We were eating dinner one night when Kevin's "family phone" rang. He groaned, picked up his glass of wine, and closeted himself in his study. He emerged looking grim. "It wasn't my mother. It was my brother Finbar. He's says he feels terrible and he's checking into Montefiore Hospital tomorrow for tests."

"Oh no, the children! What if . . ."

"Nothing's going to happen! It can't!" Kevin refilled his glass, and we finished dinner in silence.

Finbar was a widower, raising six children alone. We'd never met, but remembering my father's struggles raising three children alone, and my fears as a child, always worrying that something would happen to him, I couldn't wipe the thought from my mind.

Kevin went to see him in the hospital the next day, but the tests still hadn't come through. "I don't like the way he looks," he said. "He hangs his head to one side in the most peculiar way. He's not in any pain, so I don't know why."

A few days later, he got a doctor's report. The diagnosis was lymphoma; the prognosis, poor.

"The children . . . what if. . ."

"Don't say that!" Kevin screamed. "He's got to live!"

Ten days later, two weeks after he'd been hospitalized, the call came through. Finbar had died in the night.

I SAW LITTLE of Kevin the week of the wake. His mother had apparently held up well, but Kevin returned looking shaken. "Who's going to care for those kids?" he cried. "They've just about got over their mother's death, now this. . . ."

Caring for six children—two boys and four girls, ages three to fifteen—was a full-time job, and none of the Sullivans felt equipped for the burden. Those who were married had problems of their own, and those who were single suffered from what Kevin called "the Irish disease" (his own drinking excluded, of course). His brother Vincent lived alone in a rooming house, and Harry, a pale, toothless wraith who drifted around the Village lived only God knows where. This left only Kevin.

I would not have recommended him, having come to the conclusion, after eight months of marriage, that Kevin was not even equipped to handle one child, much less six. Li-lan would agree. She was tired of his moods and his tantrums, and of having to tiptoe around the house to spare his jangled nerves. Kevin had given up psychoanalysis, considering himself "cured." His hangovers were monumental, and when he couldn't make it to Columbia, I called his office, giving him every disease that could be cured in twenty-four hours. I had thought of leaving him, but this was hardly the time.

Kevin finally yielded to family pressure and agreed to assume the role of surrogate father. But he couldn't see himself living with six children, and we spent hours every night trying to find a solution—how to honor his commitment, yet maintain a distance. Should we move them out of Queens into an apartment nearby? Should we rent a brownstone and house them on separate floors? Meanwhile, he hired a housekeeper and visited the children on weekends. But the more he saw of them, the less interested he was in assuming the role of parent.

And where was I in all this? I went flying back to Dr. Schweitzer and asked what he thought I should do. He answered with one word: "Run."

I knew he was right, but I couldn't. At least, not yet.

FINBAR had been dead about a month when Kevin got a call from the police. His brother Vincent had had an "accident." Would he come to the morgue and identify the body?

After viewing the body, Kevin went to Vincent's rooming house to collect his meager belongings. Aside from rosary beads, a bottle of scotch, and a suit good enough to be buried in, there was little worth packing. As he was about to leave, he noticed a stain on the wall that looked like blood, and sticking to the stain, a patch of gray hair. Vincent was probably drunk when he fell and hit his head, and it was the sight of the hair that made Kevin lose control. He sat down on the bed and wept.

The Sullivans gathered for another wake, and Vincent joined Finbar in the family plot. Kevin's mother held up well.

THE SHOCK of their father's death had finally set in, and the children were beginning to misbehave. They were difficult and quarrelsome, and the housekeepers Kevin hired invariably left. Finbar, Jr., the ten-year old, seemed the most deeply affected. He was pale and withdrawn, had lost several pounds, and hung his head to one side, just as his father had during his final weeks of illness. Kevin was worried. "If he doesn't perk up soon," he said, after one of his visits to the children in Queens, "I'll take him for a check-up."

When Finbar continued to lose weight—seven pounds, a lot for a small boy—Kevin had him examined him by the family physician. He found nothing wrong, attributing the loss of weight to the shock of the death, and the mimicking of his father as a reaction to the loss. He was, after all, his namesake, and identification with his father was strong. The doctor prescribed a tonic, and asked to see him in another in two months.

Finbar kept losing weight, and Kevin sought a second opinion. The doctor confirmed what the first one had said. The problem was psychological and should be treated as such. What he needed was male attention, someone to act as a father. He prescribed sugar pills for their placebo effect, and suggested that Kevin spend more time with the boy.

Kevin complied. He took him to the Bronx Zoo one Sunday afternoon, but complained to me afterwards that Finbar had shown no interest in the animals. All he wanted to do was sit on a bench. "There's got to be something wrong. It can't all be in his head."

Rather than consult a third doctor, Kevin brought him to Montefiore, the same hospital where his father died. He'd lost nine pounds and was skin and bones. The doctors insisted he remain for tests.

Several days later, the results came through: leukemia. The disease had gone undetected, the doctors claimed, because it was difficult to diagnose in children. Kevin was distraught. I cradled his head in my arms as he sobbed. "Where is God?" he cried. "How can He do this to an innocent child!"

Finbar failed rapidly. In less than two weeks, three months to the day of his father's death, young Finbar died.

THE UNION LEFT Limelight a shambles. It had finally given up on organizing the coffeehouses (Posman had also given up on me), but the damage had already been done. During the months of negotiations, the staff fell apart and half, including Fong, quit. I had tried several managers but none worked out. The only one who showed promise was Malcolm Morley, an Englishman who looked like a butler and painted on the side. I didn't take him seriously as an artist (wasn't *everyone* in the Village doing something on the side?) and was annoyed when he quit and took one of the milk-glass tabletops to use as a palette. (Years later, when Malcolm became famous and his paintings were selling for tens of thousands, I wondered whether he was still using my table top.)

At home, nothing had changed. Kevin was no closer to deciding what to do about the children, and there was little I could do but lend support. I spent the nights he was in Queens at Limelight, trying to get it back in shape. The gallery was my mainstay. When I immersed myself in photography, I could forget the troubles at home.

The high point of the spring season was the Edward Weston show, an exhibition I'd been angling for since 1955. The arrangements had been made through Weston's son Brett, Weston having died of Parkinson's disease in 1958. Brett wanted a show of his own, and I'd had to walk a fine line, trying to get his father's work while holding him off. It was not that he didn't deserve a show. But like so many sons who rival illustrious fathers, he suffered by comparison.

Brett was driving cross-country and was due to arrive a few days before the opening. He was bringing along additional prints (and, I suspected, a group of his own). When he didn't arrive and there was no message or call, I was afraid he'd had an accident en route. When I wasn't worrying about Brett, I was worrying about the Edward Westons, picturing them strewn across the highway. Then, just as we were closing, a man who could only be Brett Weston walked through the door. He had tanned, weathered skin and a Westerner's stride, and he was outfitted as if he'd been camping out. The only thing missing was a horse.

He blamed the delay on the New York police: "The minute I hit town, I pulled into a parking lot and went to get something to eat. When I got back to the car, it was surrounded by cops. Someone had spotted my gun lying on the seat. They took me to the station house, and I had a tough time getting out. I'd come clear across the country with my gun in full view, and as soon as I hit New York, I'm pulled in. What kind of a town is this, anyway?"

I was relieved that he—and the photographs—were safe. He brought fifty in all, including several never exhibited before. There was a selection of work from the 1920s and 1930s, a group from the Point Lobos series in the 1940s, and a version of the peppers I'd never seen. Also included were several prints from the "backyard series," made when the coast was off limits during World War II.

There were nudes, of course, all of them "discreet"—no frontal views, not a wisp of pubic hair. Ever since his retrospective exhibition at the Museum of Modern Art in 1946, Weston became cautious about showing nudes. Several trustees, concerned with public reaction, had objected to his frontal nudes. It was only through the intervention of René d'Harnoncourt, the director of the museum, that they were finally hung, though on a wall where they were less likely to be seen.

Weston had responded with a letter to Nancy Newhall, the curator of the show: "By all means tell your board that P.H. (pubic hair) has definitely been part of my development as an artist. Tell them it has been the most important part, that I like it brown, black, red or golden, curly or straight, all sizes and shapes." Yet the incident had an effect, and since "erotic" material was banned from the mail, he chose to play it safe, scrutinizing each print with a magnifying glass, checking for errant stray hairs.

These same considerations kept me from organizing an exhibition of nudes, although I had thought about it many times. I didn't want to risk being shut down by the police, and I worried too about the type of audience a show of this kind would attract.

The Weston exhibition was a huge success. The New York Times ran an article entitled "Weston's World" in the Sunday magazine and reproduced eight of the images. Brett had raised the price of the prints from fifty dollars to seventy-five, yet over half were sold. The gallery was crowded during the entire five weeks, and even those who disparaged photography had to agree: Edward Weston was an artist and a master.

Lisette disagreed. "Weston is no photographer!" she announced one night. I'd grown accustomed to her outrageous remarks, but this one I found preposterous. Had she disliked him personally? The way she felt about a photographer often colored her opinion, and I could see where the two might have clashed. She had met Edward Weston on one of her trips out west and visited him in his cabin in the woods. But all she had to say about it was, "Wherever you looked there was a cat." (She claimed there were hundreds, others reported fifty.)

"Now there's a photographer," she said, pointing to an attractive young woman who had just walked in. She had a small, pert face and close-cropped hair and was carrying a bulging gadget bag. "Come, I'd like you to meet her. She's slightly mad, but she has a very great talent. Remember her name. You'll be hearing about her in the future." Eventually I did: Diane Arbus.

WESTON was followed by Gordon Parks, the only black photographer who had been able to crack Life and the first in the country to be recognized as a professional. Lew had arranged to exhibit his photographs of teenage gangs, a powerful series about a growing menace in both black neighborhoods and white. After Parks, we showed the experimental color of a little-known photographer, Jack Smith.

I appeared at Limelight less and less, too unhappy to put on a smiling face. Some nights I managed, and on one of these nights Grace Mayer appeared, accompanied by a tall, thin, sharp-nosed young man, one of the candidates for Steichen's job. Steichen had decided to step down after fifteen years, and the museum was conducting a search for a successor. Anyone following Steichen would look pale indeed. Grace had a voice in the decision-making process, and one could safely assume, seeing her squiring this young man about, that he was the one she favored.

"This is John Szarkowski," she said beaming, and turning to the young man, who seemed ill at ease, she swept the room with an outstretched arm. "This is the place to meet photographers, John. *Everybody* comes to Lime-light." I offered to introduce him to several right then—Lisette was sitting just a few tables away—but Grace seemed reluctant to relinquish her charge. She led him to the gallery and after looking at the exhibition, they left.

Word spread through the room. Who *is* this what's-his-name? Where did they find him—in Indian country? Why not a New Yorker, someone in the know? How can a young guy like that step into Steichen's shoes?

A couple of days later, Szarkowski reappeared. He looked around nervously, as if wondering where to alight, and seemed relieved when I asked him to join me for coffee. I glanced around the room, making a mental list of those he should meet, but he suggested we leave and go somewhere for a drink.

We crossed the street to the Riviera Bar, and after a martini he looked more relaxed. He was bright and eloquent, and whatever doubts I'd had were dispelled. He was passionate about photography, had a strong point of view, and was not the nonentity that many presumed. I wasn't familiar with his photography, but I'd heard about his book, *The Idea of Louis Sullivan*, a project he'd completed on a Guggenheim Fellowship.

"And speaking of Louis Sullivan," Szarkowski said, "there's a building of his right here in New York. I don't remember the address, but it's in the manufacturing district, somewhere around Bleecker Street. Let's go find it."

We hopped a cab, got out on West Broadway, and prowled the area around Spring and Prince, a section of the city that would one day be Soho, but which was now mostly warehouses and industrial lofts. The streets were deserted. A rat scuttled by. "Don't look down, look up!" he admonished, and as I gazed at the facades of the buildings we passed—old cast-iron structures, many quite ornate—I began to see the area with new eyes.

At Bleecker, near Crosby, he let out a whoop. There it was, the old Bayard building, designed by Louis Sullivan in 1897, the lone example of his work in New York. It had an elegance and simplicity the others around it lacked, its decorative elements more subtle and refined. Twelve stories high, a sky-scraper in its day, it had the added distinction of being constructed with steel. Szarkowski expounded on its virtues at length, and on the way back to Limelight, I was treated to a lecture on the work of Louis Sullivan.

He hesitated at the door. He was in no mood to meet photographers, and besides, there was no hurry. Were he appointed director of the Photography Department (which he was two years later, in 1962), he'd eventually meet them all. "Regardless of what happens at the Museum of Modern Art, he said, "visiting that building was worth the trip to New York."

ALL THE REVERSES of the past two years—the Mafia, the union, my un-happy marriage, and all the deaths—had taken their toll. I could no longer handle the problems, and for the first time in years, Limelight was in debt. Bill collectors and process servers were on my trail, and I was beginning to feel like a criminal on the run. When I wasn't ducking into the ladies' room or fleeing to the basement, I was plotting new routes to elude them on the street.

The summer had been slow, and to catch up on bills, I tried pawning a few personal possessions. But I was shocked to discover how little of what I owned had monetary value: my typewriter was of prewar vintage, the "emerald" lavaliere that had belonged to my mother turned out to be glass, and the paintings I'd purchased from artist friends were of little interest to pawn brokers. And they were even less interested in photographs.

I woke up each morning with a boulder on my chest and could hardly lift myself out of bed. My arms were heavy, my legs leaden, and I had to force myself through the day. The worse things got, the less I was able to cope. Bankruptcy was an option, but it was considered a disgrace in these prosperous times, and it was not a route I wanted to take without exploring alternatives.

The most obvious solution was to sell the place, a decision I found hard to face. I thought back seven years to something Sheinfeld said when I signed the lease. "Some day you may want out." I had reached that point. I was tired of struggling and wanted out. I wanted out from all the burdens that Limelight imposed. And I also wanted out of the marriage. I still cared for Kevin and felt for his plight. But since he'd finally decided what to do—or what *not* to do—about the children, I felt free to think about leaving. He had come to the conclusion, after deliberating for months, that he was un-equipped to father five orphans; children got on his nerves. But he would continue in his role as visiting uncle and keep tabs on them by phone. The children, meanwhile, had worked things out among themselves. The oldest of the five, a girl of fifteen, was planning to marry in a year or so, and she and her husband intended to raise her four-year-old brother. Her three younger sisters would fend for themselves, with the help of a housekeeper hired by the estate. A sorry solution, but in the light of Kevin's tempera-ment and his inability to live with others, I believed they were spared.

Parting with Limelight I knew would be traumatic. There were many more photographers whose work I wanted to show, and many ideas for ex-hibitions that I had not yet explored. I hadn't completed the full ten years, and while I would have liked to see the gallery go on, I was afraid it might fall into the wrong hands. A new owner might use it as a publicity gimmick instead of a showplace for serious work, so rather than take that chance, I decided to close the gallery as a condition of the sale.

Provided, of course, that there was a sale. Under the conditions imposed by Big Ben—I needed his permission to transfer the lease—it didn't seem likely that I would find a buyer. Rents were rising all over the Village, and if Limelight closed, as he no doubt hoped it would, he could get thousands for the place, not hundreds.

But at least I had to try. I inserted an ad in the *New York Times* and got quite a few calls, most from businessmen attracted by the space and low rent. But none wanted to keep it as a coffeehouse. One wanted to turn it into a fast-food joint ("Limelight hamburgers, ain't that an idea?"), another a bowling alley, and another, a penny arcade. And they all lost interest when they heard of the problem with the landlord and the lease.

Christmas was dismal. I went through the motions—the tree, the gifts, a dinner of roast goose, but my heart wasn't in it. I found it hard to feign joy when Li-lan presented me with a dog she'd adopted from the pound, pre-paring me for the day when Penny shed the mortal coil. I was touched by her concern, but I didn't look forward to the prospect of walking two dogs in the interim. (Penny was ten and lived five more years.) Kevin was none too happy with another yapping dog, but since I was planning to leave him in a couple of months, it didn't much matter how he felt.

While clearing away the wrappings and the tinsel, I thought back to the Christmas of 1954 when I was faced with the same grim prospect: bankruptcy. Then I was saved by a miracle; was I entitled to another one? Limelight was falling apart. The roof was leaking, pipes were bursting, and the floor was buckling in spots. The insurance company had refused to renew my policy, and if someone were to trip and break a leg, I would be personally liable. My credit was gone, and in order to pay cash for provisions, I'd dipped into the money set aside as withholding taxes. I'd been summoned to the office of the city collector, and unless I paid up, I'd be guilty of a federal offense.

Then the miracle occurred. Les Lone and Manny Roth, the owners of the Cafe Wha' on Macdougal Street. heard that Limelight was for sale and approached me with a deal. They offered just enough money to pay back bills, twelve thousand dollars, a fraction of the real value had there been no snags. Though this didn't cover the bank loan I'd made (which I would have to repay over the next few years), I jumped at the chance. They intended to keep Limelight just as it was, except for the gallery, which they agreed to close. They would not be intimidated by Big Ben; if necessary, they would take him to court.

After accepting the offer, it was hard to appear at Limelight and act as though nothing was amiss. I found it particularly painful to walk into the gallery, though the current exhibition — by the nineteenth-century photographer Julia Margaret Cameron — was special and rare and one that I was proud of. I had always been interested in the lives of unique women, and if the gallery had to close, I was glad it would close with the work of a gifted woman.

I tried not to let on that anything was brewing the day Beaumont Newhall called and said he was in town. He wanted to buy the portrait of Mrs. Duckworth (the mother of Virginia Woolf), and hoped to see it that same afternoon. Three of the Camerons had already been sold, and since he was buying it for himself, not for George Eastman House, I dispensed with the commission, reducing the price from sixty-five dollars to forty-five. It was Limelight Gallery's last sale.

I was not up to farewells. I said nothing to anyone but Deschin about selling Limelight and stayed at home while the negotiations were going on. The day the papers were finally signed, I slipped into the basement and retrieved various items I'd stored there. On January 31, 1961, just seven years after I signed the lease, I turned the key in the door and walked away.

EPILOGUE

Whatever small virtues I might possess, the gift of prophecy is evidently not one of them. If anyone had told me on the day I sold (or, rather, abandoned) Limelight that I would be sitting here some thirty-five years later pecking away at a keyboard, recollecting those heady (and difficult) days as an inadvertent "pioneer," I would have scoffed. I'd never been one to dwell on the past—the present was always of much greater interest—but here I sit, in my apartment in Greenwich Village, sorting through clippings and letters and diary entries, re-creating a time and a place and a part of my life that in some strange way has come full circle.

The transition from public to private life wasn't easy. I missed Limelight. I missed the activity, the people, the feeling of theater, never knowing what each night would bring. But what I missed most of all was the gallery. Though it was supposed to close as a condition of the sale, I was distressed when the new owners reneged on our agreement and decided to keep it going. The outcry that followed Deschin's announcement of its closing in the New York Times had given them pause, and they decided that the gallery might be useful after all, if only for publicity value.

Most of the exhibitions were awful. What also hurt was the neglect of the space—dirty panels, flaking paint, holes from thumbtacks, burned-out light bulbs. Deschin stopped reviewing the shows, and no longer seeing the name Limelight in print, the owners dismantled the gallery and put tables in its place.

They had other problems too. Big Ben refused to transfer the lease, and

Helen Gee, Greeenwich Village, 1993, by Frank Paulin.

though I never learned the full story (I suspected they were running scared), Limelight was put up for sale within the year. The next owners had clout with Big Ben (who had upped the rent to the thousands) and apparently with the State Liquor Authority as well. They installed a bar, changed the decor, and soon nothing was left of Limelight but the name. Jean Shepherd moved in with his radio show, and the clientele changed completely. Several years later it was sold again, and it finally ended up as a transvestite bar with a heavy drug scene. It was closed by the police in 1971.

As for me, I went on to other things. I left Kevin, moved to a brownstone in the West Village, and to regain my health and lift out of the depression I sank into after the sale, I joined a gym and worked out with weights. I also studied yoga and tai chi ch'uan (disciplines new to America at the time) and gradually got on my feet. To make a living, I became active in the art world and as an art consultant working with painting and sculpture, organized exhibitions, curated shows, and developed private and corporate collections. Few of my clients were interested in photography, and after a photo mural I'd proposed for a wall in the World Trade Center was rejected for not being "art," I realized that photography still had a way to go. I also spent years reviving interest in Yun Gee's work, forgotten during his twenty years of mental illness. Since Yun's death in 1963, there have been five museum retrospectives.

Li-lan grew up and became a painter herself. Largely self-taught, she developed a style uniquely her own and exhibited both here and abroad. She married the Japanese artist Masuo Ikeda, whom she met in New York in 1965 during his one-person exhibition at the Museum of Modern Art. I visited them in Tokyo several times during their ten-year marriage, and through Masuo I became involved in the Japanese art world. I built several major corporate collections and also worked with the Tokyo Shimbun, a newspaper that sponsors museum exhibitions, and assisted in organizing several large shows. In 1977, I realized a life-long dream and spent a month in the People's Republic of China, and, more recently, a week in Taiwan in connection with an exhibition of Yun's work at the Taipei Museum of Fine Arts.

During this time I had been watching photography from the sidelines. I rooted for Lee Witkin when he opened a small gallery on a shoestring in 1969 and saw it become the first *commercially* successful photography gallery in New York. I also watched as Tennyson Schad, an attorney by trade, opened the Light Gallery in 1973, a gallery which, under several different directors during its ten-year life, made a substantial contribution to the acceptance of art photography. The auction houses took note, and I watched (with considerable amazement) as photography became a collectable, prices rising each year. (Who would have imagined *this* in the 1950s?) I also watched the development of a hierarchy, parallel to that of the art world, of critics, curators, historians, and dealers. More and more schools offered courses in photography, and, most heartening of all, about half of the students were women. I watched too as photography itself changed, reflecting changes in technology, society, and the world as a whole.

No longer content with sitting on the sidelines, I edged back to the field of photography. Choosing not to become a dealer, I took the less lucrative but ultimately more satisfying route of teaching, curating, lecturing, and writing. In 1979, I organized the exhibition *Stieglitz and the Photo Secession* for the New Jersey State Museum, subsequently shown at the National Arts Club in New York (where Stieglitz launched the Photo Secession in 1902). In 1980, I curated *Photography of the Fifties: An American Perspective* for the Center for Creative Photography, Tucson. It was shown at the International Center for Photography in New York and traveled for two years.

It's been a fascinating time, though not without setbacks. Despite reasonably good health, I developed two serious illnesses in recent years. In 1991 I was in St. Vincent's Hospital with acute pneumonia at the same time that Robert Frank was a patient there too. But being on life support, I couldn't reach past all the hoses and wires to pick up a phone and invite him to my room. After another illness, I recovered a second time, and as Robert would say, "Life dances on. . . ."

I only hope that when I'm cut down for good, I'll be caught in the middle of a jig.

LIMELIGHT CHRONOLOGY

1954

Joseph Breitenbach, *Korea*, May 13–June 27

Rudolph Burckhardt, June 29–August 15

Louis Stettner, August 17–September 27

Minor White, September 28–November 5

Grant La Farge, *New England in the 1890s*, November 6–30

Great Photographs: Berenice Abbott, Ansel Adams, Edouard Boubat, Bill Brandt, Brassai, Manuel Alvarez Bravo, Harry Callahan, Imogen Cunningham, Robert Doisneau, Robert Frank, Izis, Lisette Model, Gotthard Schuh, W. Eugene Smith, Paul Strand, Jacob Tuggener, Sabine Weiss, Edward Weston, Minor White, December 1–30

1955

David Vestal, January 3–February 14

Arnold Newman, February 15–March 19

Eliot Porter, March 21–April 17

Alfred Stieglitz/Dorothy Norman, *Portraits of Each Other*, April 19–May 7

Dan Weiner, *Italy*, May 10–June 7

Suzy Harris, June 10–July 25

Group Show: 14 *Photographers*, July 28–September 2

Wyn Bullock, September 5–October 8

Moholy-Nagy, October 11–November 19

Edouard Boubat, November 22–December 31

1956

Leon Levinstein, *New York*, January 3–February 11

Ansel Adams, February 14–March 31

Esther Bubley, April 3–May 5

Imogen Cunningham, May 8–June 25

Sabine Weiss, June 28–July 29

Footlights and Spotlights: Theatrical Photographs of the American Stage, 1860–1900, loan exhibition from George Eastman House, August 1–September 19

Ken Heyman, September 21–October 28

Dan Weiner, *South Africa*, October 30–December 2

Eugene Atget, December 4–January 6

1957

Izis, January 8–February 17

Frank Paulin, February 19–April 2

Eliot Porter/Ellen Auerbach, *Madonnas and Marketplaces*, April 4–May 19

Elliott Erwitt, May 24–July 7

Morris H. Jaffe, July 9–August 18

Lyrical and Accurate, loan exhibition from George Eastman House, designed by Minor White, August 20–September 28

W. Eugene Smith, October 1–November 10

John Cohen, *Peru*, November 12–December 15

Berenice Abbott, *Portraits of the Twenties*, December 17–January 26

1958

David Seymour, *Chim's Children*, January 28–February 25

Rudolph Burckhardt/George Montgomery, February 27–April 10

Ken Heyman, *Bali, Japan, Hong Kong*, April 12–May 25

Bert Stern, May 27–July 20

James Karales, *Rendville, U.S.A.*, July 24–August 31

Group Show, September 3–30

Harold Feinstein, October 2–November 15

Gerda Peterich, *Dance Portraits*, November 18–December 31

1959
Robert Doisneau, January 5–February 28
Harry Lapow, March 3–April 12
Dan Weiner, *Russia and Eastern Europe*, April 14–May 12
The History of Photography, loan exhibition from George Eastman House,
May 15–June 30
Group Show: *Seven Europeans*, July 2–August 13
Group Show: *Images of Love*, August 15–September 30
Brassai, *The Eye of Paris*, October 5–31
Group Show, November 2–December 13
Louis Faurer, December 15–January 18

1960
Photographs by Professors: Lou Block, Van Deren Coke, Allen Downes,
Walter Rosenblum, Aaron Siskind, Henry Holmes Smith, Minor White,
January 19–February 29
Ralph Hattersley, March 1–27
Jerry Liebling, April 1–May 15
Edward Weston, May 17–June 26
Gordon Parks, June 28–August 7
Jack Smith, August 9–September 11
Group Show, September 13–October 16
Claudia Andujar, October 18–November 8
Paul Caponigro/Minor White, November 10–December 14
Julia Margaret Cameron, December 16–January 31, 1961

INDEX

References to illustrations are printed in boldface type.

Abbe, Kathryn, 157
Abbott, Berenice, 24, **192,** 192–95,
    248; described, 189–91; exhibition
    at Limelight, 86–87, 90, 217–20
Adams, Ansel, 24, 105, 248–50; exhi-
    bition at Limelight, 86–87, 153–56,
    269; quoted, 76, 154
Admiral, Virginia (De Niro's mother),
    239, 242
Agee, James, 115–16
Agee, Mia, 116
Alsberg, Cora. *See* Wright, Cora
    Alsberg
Americans, The (Frank), 250–54;
    preparations for shooting, 110–18
American Society of Magazine Pho-
    tographers, 64
Ansco, sponsors peacock dinner,
    237–39
Aperture (journal), 66, 74, 103–4
Arbus, Diane, 283
Art Institute of Chicago, 230
Atget, Eugene, 193–95, 213
Auerbach, Ellen, 204–9, 269; photo-
    graph by, **205**
Avedon, Richard, 24, 248–49

Baldwin, James, 254–55
Barry, Les, 252
Barzun, Jacques, 267, 270
Bassman, Lillian, 157
Bayard building, 284–85
Beats, 250–53
Beauchamp, Anthony, 132
Beraud-Villars, Marie-Jean, 164
Bernstein, Lou, 23
Berryman, John, 266
Big Ben (Limelight landlord), 30–31,
    226, 286–90 passim
bikers, 77
Block, Lou, 272
Bloom, Claire, 236
Blue Mill Tavern, 74, 80
bohoes (pre-Beatniks), 70–74, 77–86
bookies, 137–39, 162–64, 224–33
Borchers, Bob (Limelight manager),
    93–94, 133–39 passim, 172, 196
Boubat, Edouard, 42, 153–54; ex-
    hibition at Limelight, 86, 90,
    150
Bourjaily, Vance, 145
Bourke-White, Margaret, 108, 157
Boys, the, 137–39, 162–64, 224–33

Brandt, Bill, 42; exhibition at Limelight, 86–87, 90
Brassai, 164; exhibition at Limelight, 86, 90, 272
Bravo, Manuel Alvarez, 164; exhibition at Limelight, 86, 173–74
Brecht, Berthold, 43
Breitenbach, Joseph, exhibition at Limelight, 43, 48–52, **51,** 64–66
Brodovitch, Alexey, 16, 111
Brooklyn Museum, 68
Brooks, Elizabeth (Helen's cleaning woman), 269–72
Bubley, Esther, 108, 157
Bullock, Wynn, 105, 156
Bunnell, Peter, 160
Burckhardt, Rudolph, exhibition at Limelight, 66–68, **67**
Burden, Shirley, 164

Callahan, Harry, 148; exhibition at Limelight, 86, 90
Callem, Maude, 177–78
Calomiris, Angela, 14
Camera Club of New York, 68
Cameron, Julia Margaret, 287
Capa, Cornell, 63
Capa, Robert, 230, 243
Cartier-Bresson, Henri, 248–50, **251,** 256
cats, at Limelight, 62–63
Cedar Tavern, 114–15
Chaplin, Charlie, 48
Chemex coffeepot, 34, 62
Chi, Chen, quoted, 102
Civil Rights movement, 231, 244, 252
coffeehouses, emergence of, in New York, 5
Coffee Mill (coffeehouse), 5, 29
Cohen, John, 64; photograph by, **98**
Coke, Van Deren, 148, 272
Cole, William, 254

Collins, Al, 128–30
Communism. *See* McCarthyism
Compo, 105
Conley, Bob, 270–72
Conley, Mary Jane, 271
Cornell, Joseph, 66
Cunningham, Imogen, 156–61, **158,** 248; exhibition at Limelight, 86–87, 269

Dahl-Wolfe, Louise, 157
Dain, Martin, 64
Danielson, Pehr (Limelight manager), 226, 232, 256
Danzig, Jerry, 64
Davidson, Bruce, 269
Davis, Stuart, 160
DeCarava, Anne, 146–48
DeCarava, Roy, 146–48, 274
de Kooning, Elaine, 157
de Kooning, William, 211
Denby, Edwin, 66
De Niro, Robert, 239, 242
Deren, Maya, 256
de Reuss, Princess Paule, 190–91
Deschin, Jacob (Jack), **65,** 69n, 125, **241,** 245, 288–89; as Helen's adviser, 82–83, 119, 142–43, 146–47, 215, 238; photograph by, **67;** quoted, 41, 105, 107, 147–48, 208–9, 210; reviews by, of Limelight exhibitions, 64–69, 80, 87, 172, 194, 269
Desfor, Irving "Doc," 228, 238
d'Harnoncourt, René, 282
Diogenes IV, 164
Diogenes with a Camera III, 164
Doisneau, Robert, exhibition at Limelight, 86, 90, 242–43
Downes, Allen, 272
Downes, Bruce, quoted, 252
drugs, 77–84

Duchess of Windsor, 132
Duncan, David Douglas, 43
Durniak, John, quoted, 252

Eidlitz, Dorothy Meigs (collector), 89–90, 161
Eisenstaedt, Alfred, 248–49
Emerson, Peter Henry, 213
Engel, Morris, 64
English, Frances, 14
English, John, 13–15, 85, 110, 132, 153
Erwitt, Elliott, 73, 210–11
Evans, Walker, 85, 86, 110–17, 164

Fagan, Pat (Limelight bouncer), 81–86, 91–92
Falk, Sam, **65,** 82
Family of Man, The: Helen visits, with Steichen, 99–103; impact of, on photography, 95–97, 103–7, 273; opening of, 95–100, 164
Fancher, Edwin (Ed), 144–45, 170
Faurer, Louis, 272
Feiffer, Jules, 254
Feinstein, Harold, 64
Fellig, Arthur (Weegee), **234,** 235–37
Fong (Limelight chef), 197–99, 221, 238–39, 262–63, 280
Footlights and Spotlights: Theatrical Photographs of the American Stage, 1860–1900, 171–72
Frank, Andrea, 55
Frank, Mary, 37, 41–42, 55, 97, 113; photographs of, 100–101, 150; as sculptor, 211
Frank, Pablo, 41–42; photograph of, 150
Frank, Robert, 37, 55, **98,** 211, 248, 292; exhibition at Limelight, 86–87, 90; and The Family of Man, 97–101 passim; meetings between, and Helen, 40–42, 46, 84–85, 88–89,

148–49; photographs America, 110–18, 250–54
Friedlander, Lee, 64
Frissell, Toni, 157

galleries, photograph, 5, 68–69, 119, 122, 146–48, 291. See also Limelight
Garbo, Greta, 132
Garnett, William, 164
Gee, Helen, **12, 23, 44, 50, 51, 57, 60, 131, 240, 290**
Gee, Li-lan, **12,** 13–15, **45,** 48–53 passim, **126,** 223, 286, 291; and Bobby De Niro, 239, 242; and the Boys, 137, 162–63, 227; and Steichen, 165–67; wins trip with Helen, 126–30, 155–56
Gee, Yun, 8–13, **9,** 18, 190–91, 291
Gee v. Yee, 31–32
George Eastman House, 74, 155, 171
Gill, Leslie, 157
Gnant, Rob, 268
Goldsmith, Arthur, quoted, 253
Gordon, Morris, **65**
Gould, Joe, 71
Graves, Morris, 161
Great Photographs, 73–74, 86–90
Greenberg, Clement, 256
Grossman, Miriam, 25, 49–52
Grossman, Sid, 23–26, **24,** 49–52, 148, 150, 153
Guss, Louis, 267–68

Haas, Ernst, 248–49
Halsman, Philippe, 63, **65,** 73, 248–49
Hammid, Hella, 64
Hansberry, Lorraine, 254
Harbutt, Charles, 153
Harrington, Michael, 145
Harris, Suzy, 64
Hart, John Barkley, 160–61, 172
Hartigan, Vincent, 154

Hartman, Erich, 73
Haven, Kathleen, 103, 274–75
Hayes, Richard, 170
Heath, David, 64
Hellerman, Freddy, 256
Heyman, David, 175
Heyman, Ken, 173–75, 247; photograph by, **246**
Hiss, Alger, 256
Hoban, Tana, 108
Houseman, John, 256
House Un-American Activities Committee, 39, 116. See also McCarthyism
Hudson Park Library, 68–69, 69n
Hughes, Langston, 147
Hujar, Peter, 160
Hyman, Earle, 170

Ikeda, Masuo, 291
Institute of Design in Chicago, 140, 141
Iron Curtain, photographs from behind, 268–69
Izis, exhibition at Limelight, 86, 90

Jacobs, Ray, 64
Jaffe, Morris, 64, 183–84; photograph by, **126**
Japan, Steichen's visit to, 186–87
Japanese-American Relocation Center, 154
Jewell, Edward Alden, quoted, 191
Joyce, James, quoted, 100
Julien Levy Gallery. See Levy, Julien

Kalisher, Simpson, 64
Kanaga, Consuela, photograph by, **158**
Kaplan, Sid, 64
Karales, James, 213–14, 231; photograph by, **179**
Karsh, Yousuf, 248–49
Kerouac, Jack, 250

Kinzer, H. M. (Mike), 178–80, 228; quoted, 253
Kirstein, Lincoln, 160
Klein, William, 253
Knight, John Adam, 64, 238, **241**
Koch, Ed, 258
Kodak Information Center, 68
Korea, 43, 64–66
Kramer, Hilton, 106–7

La Farge, Grant, 73, 83
La Farge, John, 73
Lange, Dorothea, 86, 108, 248
Lange, Hope, 127, 129
Langer, Don, 238; quoted, 97
Larsen, Hazel Frieda, 108
Lavine, Arthur, 64, 105; photographs by, **29, 43–47, 50–51, 57–61, 65, 131**
lawsuits, 31–32, 175–76
Leen, Nina, 157
Leslie, Alfred, 113–15
Levinstein, Leon, 64, 130; exhibition at Limelight, 150, 153
Levitt, Helen, 24, 108, 248
Levy, Julien, 5, 87, 122, 191, 193, 195n
Lewis, Margery, 212
Leyton, Doris, 173–74
Liberman, Alexander, 111
Limelight, **50, 67;** actors at, 169; attempt to unionize, 257–65, 281; bohoes at, 70–74, 77–86; cats at, 62–63; exhibitions at (see Limelight, first exhibition at; names of individual exhibitors); first exhibition at, 40–43, 49–52, **51;** floor plan of, **33;** idea for, conceived, 3–5; as "intellectual coffeehouse," 255–56; lawsuits against, 175–76; liquor license for, 260, 265; name for, considered, 46–48; opening night at, 55–62, **58–61;** before reno-

Limelight (continued)
vation, **29;** renovation of, 27–39,
43–47, 46–48; sale of, 285–90;
staff of, 72–73, 197–99, 220–23
Lone, Les, purchases Limelight, 287
Lowe, Jacques, 269
Lynes, George Platt, 160
Lyrical and Accurate, 213

Madonnas and Marketplaces, 206–9
Mafia, 138–39
Mailer, Adele, 255
Mailer, Norman, 144–45, 255
Maisel, Jay, 269
Marin, John, 120
Marquis, Jean, 268
Martin, Tulio, 133–34
Martinez, Romeo E., 268
Mather, Magarethe, 157
Mayer, Grace, 199–201, **200,** 228,
245–47, 274–76, 283–84
McAlpin, David, 154
McCall's, 132–34, 153
McCarthyism, 14, 24, 38–39, 92, 244
McCausland, Elizabeth, 189
McLaughlin, Frances, 157
Mead, Margaret, 174–75
Meatyard, Eugene, 148
Menninger, Dr. Karl, 174–75
Metcalf, Addison, 159
Mia (Helen's cat), **126**
Michalik, Rozena, 268
Mikoda, Phil, 237–39
Mili, Gjon, 248–49
Miller, Ralph "Skip," 238
Miller, Wayne, 97, 103, 109, 245–46;
photograph by, **96**
Mirin, May, 64
Mischa (Limelight manager), 197–99,
220
Model, Evsa, 21–22, 63, 73; Helen's
first meeting with, 17–18

Model, Lisette, **23,** 24, 63, 73, 248;
and Abbott, 189–90, 217–18; criti-
cism by, 95–97, 143, 283; and
Cunningham, 160–61; exhibition
at Limelight, 86–87, 90; as Helen's
teacher, 3, 16–17, 19–22; quoted,
273; studio of, **19**
Modotti, Tina, 157
Moholy-Nagy, Laszlo, 140–46, 150
Moholy-Nagy, Sybil, 140–44
Morales, Adele, 145
Morgan, Barbara, 24, 104
Morley, Malcolm, 281
Mostel, Zero, 256
Mounicq, Jean, 268
Moynihan, Daniel (Pat), 266
Murat, Princess Eugénie, 219
Murray, William, 145
Museum of Modern Art, 8, 16–17, 68,
87, 282; and Ansel Adams, 154–55;
opening of, 122; photographs first
exhibited at, 191; technical advice
from, 46, 52. See also *Family of Man,
The*; Steichen, Edward
Museum of Natural History, 68
Museum of the City of New York, 68

Naylor, Genevieve, 157
Nettleton, Lois, 239, **241**
Neves, Manuel (restaurateur), 74, 81,
86, 88
Newhall, Beaumont, 74, 154–55, 287
Newhall, Nancy, 154–55, 282; quoted,
76–77
Newman, Arnold, 63, 73, 119, 154
Newman, Gus, 63
New School for Social Research, 16,
273
Noguchi, Isamu, 256
Nonnamaker, Queen (Helen's secre-
tary), 15, 40, 48, 90, 99, 107, 112,
133–34

Norman, Dorothy, 103–4, 118–25
Norman, Edward, 120

Obies, 169–71
Obsatz, Victor, 64
O'Connor, Frank, 254
Off Broadway, 168–72
O'Keeffe, Georgia, 119–25, 157
Oriental Exclusion Act, 8
Orkin, Ruth, 64

Paige, Geraldine, 171
Parks, Gordon, 283
Parrella, Lew, 64, 73, **263**, 263–64, 268–69; quoted, 208
Paton, Alan, 244
Paulin, Frank, 153; photographs by, **251, 263, 290**
peacock dinner, 237–39, **240–41**
Penn, Irving, 248–49
Penny (Helen's dog), 52–53, **126**
Perelman, S. J., 254
photograms, 141–43
photographers, ten greatest, in *Popular Photography* poll, 248–50
Photographer's Place, A, 146–48
Photographs by Professors, 272–73
Photographs from the Museum Collection, 245
photography: changes of, in later years, 273, 291–2; color, 201–3; first exhibition, 191; impact on, by *The Family of Man*, 95–97, 103–7, 273; pricing, 87. *See also* photojournalism
photojournalism, 75, 156–57, 177–78, 243–44
Photo League, 14, 23–24, 147, 244
photomontage, 141–42, 190–91
Place, the (site of Limelight), 27–31
Polaroid, 155
Pollack, Peter, 230; photograph by, **192**

Popular Photography, poll conducted by, 248–50
Porter, Eliot, 119, 154, 204–9, **205**, 269
Portraits of Each Other, 118–25
Pratt, David, 171–72

Radkai, Paul, 16
Rado, Charles, 225
Rapho-Guillumette, 225
Rausser, Fernand, 268
Rendville, USA, 231
Reynolds, Charles, quoted, 252–53
Rienzi (coffeehouse), 5, 29
Rivera, Diego, 191
Rohan, Pierre de. *See* Knight, John Adam
Roiter, Fulvio, 268
Rolke, Tadeusz, 268
Rolleiflex (camera), 16–17, 20, 151
Romano (real estate agent), 28–30, 134–35
Romany Marie, 71
Rosenberg, Ethel, 48
Rosenberg, Harold, 256
Rosenberg, Julius, 48
Rosenblum, Walter, 24, 148, 213, 272
Rosset, Barney, 250
Roth, Manny, purchases Limelight, 287
Rothman, Michael, 257–65
Rothschild, Norman, 64, 238
Rubin, Moe (contractor), 32–33, 36–39, 46
Rudolph, Paul, 101
Russia and Eastern Europe, 244

Saarinen, Aline B., quoted, 106
Sam (Helen's accountant), 32, 37–39, 89, 258, 262
Sander, August, 164
Sarony, Napoleon, 171–72

Scacheri, Mabel, 64, 238
Schad, Tennyson, 291
Schapiro, Meyer, 111, 256
Schenk, Gustave, 164
Schlumbohm, Dr. (inventor), 34–35
Schuh, Gotthard, 42; exhibition at
    Limelight, 86–87
Schwartz, Delmore, 266
Schweitzer, Albert, 182–84, 184n, 212
Schweitzer, Ernst (Helen's psychoana-
    lyst), 183–84, 184n, 279
Seldes, Gilbert, 145
Seligman, Paul, 64; photograph by,
    234
Seymour, David "Chim," 230
Shapiro, "Sky," 46
Sheehan, Tim, 166, 232–33
Sheeler, Charles, 160, 190
Sheinfeld, Meyer (Helen's attorney),
    30–31, 136–37, 285
Shepherd, Jean, 169, 239, **241**, 290
Sierra Club, 155
Silver, Walt, 64
Silverstein, Shel, 254
Simon, Jesse, 258–59
Siskind, Aaron, 24, 142, 256, 272
Six Women Photographers, 108
Smith, Carmen, 215
Smith, Henry Holmes, 272
Smith, Howard, 172
Smith, Jack, 283
Smith, W. Eugene, 24, **179,** 231,
    243–44, 248–50; exhibition at
    Limelight, 86–87, 90, 212–16; and
    The Family of Man, 102, 105; personal
    life, 176–84
Snake Eyes (drug dealer), 77–84
Somoroff, Ben, 132–33
Spanish Village, 178, 182
Spector, Seymour ("Sy"), 238
Stanley, Kim, 171

Starr, Nina Howell, photograph by,
    200
Stashin, Leo, 64
Steichen, Edward, 25, 86–87, **96,** 111,
    146, 153, 191, **246,** 273; at Museum
    of Modern Art, 68, 155, 283–84;
    personal life, 106–9, 164–66, 185–
    89, 199–203, 245–47, 274–76;
    quoted, 95. See also Family of Man,
    The
Steichen, Joanna, 275–76
Steiger, Rod, 236
Stern, Bert, 230–31
Stettner, Louis, 64; exhibition at
    Limelight, 72
Stieglitz, Alfred, 5, 76, 87, 114, 213;
    exhibition at Limelight, 118–25
Strand, Paul, 24; exhibition at Lime-
    light, 86–87
Sullivan, Finbar, 277–79
Sullivan, Finbar, Jr., 279–80
Sullivan, Kevin, 227, 239, **241,** 266–73,
    277–80, 285–86, 290
Sullivan, Louis, 283–84
Sullivan, Vincent, 279
Swenson, May, 256
Szarkowski, John, 284

Tallmer, Jerry, 46–48, **47,** 78, 144–45,
    169–70, 267
Tallmer, Peggy, 32–35, **44,** 46, **47,**
    48–52 passim, **58,** 78–79, 145
Tuggener, Jacob, exhibition at Lime-
    light, 86
Twice a Year (journal), 120
"291" gallery, 5

union, labor, targets Limelight,
    256–65, 281
United States Reconstruction Agency,
    43

University of Maine, 154

Van Sickle, Kenneth, 229
Vestal, David, 64, 165; photographs by, **19, 24**
Viehler, Alice, 69n
Village Camera Club, 64, 68, 73, 181
Village Voice, 143–48, 153, 160–61, 228–29, 254; sponsors Obies, 169–71

Wallowitch, Ed, 64
Weegee, **234,** 235–37
Weiner, Dan, 73, 119, **243,** 243–44
Weiner, Sandra, photograph by, **243**
Weiss, Sabine, exhibition at Limelight, 86, 157
Weston, Brett, 281–83
Weston, Edward, 24, 76, 157; exhibition at Limelight, 86–87, 281–83
Whelan Studios (American Photograph Corporation), 10–13
White, Minor, **75,** 153, 165, 213, 256;

as editor of *Aperture*, 66, 103–4; exhibition at Limelight, 74–77, 80, 86–87, 90, 156, 272
Wilcox, John, 145
Wimmer family, **6,** 7–8
Winchell, Walter, 92
Winogrand, Gary, 253
Winters, Shelley, 170–71
Witkin, Lee, 291
Wolf, Dan, 144–45, 170
women photographers, 108, 156–57, 248. *See also names of individual photographers*
World War II, images from, in The Family of Man, 102
Wright, Cora Alsberg, 104–5, 228, 238
Wright, George, 146–48, 238, **241;** quoted, 104–5; reviews by, of Limelight exhibitions, 142, 153, 194–95, 210

Yee, Tom, 31

Zanutto, James, quoted, 252